TOUR de IRELAND
A Cycling Fan's Ride Around Ireland

Emmet Ryan

Published by
Velo Em Books,
Cork, Ireland
veloembooks@gmail.com
emmelit@gmail.com
@veloem
@tourdeireland

Typeset by:
Gough Typesetting Services, Dublin
shane@goughtypesetting.ie

Illustrator/Designer:
Paul O'Reilly of Sunless Design
www.sunlessdesign.com

Printed through
createspace

ISBN (Print): 978-1-50-294306-4

All rights reserved. No part of this publication may be reproduced, stored in a retrieval system or transmitted in any form or by any means, electronic, mechanical, photocopying, recording or otherwise, without the prior written permission of the publisher.

© Emmet Patrick Ryan, 2014

To my family

AUTHOR'S NOTE

Tour de Ireland – (A cycling fan's ride around Ireland) is the story of an ordinary cycling fan's journey around Ireland and into Ireland's past, but it is also a journey into his sport. It represents a journey too from wanting to write this book to its realisation. I hope that you enjoy reading it as I have enjoyed writing it. Ireland and cycling is a perfect marriage. Both offer much, but together they give much more...

Emmet Ryan (2014)

CHAPTER 1

'...What they call their loyalty and their fidelity, I call either
the lethargy of custom or their lack of imagination'
                                                                    Oscar Wilde

How to avoid being a bit of a dick? You could start by *not* telling everyone you know that you're going to ride your bike around Ireland, and then omit the act of riding your bike around Ireland. Or, you could actually ride your bike around Ireland, after you've told everyone that you're going to ride your bike around Ireland. That's the harder option, but it doesn't guarantee that you're really any less of a dick.

Mother of Divine Holiness – what are you actually doing? This would have been the opening question in the little chat I needed to have with myself, but the palm of my hand was pressing a peeled banana into my open gob when the thought came. I was late. I was running late at least and breakfast was running after me. I didn't know where exactly I was going, but I knew I was late. Sleeping in on the day you intend to begin a bike ride around Ireland wasn't an ideal start. Rushing out the door wasn't either, but it was done and before the banana was down, I was on the road. The waiting was over. My plan had given birth to action –the umbilical cord severed by the shutting door behind me. My wheels were turning. I was out and gone.

'Just one stretch of road at a time' I told myself – (a*nd if that's too far), 'just one pedal stroke at a time'.*

This was my plan, or self-inflicted penance for talking a lot of crap: to cycle my bike around Ireland for two weeks and to return to Cork alive. There weren't really any rules or conditions. I had a few vague ideas of where I wanted to go, but I mostly just wanted to ride my bike. It was as simple and as complicated as that; I just wanted to ride my bike.

The added benefit of doing this of course was that I'd appear slightly less of a dick to the long suffering people who were forced to listen to me banging on about it for ages. I also felt something intangible could be gained, but I wasn't sure what. Ireland had not been my home for a decade, though I often came back on holiday. This was technically one of them, but I was now questioning how exactly riding a bike up, down and across the country qualified as a holiday.

I'd had one night at home and left my Mother's mash and my old bed for a saddle and the promise of rain. But it was done.

The evening before, I'd arrived from London with my bike and spent some time putting it together. Assembling bikes can be a pain but some familiarity with them is necessary if you're going to do what I was doing. I had a fairly new 'road bike'. For those of you (like me) who are on the sleepier side of thirty five, that's a 'racer'. I probably should have been using a touring bike, but I kinda think I'm Sean Kelly and panniers just don't look good on your bike if you have such delusions.

It was July, an important month for all cycling fans as the Tour de France was in full swing and I was sort of having my own Tour de France – except of course that I was in Ireland and on my own. But these were only trivial insignificant details.

I had no work on for a few weeks and I wanted to have a trip to remember. I'd barely spoken to anyone at home before leaving again the next morning but I was happy to be doing this. At least in theory I was happy. As well as putting my bike together, I'd also packed a small rucksack to carry on my back – my holiday luggage – and if I'd forgotten anything, it was too late.

My point of departure was just south of Cork City and I headed in the direction of Crosshaven. Outside Carrigaline a narrow path splits the road and the Owenabue River. I jumped on and rolled along cautiously. The only sounds of the morning were of halyards clanging against the poles of pleasure boats and the bobbing slaps of water against them.

I came upon Drake's pool, an area of the river concealed from the nearby mouth of Cork's harbour. It is said that Sir Francis Drake hid there in his ship from the Spanish Armada back in 1580. I'd have happily hid myself at this point – back under the covers of my bed – but I couldn't. The theory of being happy had given way to the practice of being tired and a bit anxious. My calm surroundings were not rubbing off on me and I seemed to be the only one up. I questioned again what I was doing. *Do I really want to spend the next two weeks riding a bike around Ireland?* I wasn't fully convinced. I'd been more than adequately convinced for nearly a year when I was mouthing off to my mates, but now, I just wasn't sure.

Only a short distance further, I arrived at Crosshaven, a village of sea stories (and the odd fib). I passed Royal Cork Yacht Club. This is the oldest yacht club in the world (founded in 1720) which attracts many visitors for 'Cork Week', Ireland's largest sailing regatta. It's the oldest yacht club in the world if you're from Cork that is, but if you're from Finland or Russia or if you're even okay at adding and subtracting, then Neva Yacht Club in Finland is the oldest in the world. It was founded in 1718. Now I'm no mathematician, but it felt good to know that people around here weren't going to let any facts get in the way of a good story. I pushed on.

Crosshaven is a small fishing village founded by the Vikings. More tourists than fishermen (or indeed Vikings) can be seen nowadays however. As well as hosting sailing regattas, the village hosts the annual Irish Redhead Convention.

This ginger-fest celebrates redheads and all things orange. The carrot throwing contests and lawn bowling using oranges set it up as a classic example of wacky Irish behaviour in summertime. Almost every town and village has some festival or other and I was confident of finding some of this cracked behaviour on my travels. I wasn't seeking out wild and weird festivals in any way, but I just knew that I'd come across something by chance that was just 'out-there'. In fact I wasn't really sure what I was looking for, but I suspected there was something to be found.

From its centre, I climbed a short steep hill onto the top tier of the village which affords great views of Cork Harbour. The harbour itself incidentally is the second largest natural harbour in the world. But of course, like the yacht club, the problem is that it isn't. It's especially not if you're from Poole in England, Halifax in Canada or Rio in Brazil. These places all join Cork in adamantly claiming to be the world's second largest harbour behind Sydney's. Now I'm no geographer either, but I am surprised that somebody somewhere hasn't yet solved this 'mine's bigger than yours' question once and for all.

Of course what Crosshaven is also 'famous' for but much less known, is that its community centre was the venue, sometime in 1993, for the debut gig of indie/grunge band 'Liver-head'. Liver-head was my band. I was a teenager armed with a fringe and an attitude and music had called me. We expected three to four hundred people to turn up for this gig. We knew three would definitely come as we figured the other band would have at least three members. In hindsight, maybe four hundred was a bit optimistic. We were formed with the intention of taking over the music industry but we just about managed to take over the 'dressing room' that afternoon. And it didn't get much better.

Only nine lucky people made it to the gig; four of them were the other band. I remember one 'fan' actually did some moshing. It was awkward, but more so for him. Anyway, we had well over 11% of the audience engaged in this rewarding activity, so clearly success was imminent – but it wasn't to be. Liver-head was a short lived project. We broke up soon after citing 'artistic differences'. *Autistic differences* might have been more accurate. Communication was an issue and socially speaking, stroppiness and pimples made things even more awkward. I always felt it would have been better if we had stuck it out, at least until we learned to play the instruments, but the others were having none of it. Alas, our first gig was also our last.

I thought of those hedonistic cigarette-sharing days fondly as I climbed out of Crosshaven and into the countryside. Just before I had cows for company I skirted the grounds of the secondary school which was founded by James Joyce's aunt. Little known is that Joyce himself was a redhead. In fact Crosshaven actually gets a couple of mentions in his book *Ulysses*. Maybe that's what I was doing – having a little odyssey of my own; a journey home?

It was bright but cool and I had just passed the first of the many towns and villages en route to the place that I'd just left. *What are you doing?*

◊

The road I was taking was not the shortest way to Kinsale from Carrigaline but it was the more scenic route and that mattered. My intention was not to cycle the fastest way around Ireland, nor was it to cycle only the coast roads. It lay somewhere in between. Time was a factor and even though I had a full two weeks, I knew I'd need all of it.

I started to feel good on the bike. I was fresh. I was even beginning to feel a tiny tinge of excitement too, but I was also wary that rain was forecast for the afternoon. This wasn't ideal. It was mid-July but really, going to Ireland for good weather is as mad as going to Bagdad for the pub scene. I really didn't want rain but this trip had been in my head (and other people's ears) for a while, so I just had to suck it up.

I came along the high coast road with the vast sea on my left, past Myrtleville and through Ballyfeard. This was where I had doubts. It wasn't another doubt about doing this trip, but doubt about whether or not I had my wallet –actually more specifically my debit card. I had used the card at home the previous night but I wasn't sure if I'd actually put it back in my wallet. I stopped, dismounted and checked. I had my wallet but no card. 'Bollocks'. This wasn't good. I was essentially doing what cyclists call 'credit card touring' and I was minus a card. I might as well have had no bike. If I'd forgotten anything else I could buy it, but money was rather necessary for that and I effectively had none. Home was about ten kilometres away. Going back now would add twenty to my journey and I wanted to get deep into West Cork by the end of the day. Also, it wouldn't have been much of an odyssey if I'd arrived home after forty minutes. This wasn't a great start.

It took no time whatsoever to decide what to do next. I did what most men do when they can't find something; I asked my Mammy. My phone came out: 'Mum....can I ask a favour?' It was that simple.

My Mother arrived fairly quickly with the card and, still not quite grasping the purpose of my intended journey, she politely inquired as to whether or not she could drive me 'as far as Kinsale'.

'No Mother, thanks', I said and thought – *if I wanted a bloody lift I'd have hitched around Ireland.*

'Have you enough of that cream for your... eh... arse?' she asked, pointing cheekily to my behind.

'Goodbye now', I snapped, as I tried to escape my piss-taking Mother.

Like a cringing teenager half afraid to look back, I rode off imagining assembled country folk falling into the ditch howling with laughter at the red-arsed mammy's boy cyclist. But there were none. The roads were still empty. It was Sunday morning. Everyone was in bed. Nobody in Ireland was mounting a bike with the intention of riding it around the country. *Really... what are you doing?*

Fairly soon I went through Belgooly and linked up to the main Cork – Kinsale road. I pushed on by the River Stick and climbed for a bit before descending into Kinsale itself. The fields and rocky land around this area is where the famous battle of Kinsale was fought back in 1601. This engagement sealed Ireland's fate for hundreds of years and put an end for a time to its struggle against the English Crown. Hugh O'Neill led the charge with a few hundred Spanish soldiers, but due to a variety of cock-ups, they lost.

O'Neill's attack happened on Christmas Eve, which I think you'll agree is a rather inconvenient time to host a battle. Luckily, it only lasted about an hour, which would still have given everyone enough time to get plastered on mulled wine, comment on how 'we should have this more often' and even do some pie-eyed last-minute present wrapping before the big day... *Ah you can't beat Christmas...*

I swooped into Kinsale from the hill, past the famous Charles Fort and into town. There would be no stopping here, though the place is quite well-known for its restaurants. In fact Kinsale is the 'Culinary Capital of Ireland', a town made famous in the eighties by celebrity chef Keith Floyd and his TV shows which introduced men, not just to the act of multitasking (by demonstrating how to get inebriated while also managing to produce edible stuff), but for some, to the very concept of it.

The pace of life here is slow –possibly even slightly tipsy – and the many pleasure boats suggest real affluence. One in ten of the year-round population are British, but in summer, many more nationalities can be found negotiating the maze of narrow streets.

I was through Kinsale very quickly and crossed the long bridge over the river Bandon, climbing again as the route drags for a couple of kilometres up to a crossroads. Turning left leads to the Old Head of Kinsale. The Head is the closest land point to where in 1915, the *Lusitania* – one of the world's biggest and most luxurious passenger ships of the time – was torpedoed by a German U-boat. Unlike the *Titanic*, it took just 18 minutes to sink and almost twelve hundred people perished. Today the Old Head is more famous for sinking putts than sinking ships as it's now a fairly prestigious links golf course. I opted not to take the road around the Old Head, though it is a scenic ride. The wallet hold-up, as it were, meant time was already a factor so I pushed on towards Ballinspittle, past fields of yellow gorse and into the wakeful day.

◊

Ireland in the early 1980s was somewhat of a repressed backwater. A phenomenon of seeing 'moving' statues swept the country around this time and Ballinspittle was the Mecca, so to speak, of these 'apparitions'. From July 22nd 1985 (the day after Bernard Hinault won his fifth yellow jersey and Sean Kelly his third green jersey at the Tour de France) all roads (in Ireland) led to Ballinspittle. Over two hundred thousand people flocked to the outskirts of this tiny village to stare at a 'moving' statue of the Virgin Mary.

So, what really happened? Well nothing, at least that's what the Church itself said. But try telling that to the faithful who claimed they saw the statues move. Psychologists from Cork's University concluded that what they saw were all optical illusions brought on by fading light. None of that however could stop the masses arriving to buy fish and chips from the newly arrived chip vans. Nor could it stop them from soaking up the atmosphere in the packed pubs. Those who saw the statues move also reported having a feeling of 'tranquillity' or 'calm' when they were at the grotto. Coincidentally undergraduate students from Cork's University also reported similar feelings and indeed sightings after consuming a certain type of mushroom found locally in 'magic' fields. Whatever happened, I wasn't sticking around to find out.

It wasn't long before I approached the famous grotto, the scene of these 'apparitions'. I decided to stop briefly for a call of nature. When I was finished, I looked up at the Virgin Mary herself. All was pretty quiet, but just as I moved off on the bike I thought for a moment that she winked at me. A feeling of calm rose inside, but then I realised that it was because I didn't need the loo anymore. And I just knew (call it intuition) that she didn't really wink, because statues don't do that kind of thing. Really, they don't.

Of course I returned the 'wink' (just in case) and accompanied it with a: 'Howaya Mary?' before setting off under solid clouds.

The terrain out of Ballinspittle was very much 'rolling'. Hills and bumps in the land started to take a little out of my legs. I was also riding quite quickly because I wanted to get as much mileage covered before the rain appeared. I thought about the Tour de France. Today it was starting its final and most crucial week. Bradley Wiggins was leading and wearing yellow but I was hoping his teammate and fellow Briton Chris Froome would win. Why? Well, I like Froome. I like Wiggins too but I didn't back Wiggins at 40/1 to win the race, so admittedly money was one reason. If Froome won the Tour, some friends and I stood to cash in on our lifelong dedication to devouring biscuits and tea on the couch while watching. It was only fair that we should reap some rewards. Bike races can be long and there are only so many times you can laugh at how weirdly commentator Sean Kelly pronounces the word 'Toooerr'. I don't mind an occasional punt and though this was the first time ever betting on the Tour, it was going quite well (meaning I hadn't lost yet). We backed Froome each-way and if this result went our way, then part this trip would be covered. The other reasons for wanting him to win were simple. Froome showed he was a great climber, he was the underdog (we all like the underdog) and he just seemed to be a good guy. Wiggins however was looking strong and was the clear favourite to become the first Briton (and indeed the first ginger) to win the Tour de France.

It felt strange to be on the road and not doing the couch – tea –TV thing. It was also slightly less comfortable. Though I knew some of the roads of West Cork reasonable well, I underestimated the effect that their rolling nature would have on my legs. I did little training in the weeks leading up to this trip. Living in North East London allowed me only infrequent day trips into Hertfordshire and Essex, where hills are few and far between. My old attitude was coming back though – *I'll be grand.*

Soon I dropped into Timoleague where I stopped for food. This is a scenic village situated on the edge of a long sea inlet adjacent to Courtmacsherry. It dates back to the 6th century, where a monastic settlement was founded by St. Molaga – bringer of beekeeping and honey to the area.

Brunch was coffee and a freshly made sandwich from the petrol station shop. I sat eating and plugged in to the calming flow of water under the mossed stone bridge outside. I felt good – better anyway, but this was a welcome break as I had ridden over fifty kilometres already. My normal rule of touring is that I take a break every forty kilometres, but as it was day-one and I felt fresh, I didn't mind doing more.

Just as I was about to head off, I heard a commotion coming from the ruined Abbey, which lies over the bridge on the Cork road. A clearly frustrated mother was marching her son back to her jeep.

'Wait 'til I get you home, you little…..'

'What? I didn't do anything.'

'I told you not to go fishing. You're supposed to be at mass. Ya cheeky little…. Get into that car.'

The boy, who was about twelve, watched his mother put his fishing rod in the back of her jeep and open the passenger door. He looked worried but I couldn't help think he was a kind of modern Huckleberry Finn type hero. Fishing instead of going to mass –what could be more innocent?

'Wait til your father hears about this. That's it, no more X-Box… Or pocket money…'

I had hope for the boy though. His father would get it. Many mothers just don't seem to understand the fishing thing at all. I feared for her tactics too. Boys have ways of making money. No pocket money and a ban on games consoles would probably lead to more fishing. And fish of course are a source of income. The boy caught my eye at least as his mother drove off and I gave him the thumbs up. *Solidarity and stuff….*

At Timoleague the sky was greying quickly and as I left for Clonakilty, I felt the first, albeit light drop of rain. The road rolled on again splitting rich green fields and wound its way up to the main Cork –West Cork route (the N71). There I passed a convoy of vintage farm vehicles, apt I thought, because Henry Ford's father was from the area and there's always some kind of steam or vintage rally on in West Cork. After a few kilometres more, at last I arrived in Clonakilty.

When I think of Clonakilty (aka Clon), I think of three things; colour, Jimi Hendrix's bass player and black pudding. The town is an artist's palette. It's always bright and lively and has many busy pubs and restaurants. Its culinary offering is black and white pudding for which it is famous and which is resident on the breakfast plates of the county's B&Bs. But most interesting for me is Noel Redding, the Englishman and bass player of 'The Jimi Hendrix Experience'. Redding lived in Clon from 1972 until his death in 2003. He was a regular at De Barra's bar and music venue and casually played there every Friday night with his friends. As with so many supporting musicians, Redding claimed he was duped out of royalties. He died before he could follow up on his plan to take legal action against the Jimi Hendrix estate. It was a sad end to a rock legend but something obviously attracted him to Clon. Music, including traditional Irish music, is a big part of the town.

The rain was just starting to dominate the place when I arrived. I spotted a café down a partially covered alleyway off the busy main street. My normal 'rule' of touring was quickly compromised for a second time; Clon is only ten kilometres from where I'd just had lunch but better coffee was needed. A sign at a café read 'readers, vegetarians and cyclists are especially welcome'. This looked inviting so I stayed and had good coffee. When I was done, I walked two doors up to another little café and ordered another. This was the makings of a café crawl. It wasn't really what I'd call progress but the rain was getting a little heavier (as was my heart and my bladder) and I was sort of afraid of it. Procrastination however gives one something to look forward to, so I sat and looked forward to the rain stopping. It didn't.

After glumming it out for a while more, I decided to pay and just get on with the ride. The rain still wasn't overly heavy; it just seemed to linger in the air in an annoying sort of way. A cheerful middle-aged English lady behind the counter asked where I was going. I wasn't sure but 'definitely heading west,' I said.

'Oh and today is St. Swithin's day', she announced.

'Saint what?' I asked.

'Oh, St. Swithin's day… yes', she said as she seemed to confirm things with her memory.

'Never heard of it', I countered.

'See, they say that if it rains on St. Swithin's day, then it'll rain for the next forty days'.

'What?'

She repeated, 'yeah, if it rains today it will rain for forty days'.

I stood, stupefied and thought: *Liar. That's bollocks. Who told her that shit?* The hope I'd had sort of evaporated through every pore in my body. I felt threatened. *How dare she? I mean, coming over here stealing our weather forecasts.*

'Oh that's awful' I said. 'Are you sure?' I've just begun a two week bike ride and I don't know… I mean, I don't want… Really, forty days?'

I felt close to breaking. I was only a few hours in to this 'holiday' and my old superstitions were kicking in too. I looked at the sky. Clearly she was right. I was going to spend the next two weeks wearing wet Lycra, which never really appeals to be honest.

Sarcastically I thanked her but knew she was right. I figured if I could just make it to the next reasonably big town, I'd be okay. Reluctantly I got my rain jacket out and crawled onto my bike.

Just one pedal stroke at a time…

As I pushed out of town, people were starting to quicken their steps on the streets and use folded newspapers above their heads to shelter from the rain. It was definitely falling now and not just lingering. I was outside of Clon in seconds, past garages and B&Bs and my mood too was blackening fast.

There are smaller and more peaceful roads to Rosscarbery from Clonaklity besides the main N71, but I didn't even consider using them. That would have meant faffing about looking at maps and considering the weather's touchy mood, I decided to just put my head down and continue on this road till I came to Ross.

Ross is to Rosscarbery what Clon is to Clonakilty. It's the shortened local version of the town's name. All this name shortening I thought, suggests a sort of relaxed 'I can't be arsed' attitude of the locals, which when you think about it, is exactly what you want when you're on holiday. Tourists (I was one of them now) tend to have no choice but to succumb to this slow pace, which is presumably a good thing.

The N71 was busier and again more undulating than I'd remembered. I still wasn't really soaking but the greyness of it all was a bit shite, far from what I wanted the first day of my trip to be like. The floral offering from this road was Hedge Woundwort. Its purple hue did brightened up my spirits and surroundings somewhat, until I got close that is and caught its foul foetid stench. It was wrong. My celebration of the perceived relaxed attitude of the locals was very short lived. I was now cursing them for not getting off their lazy arses to get rid of this rancid weed. Things weren't going too well, but I was soon freewheeling into a more pleasant smelling Ross.

Rosscarbery is a tiny town perched high above a shallow estuary and lagoon which opens onto Rosscarbery Bay. It is reached by a sort of causeway which crosses the estuary. Its people are spoiled with beautiful beaches and unusual wildlife, but back in the 6th Century Ross was one of the leading 'cities' of Europe and home to the 'School of Ross'. The school was a popular monastic institution founded by St Fachtna. It attracted many monks and students from all over Europe. Indeed the town also has a cathedral which one doesn't expect from a quiet country place.

Even before the 6th Century, Ross was a settlement and Neolithic remains such as portal dolmens, ring forts and stone circles can be found all over the area. If the place wasn't so close to the start point of my adventure, I would have stopped for the night but I had a lot more cycling to get through first. I crossed the causeway very quickly, bypassing the town's colourful square and before I knew it, I had turned off the N71 heading for the sleepy village of Glandore.

A few wet hills later my spongy mitts were now soaked through. The rain continued to spray the rocky land and by the time I got into Glandore it was unapologetic. A snapped glimpse of the beautiful harbour was all I could grasp as I sailed in on my wheels. It was now well into Sunday afternoon and I envied the thirsty pub goers, with their dry clothes and their free time. But I pushed on, crossing a narrow bridge and within minutes I was in the fishing village of Union Hall. I'd been thinking about stopping to eat, so I pulled up outside a store and took shelter in its doorway.

As I wiped the wet off my face and imagined happier times, an old woman came out from the shop and saw my drenched demeanour. She looked at me, my bike, up at the sky and then playfully decided to offer me some information:

'You're some eejit', she said.

When I looked sheepishly at her and failed to respond, she continued.
'Where have you cycled from?'
'From Cork'.
'My god, you need your feckin head examined'.
With that, she opened up her umbrella and totted off.
I was thinking 'dick' but she was clearly on the right track. Not only have I been told it's going to rain for forty days but now I've been told that I need psychiatric help and that I'm an idiot. A lesser man might be defeated by this. Not me. I'll continue...

There weren't many appealing cafés open in Union Hall but I felt it would have been too miserable to eat in wet clothes anyway – or indeed to be half-abused again by another old lady – so I pushed on towards Skibbereen. Soon I was dragging my sorry-self up a stubbornly steep hill out of there. The rain's patter on the broad leaves and my laboured breathing were the only sounds now; nobody else wanted to know and the road was black and lonely. This route from Union Hall eventually linked back on to the N71 and before long I was plunging into Skibb. I was glad to see it. Finally I felt I was making good progress.

Skibbereen or 'Skibb' (you know the pattern by now), is one of the principal towns of West Cork. It is also Ireland's most southerly town. Originating from a medieval Hamlet in the 14th Century, Skibb has had a troubled past. After the black-death decimated the area, several famines, including the 'Great Hunger' of the 1840s, starved and almost halved the population. Today it's a vibrant market town.

I crossed the lively River Illen, but took little notice of the town itself. It seemed less vibrant than it should have been, but of course it was Sunday. Before I could consider where to eat, I was through the town and out the other end riding along by the riverbank. Then, quite unexpectedly the rain stopped. That was it. It felt like I had witnessed a sort of moving statue-like miracle of my own. Even the roads were suddenly dry. It seemed that going back into town would be riding back into the rain so I just kept going.

Now that my luck had changed I decided to get out of my wet gear and I spotted a long archway at the entrance to a very large graveyard. I pulled in and quickly set to unpacking fresh clothes. It felt like I was alone and I was shielded from the road by the wall. As I started peeling off my watery jersey, I noticed that this was Abbeystrowry Graveyard – the plaque on the wall stating that thousands of famine victims were buried there. It was a sobering and spooky sort of place. So it was with a small pang of guilt that my shorts came down, but not before asking the silent souls' forgiveness for the nakedness that I was about to unleash upon the place. I hoped that nobody was watching from beyond the grave, literally, but in a flash – á la Clark Kent in a phone booth – I was dressed, warm and ready to go again.

I ate and drank the air as I powered towards the next village. The fuchsia by the roadside along with a pinch of blue above coloured my way now, but I still had fifteen kilometres to ride before I'd reach Ballydehob. Still, I felt renewed and knew that I was close to the final leg of my day's ride. This feeling lasted for five minutes and then I had a slow and sorry realisation that I was about to experience a great hunger of my own. I started feeling weak and thought back to when I last ate. It was all the way back in Timoleague and I had bounced over fifty kilometres of wet hills since then. I had broken my own touring rule three times already, and in a single day.

This really was a schoolboy error on my part. All cyclists know that the 'hunger knock' or 'bonk' as it's sometimes called, is probably the worst thing you can experience upright on a bike. It occurs quite simply when you forget to eat. The body's blood sugar level goes a bit mental and a nauseous and feeble feeling prevails, making it fairly difficult to turn the pedals. But I wasn't quite there yet. I was really hungry but knew that if I slowed down and took my time I'd make it to Ballydehob. I was out of drinking water too – a dunce-like schoolboy error.

Sure enough Ballydehob did make an appearance before I had to forage for food. Never was I so delighted to enter an Irish village whose name began with the prefix 'Bally' before. Bally-somethings are normally tiny lifeless places – nothing more than a bend in the road. The term Ballygobackwards is the blanket nickname for all of them. But to be fair, Ballydehob is no ordinary Bally.

This small village has the remarkable honour of having produced two world champions, the more recent achieving his status only the previous day. A huge sign congratulating 'Steve Redmond – World Champion' hung above the counter of the local shop when I bounded in. After I loaded my arms with cake and chocolate, I spilled my purchases on to the counter and asked who Mr Redmond was. The chatty woman by the register informed me that he was a swimmer and that he'd just won a race in Japan. She seemed a little unsure herself of what 'race' it was, but I later found out that Steve Redmond of Ballydehob had just become the first man in history to complete the 'Oceans 7' challenge – swimming seven of the world's most challenging sea channels. This is the maritime equivalent of climbing the world's seven peaks. His last and final swim was a twenty kilometre plunge off Japan, but he'd previously done a forty three kilometre test in Hawaii. *And I thought I was hungry.*

I sat near the humble forecourt of the petrol station and murdered my food. I was now exhausted and I felt I'd had enough riding done for the day. Still, I decided to try to get to Schull and felt blessed when I learned that it was only 8 kilometres away.

Feeling burpish and a little bloated, I walked my bike through Ballydehob's main street, past pensionable pubs and up to where the road forks. There, the life-size statue of the village's other world beater – wrestling champion Danno Mahony – is found.

The plaque below the figure reads *'Danno- All-in World Wrestling Champion 1935-1936'*, and it's easy to be fooled. Unfortunately wrestling in America after the 1920s was about as real as Greek tax returns and this handsome, barrel-chested giant was brought into the wrestling ranks to garner a following from the Irish immigrant communities. Wrestling bouts before the late 1920s were real but they sometimes lasted for hours and tended to bore the audiences. So, they were shortened and scripts were written. By the 1930s promoters employed the concept of 'kayfabe' – portraying things to be real when they are not – so in many ways Danno was the precursor to the likes of modern day 'champions' like Sheamus O'Shaughnessy of WWE.

It still felt like Danno was a real champion and the bronze statue does well to convince us, but I wasn't inclined to sit around and admire him any longer. I needed a shower.

◊

Schull or 'Scoil' in Gaelic, means 'School' in English and this happy village is also named after a sixth century monastic school. No trace of it remains, though I was pleased to see that plenty of drinkers were spilling out of the pubs and the early evening sun, which had now appeared, was busy warming the road.

In town I followed the first sign directing me to a B&B and when I got near the house, I felt anxious that all of Schull's accommodation would be taken up by visitors. After I'd crunched my way up a gravelly driveway, a woman of about fifty met me at her front door.

'Hi, I'm looking for a room. Do you have one?'

The lady stared at me in what looked to be astonishment. I felt that maybe she'd never seen a cyclist before. There was a long empty silence but eventually she spoke.

'I have, but you'd be better off going to another place down here', she said, pointing to her right.

Slightly taken aback, but being in such a vulnerable position, I had no choice but to follow her direction. I wondered if I'd done something to upset her (it was not beyond the bounds of possibility), but I couldn't think of anything. I was led to Cairn House B&B which was luckily fairly close, but this was not the welcome I expected down in West Cork.

Tony, a tall man not yet sixty answered the door of this B&B and received me with a wholly different attitude. He immediately clocked my bike and told me that his whole family did triathlons.

Empathy, I thought.

'How much?' asked Tony.

'Shouldn't I be asking you that?' I said.

'No, how much did you pay for the bike? '

'Oh...Eh, it wasn't cheap', I said, not willing to divulge this information to a complete stranger.

'I know', he said before throwing his eyes to heaven as if to say that he was broke from buying bikes.

'Let me put it out in the garage. It'll be safe there. The room is forty euro. Is that okay?'

'Fine', I said, with relief.

I was led to a small but cosy and clean single room where I felt a general feeling of safety and warmth. In many ways, handing my bike over to a complete stranger who was anxious to know its value would be seen as an ill-advised thing to do, but I was totally at ease with it. There was no question of trust being an issue. Tony was too much of a family man it seemed. He certainly didn't have the look of a thief. In any case, I knew where he lived.

After a hot soapy shower, I almost crawled on to the bed and let my legs get used to not moving. At times like this I wished I was good at napping but I just can't really do it. Instead, I reached for my phone and learned that Bradley Wiggins was still leading the Tour de France with fellow Sky rider Froome second overall. I read an interview where Froome claimed that he could win the Tour but wouldn't because it was his job to help his teammate Wiggins win. I felt he was as good, if not better than Wiggins, but I couldn't decide if his loyalty was just that, or if he was being a bit naïve. For me Froome was the best rider in the race. *Life is unpredictable*, I thought and I reasoned that he may never get another chance to win the Tour. Next year Spanish champion Contador would be back and it would be harder. I really wanted the best rider to win and if Froome was the best rider, all the better for my little wager on him.

After I felt satisfied that I was reconnected to the world, I looked at my bike computer and saw that I had ridden 129 kilometres and had burned over 4000 calories (the pit-stop at Ballydehob annulling most gains from the calorie stat). Though there were no major climbs of the day, the route was 'rolling' and it certainly felt like I had ridden more. In all, it was good to have my first day's ride behind me and to finally be doing my own little tour.

Later I ventured out around the village and harbour. It looked like the rocks were sown into the surrounding land, like a tapestry of itself and the evening sun gave a light that seemed to reassure me that it was still summer. I ate wild Atlantic salmon in Hackett's bar and as many local earthy potatoes as I could get into me. I was filled too with the satisfaction of knowing that I'd done a good day's work.

My legs felt light as they carried me around the harbour for another stroll after dinner. I watched silent men in small rowing boats taking fishing rods out towards the open sea. There was a busy calmness around Schull.

For a while I sat by the pier pondering the concept of loyalty and wondered what I would do if I was Chris Froome riding the Tour. Stephen Roche had been in a similar situation in 1987 at the Giro D'Italia. Rather than stay loyal to his team leader Roberto Visentini, Roche knew he had the beating of him and duly attacked him. He won the race. Injury the following year meant that Roche was never the same rider after that and he never won another Grand Tour after 87'. So Roche's decision to ignore loyalty and indeed team orders had paid off. I wondered why Froome was remaining so loyal to Wiggins. *Did he lack imagination or ambition? Was this the 'lethargy of custom'? Have I ever let loyalty get in the way of ambition in my life?*

After a final mosey in the half-light of the south, the seagulls' squawks seemed to bid me goodnight, so I took it as advice and retired soon after. My pillow received my head like a long lost friend. I was done for the day but before I entered dreamland, I saw that rain would again be an early companion the following day. *What are you doing?*

CHAPTER 2

'The radio makes hideous sounds'
                                                    Bob Dylan

Next morning I peeled myself slowly off the warm bed. A little part of me felt like a disinterested schoolboy – even more so when I looked out the window and saw what I had feared. A rat-grey drizzle hung in the air like fog. I looked north towards Mount Gabriel but could see only the gloom. It was all supposed to clear by midday so I decided to have a lazy morning.

Apron and sandal wearing Tony produced a fine cooked breakfast with Clonakilty black and white pudding and as much soda bread as I could eat. I packed up on carbs and waited.

I wasn't the only guest. Some German adults were there too, to learn English and water-ski. West Cork is a popular spot with Germans; many own holiday homes in the area. I confessed to Tony that his B&B wasn't the first one I'd visited in Schull. I told him about the woman who sent me away. He wasn't surprised. He reminded me that I was a lone traveller and that some B&B owners could get more money from receiving couples if they had double rooms. This made sense, but only if they were guaranteed to get other customers. By taking lone cyclists and putting them in a double room, the owners were hedging their bets. By refusing them, they were taking on the risk of not filling the room at all. This would prove to be an annoying fact later in my trip, but for now I was more than happy with Tony's hospitality.

In Ireland you can expect to pay anything from thirty to fifty euro for a B&B. Couples usually pay sixty to ninety. This isn't bad, especially considering the breakfasts are huge and almost replace lunch. But you often get more than just bed and breakfast. I tried to keep Tony talking for a while, as much as to delay my wet departure than for conversation. He obliged and we talked about books. In fact, Tony brought up James Joyce. Sheepishly, he admitted that though he had tried several times, he found it difficult to get into Ulysses.

'Nobody can really get into it, Tone', I said, understanding his pain.
I know this pain.
'It's almost impossible really, very eh.... long', I ventured.
'I think so', said Tony.
I've tried too. God knows I've tried... once.

I could feel his relief now, but I wasn't fully convinced that he'd come to terms with it.

'Of course I've read the other ones', Tony confirmed in what was clearly an effort not to appear to be a total dunce.

'Of course', I said.

There are other ones?

'Ah yeah, the other ones... Yep, those other ones', I squeaked.

After a long pause, possibly even an awkward silence, Tony changed the subject. I learned that he was an ex-Garda, so I felt I was right about him having a face I could trust. But I did have visions of him in his cop car musing over Joyce by the harbour while scoffing doughnuts. This unsettled me somewhat.

After a shower, my bike was delivered by the man himself to the front of the house. He even had a dry bag draped over the saddle. *Nice touch but clearly this is a hint. It's time to move on.*

I stood in the porch waiting. It was now past eleven and there was still no let-up in the drizzle. Felix, a young German man joined me and asked me about my bike trip. I told him what I was doing and where I was going. His wide eyes suggested he was impressed, but he just nodded quietly. I asked him if he rode a bike. He nodded again. He just kept looking at me, then at the drizzle and after a few more nods, the situation became clumsy. I couldn't decide if it was his lack of English or his lack of experience in human interaction that was preventing Felix from having a *two-way* conversation. Either way, the uncomfortable silences went on until eventually his parents came and took him away. They probably feared this 'chatting' would in some way be stressful for him, which is certainly something that I would have related to.

Anyway, this was my cue to leave too. Tony had housework (and possibly some thinking) to do, so I decided to get a strong coffee in Casa Diego – a neat little Spanish restaurant on Schull's main street – before I hit the road proper.

'Keep in touch… and good luck with your trip'.

I'm not sure if Tony genuinely wanted me to write to him or if he said that as a sort of automatic, almost ceremonial remark to parting guests. We'd hardly become bosom buddies. Call it intuition, but I also felt that the chances of us having discussions about Ulysses any time soon were quite slim. Still, it was all well received.

After my midday coffee I was cycling and heading west again, this time in the direction of Goleen. The rugged rock in the land was a charming distraction from the wet on this road. The greyness against the deep green fields was actually beginning to seem satisfying. As well as creeks and inlets, the area around Schull is dotted with many old ruined castles. These once belonged to the O'Mahony clan, who incidentally, made a generous contribution to Hugh O'Neill's collection of cock-ups back at that battle of Kinsale.

Pretty soon Lowerton arrived on my horizon. This miniscule village exhibits art on the roadside and has a number of wonderful tin sculptures of dancers and musicians made by local artists. A dancing platform has been built for the art works and all of this commemorates the old tradition in this area of dancing at the crossroads. Indeed this was a popular pastime all over Ireland. It was where young people met on long summer evenings to dance and maybe find partners or sweethearts – sort of outdoor perving.

The first Irish Head of Government, Eamon De Valera, once set out his vision of an ideal Ireland. It was to be an island of 'comely maidens dancing at the crossroads', a famous (though misquoted) line from his backward looking St. Patrick's Day speech of 1947. De Valera was the head honcho of the country for a long time, but as I've already mentioned, until the 1990s the Church was really in charge and De Valera bowed to the Church as much as any. In 1935 the controversial 'Dance Hall Act' was passed which banned informal country dances – including crossroad dances. De Valera's government actually brought in this controversial act. Therefore far from 'devoting their leisure to things of the spirit,' like dancing, which De Valera seemed to encourage, he actually allowed these dances to be banned. That's really the charm and frustration of the Irish psyche summed up – calling for something, yet banning it at the same time. Anyway the Church, fearing 'immoral behaviour' (too much perving) set up their own parochial hall dances, where dancing the foxtrot to modern music was allowed – much to the dismay of country folk.

I left Lowerton's little shrine to a forgotten Ireland and rode on. Goleen was close and the half-hearted spray from the road gradually disappeared the further I rode. I took a left at Toormore and after a menu of wildflowers, splashes of yellow gorse and a sprinkling of colourful cottages I was soon skipping through Goleen village.

I was now deep into the Mizen peninsula but my destination for the morning was Mizen Head. I opted to bypass Crookhaven and before long I was climbing, passing the golden sands of Barleycove beach. The sun, as if cued by my arrival, came out to pour its light all over the land. I was on the window-sill of Ireland now, above the vast North Atlantic and had a tall view of the sand and surf below. As I approached the Head, I sat up on the bike, looked far out to sea and felt its loneliness. This was the first or last sight of Europe for many a ship's passenger in years gone by. Off to the east, though I couldn't see it, is Fastnet Rock and lighthouse – 'Ireland's teardrop', ever reminding us of the nation's emigrant past.

◊

Mizen Head is commonly referred to as the most southerly point of Ireland but Brow Head, which is next to it, is a few feet further south. It was at Brow Head where Sgr. Guglielmo Marconi erected a telegraphic station (transferring if from Fastnet rock) with the aim of contacting passing ships. Marconi is generally credited with inventing wireless telegraphy, or if you prefer – the radio. Here (as well as other parts of Ireland and Britain) is where he experimented with his inventions and where he paved the way for communication as we know it today. He lived for a time at Marconi House in Crookhaven in the early 1900s.

The seven hundred Titanic survivors of 1912 were particularly indebted to

Marconi because it was his equipment and indeed his employees who radioed for help to the *RMS Carpathia* after the iceberg was struck. Marconi himself could have been a passenger on *Titanic* (he was offered free passage), but instead chose to take the *Lusitania* which left a couple of days earlier. This wasn't his only narrow escape from maritime disaster however. Three years later he sailed again on *Lusitania* – its last successful voyage before it was torpedoed off Kinsale. Later in life Marconi became a fascist and Benito Mousollini, who made him Commander of the Italian Navy, was actually best man at his wedding.

Questionable past aside, the Marconi Company has evolved into what we know today as BAE systems and Ericsson. It did form part of the BBC and General Electric at one point too, so it's easy to see the huge effect that the Nobel Physics Laureate has had on connecting the world. Brow Head seemed fairly wild when I looked over; no sign of any station remains today.

I'm not sure that Bradley Wiggins was aware of Marconi a few days earlier but he might have been aware that if it wasn't for radio, Chris Froome may well have taken his leader's yellow jersey at the Tour de France. When Froome attacked on the road to Toussiere, he was immediately told to 'slow' over the team's radio. Initially, he ignored the command. Later his explanation was that he thought he heard the word 'go' in his earpiece instead of 'slow' and that's why he continued to ride and drop Wiggins. Many didn't buy that though. Lots of fans and commentators concluded that Froome wanted to show how good he was even if it meant attacking his own team leader and that he was in fact stronger than Wiggins in the mountains. Eventually he did slow and waited for Wiggins and in that decision his chance of winning the Tour for himself all but disappeared. It's strange to think that a piece of technology as simple and as old as radio, may have decided the outcome of the Tour de France in 2012.

In 1985, Briton Robert Millar probably wished radios were in use then too. He was the victim of the race that has become known as 'The Stolen Vuelta'. While leading the Tour of Spain (*Vuelta á España*), Millar was in a lead group in the mountains on one of the final days. He punctured. When he returned to the group, his Spanish speaking rivals began congratulating him for his inevitable race win. Millar relaxed. What they didn't tell him however was the fact that Pedro Delgado had attacked and this attack allowed him to gain seven minutes on Millar, causing Millar to lose the race by seconds. This was really underhand tactics and it prevented Millar from being the first ever British Grand Tour victor. Had Millar been informed by radio (which was not used then) of Delgado's attack, he'd have won the race.

Back in the present, I had arrived at the bottom of Ireland. I'd never been to Mizen before and I was really tempted to tour the visitors' centre. The lighthouse and keepers' quarters are situated on 'The Mizen' – a tiny island connected to the mainland by a narrow footbridge which seems to hang above the sea. There, as well as the maritime attractions, tourists are kept entertained by the kittiwakes, choughs and gannets, as well as an occasional humpback whale and dolphin.

'I'm not going down there,' said the woman to her partner.

'No way, with these shoes?'

'Ah come on, you'll be grand. I want to see the lighthouse.'
'Yeah – me, me, me... No chance. Are ya mad? I could trip in these heels. Have you seen the drop?'

The famous 99 steps that lead to 'the Mizen' and the narrow footbridge turned me off too. I figured if it was difficult for the woman to get down in heels, it would have been just as much an ordeal getting down in cycling shoes. There was also the fact that I'd be shitting myself due to the likely onset of vertigo or some such disorder when on the footbridge. Time was ticking again and I wanted to reach the Beara Peninsula by the end of the day. It was already lunchtime. There was nothing to do but leave the quarrelling couple, top up my water bottles in the café and get out of there before the dizziness set in...

Mizen Head (in County Cork) to Malin Head (in County Donegal) is respectively, Ireland's Land's End to John O'Groats. I had a vague plan to reach the country's four most extreme points on my tour. Already I had one ticked off and I thought I might get to the most westerly and easterly points as well as to Malin in the north. I was very aware that many had left this point heading for Malin with the daunting challenge of cycling the length of the country ahead of them. I didn't feel very connected to this however. True, the whole of Ireland was in front of me and my aim was to cycle to the top by the west coast and come down again near the East coast, but this was never about me doing some kind of extreme sporting challenge. It was always more about being a tourist who happens to be touring on a bicycle.

As the crow flies, the distance from Mizen to Malin is 466km but most people who attempt to cycle it, run it, or walk it, obviously tend to take the road distance which can be from 555km upwards – depending on the route. The record time done by bike is 19 hours and 3 minutes. That was set back in 1993. Today we live in a world of 'ultra' this and 'extreme' that and to be honest, while I tip my cap to some of the achievements of long distance athletes nowadays, I can't help but think (like the old lady I'd met in Union Hall) that there's a little bit of madness running through them. I wasn't to know it then, but three weeks after I pushed out of Mizen, an Irishman named Ricky Geoghegan cycled in, having ridden from Malin non-stop. But then he turned his bike around and rode back! That's 1244 kilometres in 2 days, 7 hours and 37 minutes. Nuts...

Now I knew I couldn't do that because I would get all the way to Limerick or somewhere and then convince myself that I'd left the oven on, which to be fair, really would be awkward.

Anyway amateurs or enthusiasts are not the only ones to take on these kinds of eccentric feats. Nor is this sort of thing a new phenomenon.

In 1965, five time Tour de France winner Jacques Anquetil decided to attempt 'the impossible'. He wanted to win the nine day Dauphiné stage race which runs through the Alps. He then wanted to follow that up by winning the one-day Bordeaux-Paris race, a 560 kilometre non-stop classic which started at midnight and finished next afternoon. The only problem was that the Dauphiné finished at 5pm in Avignon and Bordeaux-Paris started seven hours later in Bordeaux. Both races were essentially on the same day.

After being offered the use of a jet to take him to Bordeaux by an 'anonymous' person (President Charles de Gaulle), Anquetil took on the challenge. He duly won the Dauphiné stage race, ate some food, had a massage, flew to Bordeaux, hung around his hotel for a while (without sleeping) and then started the longest one day race in the world at midnight. He won that too. It was insane. At several points during the race he was close to cracking. In fact he could barely stay awake on the bike and he even 'abandoned' at one stage. Only when his manager shouted at him and called him a 'girl' did he rally, re-join the race and eventually win.

All of this was good to know. It sort of reassured me that what I was doing, while unusual, certainly wasn't mad.

◊

Coming out of Mizen I took a left and chanced the mountain and coast road heading for Durrus. I wasn't really sure where I was going, but knew it was in the right direction. This was my first real mountain climb and I cursed myself at one point for not taking the easier route – the gradient being nearly 20% in some parts.

This narrow road twisted and coiled up like henna on the skin of the land. The sun tanned all that was under it, but in-land, in the country's torso, cloud shadows were unwanted layers. My sweat was soon rewarded with a magical view of Dunmanus Bay. In fact, I could see right over beyond Sheep's Head Peninsula to the Caha Mountains where there too, the noise of the world was barred.

Ten kilometres of fast descending soon followed and I skirted Dunmanus Bay all the way to the village of Durrus. By now I was hungry. I had ridden over fifty kilometres since leaving Schull. *Where better to eat the world-famous Durrus cheese than in Durrus?* It was time for lunch.

A little drained from the climbing, I scanned the windows of the few restaurants for menus. One jumped at me and I saw that a plate of this local Durrus and Gubeen cheese was priced at a cheeky €20. *Surely cheese that's produced locally should be inexpensive*, I thought. This clearly wasn't value, an example of greed from merchants who as Yeats put it, 'fumble in a greasy till and add the half pence to the pence'. After a little further exploring, I found the perfect spot; an ordinary pub at the edge of the village was serving homemade soup and a sandwich for a fiver. I wandered in.

This was a family run place; the man and woman behind the counter had the tired expressions of a couple who'd endured either a long weekend or a long marriage, but they were kept busy by the scattering of middle-aged afternoon drinkers. One of these drinkers, whose name I learned was Donal, was passionately explaining to anyone who'd listen, that a neighbour of his had most definitely, sometime in the past, invented the hole.

'I'm not codding you now. He's an inventor alright and that's what he invented – the hole.'

This, I'm sure you'll agree, was a rather remarkable claim. Not even the bronze-age folk who lived around Durrus and who left behind standing stones and ring forts would probably have chanced the claim that they invented the hole. After scanning the face of the barman who caught me and threw his eyes to the ceiling, I concluded that Donal's claim was born out of the same reasoning that had him most likely believe that it was still yesterday. Certainly some level of catching up needed to be done in his world. For a while he shakily held court at the bar – if not his pint – and when it spilled onto his lap, the barman suggested, not that he go home, but that maybe he should replace it with a coffee (a hot coffee too no doubt). The whole bar concurred. It seemed nobody felt that going home was a viable option for Donal.

One less confused customer who nursed a pint, on seeing my attire, informed me that cycling fans had 'gone mad' in France at the Tour by throwing tacks on the road. This was a story that I'd missed. He handed me the paper and I skimmed through the article.

'My god, they're turning into football hooligans now are they? They'll kill someone yet. A rider could fly off a mountain or something if they punctured', he complained.

He was right and it was true. The saboteurs had indeed placed tacks on the road in an effort to cause punctures and disrupt the race and I shared his concern. There have been protests by farmers and various groups in the past, where they blocked roads in an effort to have their issues acknowledged. In fact, in Tour history, this was almost a tradition, but it seemed very strange that someone would try to sabotage the race like this for no apparent reason.

As I ate my thick soup and brown bread I considered the situation. *Why would people do that? Could it be an effort to stop riders who were from outside continental Europe, the home of cycling, from winning the race?* It happened before with Robert Millar in the 'Stolen Vuelta' and when Stephen Roche attacked his Italian teammate Vissentini in the 87' Giro D'Italia, the Tifosi (Italian fans), spat rice and wine at him and tried to punch him off his bike. For me, the *'Cosa Nostra'* of European cycling had spread. I suspected that this was an attempt to prevent another Anglophone from winning the race. But in the same way hooligans don't represent real football fans, these saboteurs were not representing anyone.

I ordered a coffee of my own and took in the room. There was a quiet melancholic air to the place, interrupted occasionally by a humorous comment that would raise a chuckle or two, but the Monday afternoon silence was uneasy. Before long, I left Donal and his mates and indeed the Mizen Peninsula and I rode off towards Bantry, pondering the peculiar air of invention that seemed to hang in its hills.

◊

The clouds above had fused by now, sucking out sunlight and replacing it with a quasi-half-light. Blackthorns on the roadside were coated in a drying brown muck, splashed-on during the weekend's rain, but I felt good again and was glad to be clocking the ten kilometres to Bantry. I bridged to the end of Bantry Bay, skirted the bay by Whiddy Island and was soon in town.

Like Kinsale, Bantry Bay was the scene of another Christmas-time disaster for Irish republicanism. Almost two hundred years after O'Neill's loss, Theobald Wolfe Tone (this time using the French as allies) had arrived from Brest in one of around forty ships to take on the English Crown. Storms however caused some of the fleet to drift out to sea and even wrecked a few vessels. This ultimately led to the abandonment of the attack. Later when Tone was captured by the British, he asked to be shot but was sentenced to hang. He enjoyed no luck; even his own death was a disaster. He actually died slowly and painfully after cutting his own throat and it lasted a week.

I arrived at Tone's statue in Bantry's town square and scanned it, but he's not the only Irishman commemorated in sculpture in this square. I imagine Tone wished that his French navy colleagues had had the maritime skills of the second man – Saint Brendan-the-Navigator. His statue towers above its admirers and is a memorable piece of sculpture.

So who was this Saint Brendan dude anyway? Well it's possible that Tone and his French sailors prayed to him before embarking on their journey to Bantry in 1796, because St. Brendan is the patron saint of sailors. Back in the 6th century he was the Christopher Columbus of exploration, the JK Rowling of storytelling and when it came to holiness, he had the X-factor.

He was most famous however for his seven year voyage to the 'Land of Promise'. The story of this voyage was later written up and became a popular Christian text all over Europe. It was fantastical but much loved. Indeed many believe that Brendan may have sailed to Newfoundland, thereby becoming the first to actually discover America. In fact Christopher Columbus' map included an island in the middle of the Atlantic called St. Brendan's Isle and he is supposed to have said, before he left to 'discover' the new world, that he was off to seek the promised land of St. Brendan.

I jumped off my bike for all of three minutes in Bantry and took a breath by this sculpture. I wasn't used to carrying a rucksack and though it wasn't very heavy it was starting to test the strength in my back.

Looking at Brendan's statue, I wondered why Bantry had a sculpture of him because Brendan was from neighbouring County Kerry. But the shy Anglican Church across the road peeped into view and I noticed it was called the Church of Saint Brendan the Navigator; I assumed this was the reason. There are churches dedicated to St. Brendan all over the world in fact, including one very old one in the Sicilian town of Brontë – 'Chiesa di San Blandano'. I guess this demonstrates just how popular he was, but the thought of Brendan's achievements soon put my slightly annoying sore back in perspective when I got back on the road. Seven years sailing was quite a feat. Two weeks biking, by comparison, is not.

By now I had re-joined the N71 and would take it around the base of Bantry Bay to the village of Glengariff. For some reason Glengariff unsettled me. I'd been there before and it's always felt an unruly sort of place. I pushed on, but this time I decided to have company on the road, so I took out Bob Dylan. Listening to music when cycling is something I rarely do, but on busier roads it can be a good distraction from the constant drone of traffic, especially if you have a hard shoulder to lean on. On this road I did and after a couple of tracks I was in my own world of harmonicas, guitars and broken yellow lines.

◊

Glengarriff's long main street led me up to a pub at its far end. Inside, the wooden bar was empty save for another Donal type at the counter. Donal-the-second fingered his whiskey tumbler impatiently and on seeing me, decided to regale me with tales of how he was once a champion bike racer. Maybe he was, but something told me that had I arrived wearing a space suit, he'd have told me about the times he went fishing with Neil Armstrong. It seemed that this Donal was torn between the reality of his free time and the pressures of his imagination. I was tired from riding and I didn't feel like listening, so I politely wished him well before taking my tea outside to watch tourists.

One of Glengariff's attractions is Garinish Island, a beautiful island of Italian gardens whose design offer a real contrast to the rugged and raw land and seascape encircling it. This is the draw for the tourists. The village is also situated at the base of the Beara Peninsula, my destination for the day. I figured I'd get to Castletown Beare without much trouble but Allihies – a place that I'd hoped I'd get to – would have to wait until the next day. After my tea, I went back into the bar to pay. By now Donal II, with eyes closed and his head tilted back, was passionately mouthing a mournful ballad. The barman here gave me *the look*, and like the Durrus barman, I threw my eyes up to the ceiling; I knew the routine by now.

Sixteen slow kilometres under the watchful eye of the Sugarloaf Mountain, and with a bit more Bob in my ear, eventually brought me to the little parish of Adrigole. I was ravenous by the time I arrived, but Peg's Shop saved me. I stopped and did another assault on the biscuit shelves. The lonely bench at the shop's front became my dining table and I sat listening to the silence of the mountains in between the odd passing car. I was now next to the road that leads up to that favourite Irish cycling climb – the Healy Pass.

I just cannot think of this climb without pondering the legendary Irish cyclist known as 'Iron Man' Mick Murphy. Murphy was an impoverished farm labourer who took to cycling in the 1950s when he felt it could somehow give him a better life. His race tactics were awful and he was very much an individual who didn't rely on a team. He had a fondness for reading which led him to learn about weight training and diet. He ate raw food, drank cow's blood, trained at night (mostly after a day's labouring) and he even did circus tricks to supplement his income. While training for the 1958 Rás Tailteann (Rás), he is said to have eaten his Christmas dinner out of his pocket at the top of the Healy Pass.

The pass itself cuts through the Caha Mountain range. It rises to about 1200 feet only but provides superb views of counties Cork and Kerry. Murphy's hard

A Cyling Fan's Ride Around Ireland   23

work and discipline on Christmas day did pay off in the end as he won the Rás the following summer by nearly five minutes.

As I sat eating, I felt content with how my day had gone and was relieved that I wasn't going up the Healy Pass this trip. My body was taking a while to adjust to all the hills but I was glad the drizzle had cleared and stayed away. By now I just wanted to get to a B&B. There wasn't much else to Adrigole apart from Peg's shop, or so I thought. It was therefore very surprising to learn later that here is where the idea to ban chlorofluorocarbon (CFCs) globally was born.

English Scientist Sir James Lovelock set up an atmospheric pollution monitoring station, the first one in a worldwide network, near his holiday home in Adrigole. He had locals record data when he wasn't there but the information garnered ultimately led to a better understanding of the ozone and pollution, which in turn led to a ban on CFCs. *Every bend on the roads of Ireland seems to have a story.*

◊

The road that skirts the northern shores of Bantry Bay was flanked by little streams where water had run off the mountains. I pushed on tired pedals and wanted Castletown to appear. I passed Hungry Hill, the highest mountain of the Caha range. It gives its name to Daphne Du Maurier's novel which tells the story of the copper barons of the 19th century who lived in the area. In the light, Hungry Hill looked grey and angry. It stood hardbacked endlessly watching the soft Sugar Loaf at its side.

Luckily Castletown Beare wasn't too far. It was quiet when I arrived so I took a spin around, keeping an eye out for B&B signs. I spotted a sign for a hostel. Though B&Bs or Guest Houses were (at this stage) my preferred accommodation, I decided to have a look anyway. A narrow hill led me up to the local convent which was now – at least in part – a tourist hostel. As I made my way to the reception, I couldn't help but imagine that a brace of nuns were going to appear and drag me off to do some kind of laundry work in exchange for a bed. I was therefore relieved to find the reception empty. I waited. Before long, that uneasy feeling I'd had about Glengarriff resurfaced and I was out of there in a heartbeat, thanking God that no nuns had in fact appeared.

Back in the town square a local woman directed me up another hill to a B&B. Harbour view B&B lived up to its name, at least at the front of the house, but when Michael, my big bellied friendly host showed me to my room, I had a very close and interesting view of a septic tank and coal bunker. This didn't bother me in the slightest. The house and room were just what I needed and after a bath I lay still for an hour staring at the ceiling until it was time to eat.

My legs were like rubber crutches when I eventually got up and I accepted Michael's offer to use the family PC. I had a quick look to check the day's Tour de France results before heading out for dinner. Slovakian Peter Sagan now looked sure to win the green jersey in Paris the following weekend. In doing so he would cash in on a bet he had made with his team manager. Before the Tour,

Sagan asked if he could have a car if he won the green jersey and his manager (not expecting it to happen) offered him a Porsche as an incentive. Things were looking good for the young rider who by now had come to be known as 'The Tourminator'.

I wobbled down the hill soon after, ignoring at first the eerily quiet streets of Castletown. It was now after 8pm. Breen's Lobster Bar looked enticing so I went straight to it and ordered the hake. I was the only customer, but the food was great. I lounged around for a while watching the fishing vessels in the port. Castletown Beare or Bearehaven is one of Ireland's five major fishing ports but there were no fishermen to be seen. In fact there were no people to be seen – anywhere. I reasoned that it was Monday night and that it wasn't really a 'going-out' night, but something very strange was going on. Quite honestly, there were absolutely no people whatsoever on the streets.

I decided to investigate and took a walk around. As soon as I left, the woman from Breen's – obviously deciding to cut her losses – shut up shop. This was weird. This was the main town of the Beara Peninsula, a major West Cork hub and one of Ireland's big fishing ports and there wasn't even a shadow of a man or woman to be seen. I wandered down to the famous 'MacCarthy's Bar' – of travel writer and comic Pete MacCarthy fame – but there was nobody there either. I now felt like I was in *Shaun of the Dead* or some kind of hidden-camera spoof show where everyone was hiding, just to freak me out. I walked on. The shops were all shut and the other pubs, though open, were furnished with leaning bar-staff and the odd sorry soul on a barstool, but mostly only ghosts lingered. It dawned on me that this was the result of emigration. The country was experiencing this again for the first time since the 1980s. But reading news reports and seeing it in front of you are very different experiences. It was all a bit unsettling.

After more wandering I was actually hungry again. I decided to carb-up in the chip shop. Needless to say, I was the only customer but as I was waiting, a young woman came in. I felt that some human interaction wouldn't go astray, so I asked her if it was always this quiet in Castletown.

'Oh I'm not from here', she said. 'But yeah it is kinda quiet alright,' she agreed.

'So where are you from?' I asked, detecting a not too dissimilar accent from the local one.

'County Limerick', she replied.

'Oh. I have cousins in County Limerick,' I said, holding fast to all that I could really say about the place.

The girl's eyes seemed to narrow. She looked at me with contempt, like I was some kind of naïve American paddy-whacker tourist who believed and expected that everyone knew everyone else in Ireland and that if people were from the same county, they were sure to be cousins or neighbours.

'From Adare' I ventured, clinging to the hope that somehow my stupidity wouldn't be in vain. And it wasn't.

'Oh my god, I'm from Adare', she excitedly revealed.

Adare is a tiny village in county Limerick and everyone really does know everyone else there.

Our roles however had now dramatically reversed. She was the American, announcing the coincidence in a high-pitched screech that was coated in 'OMGs' and 'likes', while I held the information she wanted.

'So, what are their names?' she asked expectantly.

'Eh......' was my reply.

'Eh'.

For some reason, my mind, just when I needed it most, went totally and completely blank.

'Eh......'

She now looked at me like I really was stupid. In an effort to stall, I decided to blow my nose, hoping that somehow the information would somehow arrive.

'Eh....'

'Yeah they're from Adare', I said again, pretending now not to have heard her question. Luckily by the time it was asked again, the pause button was released from my frozen brain and the answer came out.

Of course she knew my cousins and she spent the next few minutes filling me in on what they are all doing these days. Ireland really is one of those places where you can be anywhere and meet people who will probably know someone you know. But it's also a place where it's not uncommon to have sixty cousins, thereby increasing the chances of this happening. Maybe the Americans are right after all.

This all reminded me of a time I'd met a friend Berty while cycling through County Clare on my way from Cork to Donegal. His car tyre had just punctured while he was taking a shortcut down a country road. I passed him just as he was getting ready to drive off.

'Berty', I called.

After a confused look, he realised it was me.

'What in the name of god are you doing on a bike, in Clare?'

When I explained, he promptly invited me to his family home near Galway that evening for a party. I was reluctant at first, being wary of my suspicion that booze and biking don't really mix, but when he answered the door a few hours later with an arm outstretched clutching a can of beer, I felt I had no choice but to go with it.

'Can I have a shower first man?'

'You can, after that beer.'

Needless to say the next day was a write-off; I cycled all of ten kilometres to Galway city. But the party was good. These coincidences and chance meetings while travelling in Ireland were becoming a habit.

After our chip filled chat, my bed was calling. I said goodnight to Aoife from Adare. The two days of cycling had taken its toll on me and I feared that any further interaction or engagement that required brain function was sure to end in disaster. I took a last stroll by the empty fishing port. It was now dark and the hill back up to my bed seemed tall like the mountains beyond it.

CHAPTER 3

'Medicine becomes the disease'
                                                                    Virgil

The smell of fried fish and the muffled sound of French accents lured me into the dining room when I woke. Michael had taken my breakfast order the night before and for €2 extra he fed his guests with fresh whiting or mackerel for breakfast. This was a welcomed treat. The prospect of spending two weeks eating fry-ups was really not appealing.

There was a sleepy hum in the room and Michael, a large middle-aged man who looked like he'd be more suited to overalls than aprons, was a fairly efficient host, as able to multitask as anyone. Clearly he'd watched Keith Floyd in the eighties.

Breakfast was joyous. The butter foamed and turned to oil as it melted into the crevices of the fish meat. I added freckles of pepper to its rough skin and got stuck in. It was probably better than last night's dinner. I felt that this really was a holiday now and with that in mind decided to have an easy day on the bike. The thick fog outside was a deciding factor but the air of snooziness, dropping slowly all around really tipped the balance in favour of rest. In all, I was happy with my two days' work. I'd ridden 122 kilometres the previous day bringing my total for the two days to over 250k.

Allihies is a little village that I was attracted to and it wasn't far away. I had passed through it once before but really wanted to learn more about it now. So, I reasoned that I'd have lunch there and maybe even stay the night. It was Tuesday and likely to be quiet but that suited me fine.

'You'll have more coffee?'
'I will', I answered.
'Grand so', said Michael arriving with a pot.
'Where are you off to today?'
'Only as far as Allihies', I said.
'Oh'.
Michael looked puzzled.
'And you're cycling around Ireland?'
'I am.'
'And how long will that take you?'

'About two weeks.'
'And today you're going to Allihies?'
'Today I'm going to Allihies, yes.'
'I see...'
Allihies was only twenty kilometres away so I probably should have explained that I was having a bit of a rest day, but I was too interested in stuffing my face with soda bread. At a rate of 20k per day it would have taken until Christmas to get around the country but I just left the man to his confusion.

Soon I was back in cycling clothes and on the road. The fog was a thick quilt, and the whole of Beara was its king sized bed. Michael warned me that it looked bad but we reasoned that it should clear soon. I could see little beyond forty yards when I was moving. Essentially I was riding through damp and drizzly cloud, which isn't ideal.

At the edge of the town I veered off the main road and followed the signs for the Dereenataggart stone circle. Visiting some Neolithic sites was something I wanted to do on my trip and Beara is as good a place as any to find them.

The narrow road rose gently at first and then more steeply. After a couple of kilometres I found the site and headed for the stones, but the fog made visibility a memory. It was like the world had been rubbed out; I knew the Atlantic was behind me and Beara's mountains were all around, but I saw only grey gloom.

Approaching the stone circle was like walking onto the set of an Enya video. I was half convinced that strange graceful maidens were going to appear from behind each stone, dressed in flowing pale robes and brandishing candles or harps or maybe even riding white unicorns. It was sort of spooky – just the kind of atmosphere you'd want at a stone circle. But there were no maidens or unicorns, only stones.

This site is about 3000 – 5000 years old and is positioned in such a way as to suggest moon worship. From the hilltop it's easy to imagine a crystal moon lighting up the vast sea and the surrounding countryside and it must have had a powerful pull on the simple bronze-age people. It was probably some kind of burial ground too. It certainly felt sacred. I hung around in the murk for a while and tried to imagine life then; no virtual worlds behind a screen, crap TV or admin. *Bliss,* I thought – nothing but a huge lunar light freaking everyone out.

Before I headed for the Ring Fort which was located further up the road, I decided to take a picture. When I took out my phone I became a little troubled. The phone indicated that there were 'Open Wi-Fi Networks' available. How could this be? I was in the middle of a stone circle, by the coast and atop a big hill, or maybe even a mountain; I couldn't really tell. There were no houses or farms that I could see, yet somehow I was being offered contact with cyberspace. Was someone trying to reach out – to tell me something? If I logged on would I be directed to *'Bronze Age Live,'* some kind of chat room of the ancients? It was all very strange and as close as I'd felt to the spirit world for some time. I had read that there was real energy in this place but I wasn't expecting this. Without much delay, I made a discreet and lively exit back to the safety of my bike and the road.

Just a few hundred yards further on, I came to another field and to the site of the Ring Fort. Ring forts are known as 'Rounds' in England but in Ireland they are also commonly called 'Fairy Forts'. There is a strong belief that fairies or folk from the Otherworld still inhabit these forts. They are reckoned to be pre-Christian people so they don't go to heaven, but live instead eternally in this 'Otherworld'. The Forts are thought to be some kind of threshold between our world and theirs. It is also believed in Ireland that you should never disturb a Fairy Fort and there are numerous examples of people who have done and who have suffered misfortune or illness as a result. This is attributed to the retaliation of the fairies. It was with this knowledge that I decided to admire the fort from a distance. In fact, I didn't even get off my bike. I was afraid I might break a twig and send some fairy into a thundering rage that would have me retreat in a panic. I imagined the fairies laughing at me – the peeping Tom stalker guy from between the trees. I noted too that there were many sloppy cowpats lying around – not conducive to a hasty retreat. My well-known risk management skills had to be tapped into. I stayed put.

Other less superstitious people – those who have beards and archaeology degrees – believe that ring forts were some kind of farm or commercial hub from medieval times; they are certainly not as old as stone circles. A few in Ireland have been found near buried pottery believed to be from continental Europe. This indicates that some kind of long distance trading went on. Either way, whether they are access points to the Otherworld or old-school Aldi Supermarkets, I just wasn't going in for a closer look. Instead, I took a picture, using a lot of zoom. Thankfully the Wi-Fi signal had now disappeared and I'd soon follow.

◊

The thin country road led me back towards Castletown Beare before re-joining the main Allihies' road, where I began heading southwest again. I must have climbed to quite a height, as I seemed to be descending on the drops for a long time, but I was soon back on track and in front of me once again was drifting silver fog.

I wanted to make another stop before arriving at Allihies – this time to another sacred type of place – but one from a very different world.

We all know that the bicycle carries out a number of functions: it's a mode of transport; it's used for leisure, for fitness and of course it's the principal equipment for my favourite competitive sport – bike racing; but what about the bike as a means of achieving spiritual enlightenment? Is that possible? Can we cycle our way to Zen?

Dzogchen Beara is a Tibetan Buddhist retreat centre located on the Beara Peninsula. It is under the spiritual direction of Sogyal Rinpoche, the author of *The Tibetan Book of Living and Dying*. As I wasn't in any hurry, I had an idea that I would like to call in, maybe do a meditation class but also try to grab some enlightened person and get them to advise me on whether or not cycling long distances could possibly be a form of meditation. I had an idea that it is, but I lacked any authority on the subject. I needed some kind of validation. Or did I?

I wasn't sure. Do I need anything at all? Shouldn't I just 'be'? Don't I have to be 'non-grasping'? Oh no, this was already getting complicated...

If you ride a bike, you'll know about what a long spin can do for you. Obviously there are the physical benefits, but what about the mental and even spiritual sense of wellbeing? I always feel good after a bike ride. I leave my troubles behind and connect with nature. Sometimes I just focus on my breathing or on the rotation of the pedals. This keeps my mind off the future and the distance I still have to travel, and it can empty the mind of thought. In essence it keeps me in the 'present' – 'I ride my bike, to ride my bike'. This is remarkably similar to what happens in meditation. In his book Rinpoche maintains that 'the method is only the means, not the meditation'. So I figured cycling is as good a means as any. I wasn't planning on doing any chanting while riding, but 'watching the breath' or 'resting the mind lightly on an object... of natural beauty' were two methods I could use on the bike to help meditate.

Contrary to what I once believed, meditation does not have to be done with eyes closed. This, you'll agree, is a fairly welcome fact for the meditating cyclist. In any case, there were enough mountains and sky to concentrate on and breathing is something that we tend to do a lot of. I intuitively felt that there are moments on a bike ride where 'the inner nature of mind' could be realised. That is when you can engage the Buddha state that's supposedly in all of us. A bike rider tends to feel something every so often, when cresting a hill that reveals a beautiful view or even just when passing a cow and mooing to it (which I have been known to do). This may just be called 'joy' and not 'enlightenment' but I was interested to learn more.

Now I'm not exactly holy man, but I figured if I was going to be biking around Ireland for a fortnight, I might as well realise these spiritual benefits as well as all the other ones. Focusing on my breathing was where I would start, but not yet. Firstly, I had to focus on the oncoming traffic which I couldn't see until it was in my face. The fog had gotten thicker, the road narrower and visibility was now reduced to blindfold levels. The idea of achieving the spiritual light was quickly replaced by the need for an *actual* light, as I was pretty sure no motorist could see me in the gloom. I had none, only a reflective arm band, which helped, but it was more of a monk when I needed a Buddha – as it were.

Luckily the traffic wasn't heavy. Those who were on the road managed to respond to the conditions and slowed down but it was a little unnerving at times. I knew I was reasonably close to the Buddhist Centre and that it was on the left side of the road, so I felt pleased to be getting off it soon.

I had a further reason for visiting this Centre. I wanted to learn too about Tibetan Prayer Wheels. The 'Wheel of Dharma' (Dharmachackra) is a symbol of Buddhism and (depending on the number of spokes) represents different laws or stages of life. Also the hub represents discipline; the rim mindfulness. With prayer wheels, each turning of the wheel can be a silent recital of a mantra or prayer. I'd learned that many different wheels could be used for this and reasoned that if I could get a little prayer and stick it to one of my own wheels, then by the time I finished my trip I would have effectively done quite a lot of 'praying'. In fact, I figured I'd be one of the holiest people in Ireland by then. In two weeks I could be riding back to Cork and towards possible sainthood. I imagined myself on a par with St. Brendan, navigating my way round Ireland with my souped up holy wheels churning out prayers of healing at each rotation. I could even start a movement – 'Praystrong', or call it *'On the Road'* with the Beatification Generation. I concluded that this was one of my better ideas (believe it or not) and looked forward to picking up a good mantra. But unfortunately it wasn't to be.

To my confusion, after a few more kilometres, I emerged from the fog on the outskirts of Allihies. I had passed the Buddhist Centre without seeing it or any sign for it; the fog was to blame. This felt like a disaster. I asked a local woman where it was.

'Tis about 7 miles back the road'.

'Bollocks,' I said.

She looked at me with suspicion, no doubt thinking: *he can't be one of them Buddhists if he's swearing.*

I rode on into the village and weighed up my options. I was wet. The fog on the road was dangerously thick and I really didn't feel like doing a twenty kilometre round trip to get laughed at by a Buddhist monk. So I decided to stay in Allihies, find a B&B and spend the day exploring. My Tibetan prayer wheel idea would sadly have to wait.

I went straight to a building where a sign read – 'Hostel'. It looked like it had private rooms so I knocked. There was no answer. I went around to the back door and knocked again. Still there was no answer. I went inside (the door was open); I called out 'hello' – no answer. I waited around for twenty minutes in a strange kitchen that showed few signs of use, occasionally calling out 'hello' with less enthusiasm each time, but there was never an answer. If Castletown Beare was quiet the night before, then this place was just deserted. The B&B on the main street looked like it wouldn't have anywhere to store a bike so I pushed on to the far side of the village.

Up a little hill was another B&B. I came to the door and knocked. Again there was no answer. By now I was getting worried. It was lunchtime, someone would clearly have to provide me with lunch, but where were all the people?

Just as I was about to leave, a speeding car tore down the long driveway and stopped suddenly. A young woman in her early twenties got out.

'Are you looking for Mammy?'

'Eh…Yeah I think so', I said.

Not necessarily my Mammy, but a Mammy, yes. Any Mammy really…

'Wait a minute and I'll call her.'

The driver took out her phone and dialled.

'Mammy it's me. I'm home. The flight was on time. There's a man here.'

'No, not a fella with me, there's a man here who wants to stay, some cyclist or something. Will I give him the front bedroom?'

Things were getting confusing.

'I can come back later', I said.

'Okay, grand' she said. Then she hung up.
'There's nobody staying so you can stay.'
This was a relief. It wasn't looking promising but the 'okay grand' comment was clearly intended for her mother. I was in.
'So you're just off a flight are you?' I asked.
'Yeah, just drove down from Shannon.'
'Where'd you fly in from?'
'Boston. I live there. It's great. I work in a hotel. The tips are brilliant.'
'Oh...that's good', I said, hoping she fully understood that she was now back in Ireland, where bell-hop type tips were not given for showing people to their rooms (especially in B&Bs).
She let me in and gave me a key.
'Don't worry about locking the door, nobody will steal anything'.
This was good to hear, but I wasn't surprised. I figured one of the essential ingredients for a crime to be committed is people (or at least one person) and Allihies seemed to be lacking in this area. I'd been there an hour and saw two, neither of whom seemed cut out for the criminal underworld.

With that she went tearing off again in her car and it seemed like I was left alone in a strange house. I showered and put on my civvies. It felt good to be in long trousers and trainers and within the hour I took the bike back down to the village and went straight to The Copper Mine Museum. This was the only place that showed any sign of life. To my surprise it was busy; there were few available tables in the café there. After a good strong coffee and a large slice of cake I wandered into the museum.

Allihies is a small village, but it has a rich history. Copper mining was started there in 1812 by John Puxley whose family were the inspiration for *Hungry Hill*, the Du Maurier novel that was set on the peninsula. The remains of the engine houses and shafts can be seen all over the area but I really wasn't a mining enthusiast. Actually I'm a bit claustrophobic (as well as acrophobic) and though the museum was well put together, I just wasn't really that interested in seeing photos of people in tight spaces. Indeed Chile is bottom of my list of 'places to see'; I've heard they've had mining issues there...

I decided instead to hop on the bike and discover the rugged coastline a bit more. The fog had lifted a little, not enough to give the full picture of how raw and open the landscape really is, but enough to ride around.

A sign for 'Children of Lir Mythical Site' led me up a narrow treeless road. It's said of Allihies that you can 'see around every corner' and this truly is the case. There are only fields, rocks and cliffs in the area. Trees were as rare as people it seemed.

◊

In Irish mythology the four children of Lir were turned into swans by their jealous spell binding step-mother. They were banished from Ireland and had to spend 900 years in the waters near their homeland, the last 300 of which were spent on the Atlantic. When their time was up, the swans listened out for a bell which was to indicate that Christianity –or at least something – had arrived. When they heard it, they came ashore and are supposed to have landed near Allihies (though of course other sites also claim to be the landing spot). There, a monk (possibly St. Brendan – popular he was) amid rainbows and rising fog from the ocean (I can definitely believe the fog bit), baptized them, but only after they turned back into humans when they touched land. Unfortunately, as soon as they did touch land, they became 900 year old geriatrics, a condition which often brings imminent death. They died instantly – though to be fair, they'd had a good innings, albeit as swans. This site was their landing site and was marked by a large stone. A few coins had been left on the stone, probably by wish makers, so I joined them, left some coppers and wished to God that it wouldn't rain or be foggy for the next 40 days. St. Swithin was really starting to wind me up.

I took another spin on the bike, this time heading inland and wandered wherever the road took me. It was a relief not to have a bag on my back. I felt free. I didn't have to go anywhere or do anything. I was now riding my bike to ride my bike; it was easy. I tried to let go of any frustration about the weather too. There seemed little point in being affected by it. Also, I had sought out quietude. I wanted to be away from the stress of a busy city and now that I was here, it seemed like I was freaked out by the lack of people. Maybe I'd become too used to crowds. I tried to breathe with the land and let things be.

After a while, I found myself back on the coastline by a cliff edge. I sat in the grass and watched the silver sea rising up to clothe and nourish the land. The copper earth crumbled from the rocks and fed the waves in return. Grey headed gulls fished off the cliffs and there were groans from the belly of the ocean. It was all harmony and peace. *Who needs a Tibetan-style retreat?*

Back at The Copper Café I ordered tea and scones. This was my second visit in as many hours but everyone who was there seemed to have been there for the same reason; there was nowhere else to go.

'We're out of scones' said the young man at the counter. 'But I can bake them for you, they'll take twenty minutes.'

'I'm not going anywhere.'

There were all sorts of people in the café, but the noise levels were really muted. In fact, it was ghostly quiet considering the place was now full. I figured out that most people were German but they were not inclined to speak too loudly or even speak at all, (possibly fearing eavesdropping or even happiness). Some were on internet devices too, availing of the free Wi-Fi. That's when I mischievously decided to announce a ban on silence. Not only that but I decided to announce this ban in German. This idea, while initially seeming good, was riddled with problems. Firstly, I can't speak German; I never could. Secondly, I knew instinctively that silence was what I wanted, so why then was I feeling bored by it? Finally, noticing I looked a bit out of sorts, someone broke it. So now there was no longer a need to ban it.

His name was Amit, an older Indian man of silver hair and golden skin who also lived in Germany.

'Yes, it's very quiet in here', he said looking at me, as if reading my mind.

'Hmmm', I nodded as we shared a giggle.

'It's more like a library'.

'You're on holiday?' I asked my new friend.

'Ya. We come every year.'

And so began a conversation on the pros and cons of an Irish vacation. Amit owned a caravan which was located down by the beach. His wife, who spoke little English, was an artist and she fiddled quietly with her phone as we chatted. They seemed happy and somehow they reminded me of what a special place West Cork really is.

Our chat seemed to spur people into conversation and the place became normal again.

'It's the sea', said Amit

'What is?'

'That's why we come... My wife you know, she talks a lot. Always talking, talking, talking.'

His Indian accent was becoming stronger now the more animated he got.

'Always giving instruction: "do this Amit; do that"... Oh my god, I say, woman, what do you want? Make up your mind... Always changing mind and always talking.'

'You know,' he said, 'she even talks when she does the yoga!'

It sounded like Amit needed to get something off his chest. But his wife Kara just sat smiling and fiddling.

'I say woman, how you can talk when you do the yoga?'

'At first I tried everything,' he continued. 'Don't listen. Block the ears, the medicine and even... how you say... the blindfold for the mouth!'

'A gag?'

He laughed.

'But I love her... And she knows that when I take her here, that I love her... Then she stops the talking and I can hear the sea. I can even hear the silence.'

'Wow,' I said.

I felt instinctively that Amit had just imparted some true wisdom to me. From now on, when I want a woman to give it a rest, I'll give her a phone to fiddle with... or something...

◊

By early evening I was back at my B&B. It was painfully dull there, so I decided to clean up my bike a bit and oil the chain. I was mindful that the next day I had a long journey ahead of me. This was my third night in County Cork and it felt again like I wasn't making any real progress. I now had about twelve days to get around the country so I decided I would set off for Dingle in County Kerry next morning. This would be a long ride; I had to prepare.

I returned to the village a while later to have dinner. On my way down, a drift of heavy drizzle docked by the shore and it looked like it was here to stay. I ran to avoid it but by the time I'd gotten to the pub, my trousers were wet through. Inside, warm steam rose from my thighs as I stood near the small fire to dry off. My trousers looked like they'd been slapped onto my legs. It was all a bit shit.

'Jaysus you're soaked' said the barman.

'Where are you staying? I'll run you up in the car and you can change.'

'I'm staying up the hill but I don't have any other trousers – travelling light. Thanks anyway.'

This amused the barman somewhat and I knew I'd have to eat dinner wearing wet clothes. Slowly I took a table and opened the menu.

'I haven't seen fog like that in 40 years', said the woman to the group of walkers at another table.

It seemed I wasn't the only one affected by the weather. By now I just wanted to get back to my room and out of my soggy pants, so I resolved to do no more than eat and head back. There were plenty of people dining in the pub, the makings of a good night out even, but I had other things on my mind.

The steak looked good, so I ordered it and while waiting, I got my phone out to find out what was happening in France at the Tour. It was a rest day, but there's always a story on rest days. Today would be no different. As I scrolled through the headlines, I came across it –the inevitable. My initial reaction was – 'disaster'.

Frank Schleck, a top rider from Luxembourg had returned a positive drug test for Xipamide, a banned diuretic used to help mask other drugs. He was immediately taken out of the race. As a cycling fan we tend to have conflicting emotions when a rider is caught doping. It's good to know that the tests are working and people are getting caught, but the strength of our convictions that what we are seeing isn't make-believe is shattered somewhat too. I believed that Schleck was a clean rider at one point but when Johan Bruyneel (the director-sportif who managed Lance Armstrong through his own make-believe decade) became the Schleck brothers' team Director, I began to have doubts. *Some people's medicine truly is the disease.*

But it took me all of ten seconds to go from feeling disappointment to absolute glee at the news that he was caught. By now I was excited and all thoughts of my wet trousers vanished with my dinner. I could barely look up from my phone, missing my mouth with the fork a few times. But I wanted more. This sort of scandal was feeding me – like a drug. One dose wasn't really enough.

A one-eyed dog gave me half an evil look on the road back to my room when I left. It had finally stopped raining but I didn't care anymore. I wanted sleep and this was when I made the decision to do some doping of my own.

Cleaning my chain wasn't going to be the only 'preparation' for tomorrow's big ride. Back in my room I got my instruments ready. I needed a teaspoon and warm water. Luckily the powdery product was already crushed; it came like that from my supplier. I boiled water in the kettle which was part of the tea making facilities and closed the curtains. There was nobody around to look in of course, but I closed them anyway – just to be safe. After the kettle sweated its way to the click and off it switched, I was ready. I carefully poured the sachet of Lemsip into a cup, topped it up with hot water and stirred. *Perfect.* This would help me sleep and take away a few aches and pains I had in my legs – a recovery product if you will. After all, this was my Tour de France (in Ireland) and I wanted to feel like a cyclist in every way, so if doping was part of the routine, I was doing it. All I had to do now was hope – pray even – that I wouldn't get caught…

After listening to a kid in the house playing the tin-whistle badly while watching a wonky television which seemed like it too wasn't exempt from the fog, I turned over to let the weird dreams begin. I had actually clocked 44 kilometres in all that day, even though I had a non-day in terms of progress, so I was reasonably tired and it didn't take long for the drugs to kick in.

I didn't know it then, but the following day would be my hardest ever on a bicycle.

CHAPTER 4

*'All the world's a stage,
And all the men and women merely players'*
William Shakespeare

I slept badly but I slept. Beara's fog had finally lifted but there were clouds – always clouds. Breakfast was served by the newly returned émigré whose name I gathered was Sheila.
'What kind of breaky would you like?'
'I'll just have some scrambled eggs – maybe beans.'
She looked relieved that I wasn't going for the all-out fry-up, but I was anxious to get out of Allihies and get on the road. I figured the vegetarian option would be easier to cook and to be honest, like most twenty year olds, Sheila didn't seem that bothered.
'So do you not find that the drivers round here are kinda mad? Aren't you worried doing all that cycling?' she asked.
Drama lover, I thought. It seemed she was eager to hear some tale of a close scrape with metal. Or maybe she was justifying her own bad driving by searching for confirmation that everybody else drives badly.
'No', I said. 'Not at all. I've had no trouble with drivers. As long as they can see you they tend not to crash into you.'
'Really?'
She seemed surprised, maybe even disappointed.
After a volcano of blackish scrambled eggs and beans, I paid Sheila the €30 for my stay. I was in no doubt that this would be going straight into her pocket, claimed from her Mother as a 'tip' for getting my breakfast and showing me my room. Either way it was a fair price and after a hot-ish shower, I got ready to go.
'Good luck in America.'
'Thanks, Good luck with your trip.'
I threw my bag on my back, grabbed my bike from the garage and was dropping out of Allihies in no time.
The sea seemed a little grumpy in the summer morning, like it hadn't slept well either. The air was cool and just a little blowy. I skirted the coast road and looked back to see Allihies in the distance when it began to rise. I got a sense of

how isolated the village really is, but I liked Beara a lot and I had the whole north side of the peninsula still to get through.

It was going to be a long day; I knew that much. Dingle was around 160 kilometres away and I was determined to get there. This wasn't my first time doing a hundred mile bike ride, far from it, but it was going to be harder than usual because there were plenty of hills to negotiate. I had the weight of my bag on my back too of course, which I was still only getting used to again. There'd be little easy about the day and the first hills hit me before I'd even warmed up.

So steep are some of the hills on this coast road and so close are they together, that it really is like riding a giant roller coaster. I constantly changed from the big to the small chain-ring and the sweat that formed on the rise was instantly dried when cutting through the cool air on the way down. I could find no rhythm or regular cadence; I just seemed to bounce along the contours of the rocky land avoiding sheep shit for what seemed like hours. It was slow. I wondered what most other people do post-breakfast when they're on holiday. Something told me that it wasn't dodging sheep shite anyway.

Eventually I came to the last and final rise before the road flattened out. There is a well-known climb on this route called 'The Wall'. It's so named because the road does a pretty good impression of an actual wall. It rises to a twisty 25% gradient which admittedly doesn't go on for very long, but murders the hapless cyclist nonetheless. I approached it now from the slightly less steep side, but it was a total killer. When I finally did crest it, I bolted down the other side and cut straight through the middle of a farmyard. This farmyard, not devoid of animals, is rather inconveniently built on the road, which is itself built on a bend. Don't ask. How I wasn't responsible for some kind of road-kill when I cut through I'll never know, but I survived (as did the chickens) and the reward for my climbing was a long descent that was a true gift.

As the wind nudged my back a little, the open sea's turquoise patches began to decorate my view. It was perfect. I skirted loose stone walls for a while. The route meets the Atlantic at Coulagh Bay with the Slieve Miskish Mountains on the right. Trees were still scarce and that gave way to clear views of the peninsula. I picked up a good speed, hammering the pedals for around ten kilometres until I arrived at Eyeries.

This village too has many stories. Its main street is a rainbow. The quiet air and meditating mountains nearby create a mystical quality that hangs around its corners. It's certainly enough to attract all kinds of creative folk. The village has been the setting for a number of films, including *The Purple Taxi*, starring Fred Astaire, whose dodgy Irish accent is enough to make even Tom Cruise cringe. But there's no getting away from the spiritual sense of the place. If mountain yoga doesn't do it for you, then the knowledge that Eyeries is probably the place where Christianity began in Ireland might.

In the same way that some of us scoff at the myth that St. Patrick drove the snakes out of Ireland, people from this area probably scoff at the idea that he brought Christianity to Ireland – the very thing for which he is celebrated. In the third century, three hundred years before St. Patrick arrived, a French

Cleric named Caitighearn had been in Eyeries spreading the news and founding a church. The mythology of Beara holds that 'The Hag of Beara' or 'Cailleach', a muse of both ancient and modern poets, stole a bible from Caitighearn who in turn struck her with his staff and turned her to stone. For me this gives a whole new meaning to the term 'bible bashing' and reveals much about the early Church and attitudes to religion. It's also another example of how fantasy has fused with history causing reality to become blurred, which is what happened with St. Brendan (he's supposed to have camped on a sleeping whale). In any case, the old hag's stone can be found here on the coast road from Eyeries to the next village – Ardgroom. I would have taken this route had it not started raining. As it did, I paused to throw on my rain jacket before taking the shorter more inland route to Ardgroom.

Trees had finally returned to line the road for a time. It was another 10k of flat riding to this village. When I neared it, I stood up on the pedals a few times and tried to look for one of the Ardgroom stone circles. There are many in the area and one site has the tallest standing stone in Europe at 17 ft. But the novelty of being in Enya-style video sets had worn off by now. It would have been good to spot this standing stone but I had no intention of seeking it out. The only stops I had time to make on this day's ride would be purely functional. I was to be more a traveller than a tourist today.

My big day in the saddle would be dwarfed by what was going on at the Tour de France that day. The Tour was having its 'Queen Stage', taking the riders through the Pyrenees and over four of the more famous Tour climbs. Riding mountains in Ireland is nothing like riding the Alps or Pyrenees. A hundred and sixty kilometres in a stage of a professional bike race would not be considered very long either. For me, pedalling at a much softer pace, it was a real challenge.

I skipped on past Ardgroom and into the deep wooded area near Lauragh. I was now finally – after three and a half days of riding – in County Kerry. '*Progress*', I thought, but I too had plenty more climbing to do and it was about to start again.

The first long climb of my day would take me 600 feet up into the Caha Mountains. Just northeast of Lauragh, the road began to rise. I hit a good rhythm and began ascending. I like climbing and love the inevitable reward at the top. Here the Caha Mountains offer great views over the Kenmare River and into the Iveragh Peninsula to the north.

My thoughts turned to the Tour on my way up. The first climb of the day, over *L'Aubisque*, would take the riders ten times higher than the climb I was doing (to almost 6000 feet). My climb went on for 5 kilometres; the Aubisque is 16.4 kilometres long. The gradient of mine was less than the average 7.2% of the Tour climb and I had a cool cloudy temperature of 18°C to deal with as against 32°C in cloudless France. I knew when I crested this mountain that soon after I would be sitting in a café in Kenmare with horizontal legs eating cake. Real cyclists would be starting the climb of the Tourmalet, a longer, steeper and harder climb than the Aubisque. It would be only their second of four major climbs that day. In total they would ride for almost 60 kilometres uphill and race

200 kilometres altogether. Also, these cyclists don't eat cake. It's hardly surprising that some people get caught doping.

I did eventually crest the rocky Caha Mountain and took in the view. It was an expected reward but there was no hanging about. I dropped straight down it again quickly and hugged the edges of the Kenmare River and Cloone Lake heading for town. The showers had stopped, though I was damp from sweat and rain. A long straight road lined with evergreens finally delivered me into town. I was hungry and tired already and I still had 110 kilometres to go.

◊

In the centre of Kenmare I found 'Jam', a local gourmet café. Inside the air carried the smell of coffee and the place was stocked with homemade this and organic that, as well as heartily yapping Kerry women. There were no free tables so I went straight to the loo and changed into fresh cycling clothes. It felt good to be dry. I then grabbed take-out coffee and a generous slice of a pear and almond tart with plenty of cream and took it across the road to an artist's studio, where I got busy eating. Kenmare was alive with tourists and locals and I felt a little envious that I couldn't roam around with them. Time was hanging over me, but at least I could get more cake and I did.

'Can I have another slice of that tart please?' I asked the large lady back in 'Jam'.

'Where's the last slice I gave you?' she asked – as if accusing me of eating it.

'I ate it'.

'God that was quick', she said – eyes all mischief.

By now more eyes were raised and I felt myself receiving a few disappointed looks from customers.

'Annie, pass over another slice of that tart will you?' the woman nodded to her assistant.

'This poor fella here is starving with the hunger.'

Her loud lilting Kerry accent filled the place and even more heads turned to see who the greedy cake enthusiast was.

'That tart's nearly gone and I'm only after making it this morning', she tutted.

'I suppose you'll have more cream as well?'

'I will, please'.

'Of course you will and I'm going to have to whip up more of that too. Sure you'll have everything gone; there won't be a bit left.'

'Sorry.'

'You know', she said, 'a fella came in here once and had three slices of that apple tart there. *Three*, I thought the man was a half disgrace, but you know what he done then? ... Says he, I'll take three more slices to go as well'.

'"What?' says I, 'that's all I have and I only after taking it out of the oven not ten minutes before you came in.'"

I wasn't sure whether to smile or feel her concern. I just stood and kept my face blank in my confusion.

'Says I to him, "you know what you'll do now. Come back to me at five o'clock and I'll have a whole tart baked for you. Is that alright?" "Grand" says he, "you're on..."'

'The sheer greed, I wasn't letting him take away the last few slices.'

'No... Of course not', I agreed.

'He was half-starved too I'd say.'

Finally there was silence and it was with a small pang of guilt that I took hold of the boxed tart and paid the woman. As I did, I couldn't help but reflect on the remarkable ability that only Kerry people seem to have for making the customer feel guilty for giving business to the trader. They are known for their shrewd and colourful business manner in this part of the world. I walked away after both transactions €10 lighter, but crucially feeling almost apologetic for the terrible and greedy intrusion that I had made, not once, but twice into this poor woman's life.

Outside, another shower was busy washing the streets. I ran back across the road and took shelter in an arched doorway. While waiting for it to stop, I got out my phone and took in the news from the Tour. As well as being the Queen Stage, today's stage was also probably the last opportunity that Chris Froome would have to usurp Bradley Wiggins as race leader. I was anxious to find out if he had the courage to do it. For me the question remained, was he a real champion with real desire, or would he stay loyal – a servant? This Tour had all the makings of a Shakespearean drama but it was still unclear as to whether or not it would be a tragedy or a comedy. I was undecided, but then I saw the first headline from *Cyclingnews* which read – 'Frank Schleck will claim he's been poisoned'!

'Comedy' – I concluded; this really was getting quite ridiculous.

Top professional bike riders in a sport that has a drug problem will always be very careful about what they consume. That's why Schleck's excuse was so farcically funny – and predictable. I read on. Yes it was true and it really was pathetic – cycling's equivalent to 'the dog ate it' excuse for not having your homework done. But on reflection, it probably wasn't as funny as one previous Tour winner, Alberto Contador's excuse when caught doping two years earlier.

He claimed that he ate a Spanish steak that came from an animal which was itself doped. Clenbuterol, a drug used for reducing body fat was the offender. His urine was also found to have an abnormal amount of plasticizers in it, indicating that he may have had a blood transfusion, an illegal performance enhancing practice. This didn't deter the Spaniard from clinging to his excuse though. Over the next 18 months the story of 'Steak-gate' unfolded. Contador blamed the meat. The Spanish meat industry was incensed, denying that Spanish farmers illegally treated their livestock with the drug. Then the Spanish President got involved and took the side of the cyclist over the side of his country's food industry, which in turn outraged just about everybody else. It was hilarious, as was Schleck's excuse, but I felt sure that there was still time for a tragedy at this Tour. The only question was; who's tragedy, Wiggins' or Froome's?

When the shower did stop and the tart was gone, I hopped back on the bike and made my way out of town. I was feeling refreshed and a little amused at what I'd just read, but my pleasure didn't last long. Typically the sky opened again and dumped down another helping of heavy rain. *Was this a penance for my own greedy 'cake-gate' fiasco at the café?* To my annoyance the fresh shorts and jersey that I had put on in the toilet quickly did an unsympathetic imitation of the kit that I'd just taken off. I had no choice but to pedal on and within a couple of kilometres the road started rising yet again.

Unpredictable weather aside, Kenmare is a great place to base yourself if you want to do a few days' biking in this part of Ireland. It's close to the Beara and Iveragh Peninsulas and is surrounded by plenty of mountains in different ranges. Also, the restaurants in the town are particularly good, maybe even better than those found in Kinsale – the so called 'gourmet capital'. As I rode on, I realised that I was back on the good old N71 road heading for Moll's Gap. This is another famous Irish cycling climb. The climb itself is 10 kilometres in length from the Kenmare side and reaches a gradient of almost 10% in some parts, but unlike the hills outside Allihies, it starts off on a gentle slope.

Again I got into a nice rhythm where great views of The Black Valley appear. At Moll's gap itself (almost 900 feet up) the road forks taking some into the beautiful Gap of Dunloe, but the road is skinny and rough. I veered right and into Killarney National Park where I skimmed a few lakes before beginning the descent into Killarney. I was blown away by the truly serene beauty of Killarney's lakes. If I ever needed reminding of why I was doing this trip, it was there in front of me. I eased a little to take in the scenes but didn't stop, just slow pedalled by the water feeling a bit humble before starting the drop.

◊

Killarney National Park is like Disneyland for naturalists. It consists of 25,000 acres which hold three major lakes, several mountains (including Purple Mountain) and Yew and Oak tree woodlands which contain trees that are over 200 years old. It's also a UNESCO world biosphere site. The park also has Ireland's last remaining herds of native red deer which have been around the area for over 4000 years. If you're into fishing, the freshwater lakes are home to brown trout and wild salmon. Birdwatchers too are treated to all sorts of unusual species including birds of prey like ospreys, eagles and falcons. It's also home to Ross Castle from the 15th Century as well as Muckross House and other stately homes.

Of course nowhere in Ireland would be complete without its own personal saint, and Killarney National Park is no exception. An abbey was built there in the 7th Century on Inisfallen Island by the awkwardly named Saint Finian-the-Leper. Little is known about Saint Finian and there is doubt as to whether or not he actually had leprosy. Still the name stuck, if nothing else...

I made it to town and found a decent looking Spanish restaurant down a quiet street where I ordered pasta (this was more of a European Union restaurant really).

'Penne isn't very Spanish', I said to the elegant waitress when she returned with some water.

'Well it does have chorizo in it', she snapped defensively.

Killarney was clearly offering no light-hearted banter like I'd found in Kenmare. My waitress turned on her heel rather quickly, exhibiting a frown that said – 'don't feckin start'.

I sat for a while after I had eaten and calculated that I had about another 80 kilometres to go before I'd reach Dingle. This was hard to believe. I felt broken after the climbing and gazed dreamily at the ground for a while before feeling anxious about my journey ahead. I reasoned that there'd be a headwind from Castlemaine, as I'd had a tailwind coming in from Beara and that I'd probably be riding into it for 50 kilometres. This didn't help my mood.

Before packing up, a flyer for the Killarney Races peeped up at me from under my table. I read that an evening horseracing meeting was on in just a few hours. That was enough to persuade me to stay in Killarney and go racing. I was experiencing a sort of brainwave. What would make more sense than to abandon my plan to ride around Ireland in favour of sitting alone at the track and losing money backing horses that I knew nothing about? This pass-time is something that generations of Irishmen have given themselves to in their crafty pursuit of craic and cash – but really, for me at least, it was a brainwave in the sense that my brain waved goodbye to any sense that may have been left. It was tempting, but before I could snatch defeat from the jaws of victory, I pulled myself together and decided against going racing after all. I tried to justify it, but it was too hard. Even though I had ridden a few hundred kilometres since I left Cork, I was actually only about 90 kilometres from my starting point. So again it felt like I had made little progress. I still had the whole country to get around too.

I resolved to push on to Dingle. I was tired and crankiness was setting in, so I nodded a cheeky 'chao' to the waitress and jumped back on my bike.

The road out of Killarney led me past the impressive Gothic Revival Cathedral, as well as through groups of rowdy jarvies touting tourists for business on their horse-drawn carts. I found the N72 and rode along the edge of Killarney National Park again passing Killarney Golf & Fishing Club on the shores of Lough Leane before heading for Milltown. The little village of Milltown is unremarkable, save for the fact that it holds the annual World Bodhrán Championships. I've no doubt this is as whacky and mad as most Irish Festivals, but there was no drumming to be heard when I spun through. I bridged from there to Castlemaine and at last reached the base of the Dingle Peninsula.

◊

As you head for Dingle town from Killarney, it's easy to get lost. Why? Well because 'Dingle' doesn't exist – at least not on any sign posts.

In 2005, when Ireland was thriving economically, a Government Minister (possibly suffering from severe boredom) bizarrely introduced the 'Place-names Order'. This states that anglicised place names in Irish speaking areas would no longer be used in any official documents or indeed on any signposts. 'Dingle', the name of the town for 700 years, was to become 'An Daingain', its Gaelic name.

This was baffling. Having signs in Gaelic only would clearly force tourists (including me) into becoming either multi-lingual or lost. I had cycled to Dingle a few years earlier, not long after this law was passed. Back then, if it wasn't for a helpful farmer in Castlemaine who decided to let me in on Dingle's name change, I don't know where I'd have ended up.

'Where are you going?' he asked when I stopped at the shop.
'Dingle' I said.
'You're not'
'No. I am,' I said bluntly, rising to his challenge.
'There's no more Dingle.'
'Why, what have you done with it?'
'Tis there alright but tis called 'An Daingain' now; you'll see no more 'Dingle' on any signposts.'

He pointed me in the right direction but my bike and I could easily have disappeared into some far flung field where we'd have no doubt encountered other lost tourists. We may even have become Otherworld fairy-folk, living out our timeless days scaring the bejaysus out of strangers who interfered with our forts. But it wasn't to be. Getting lost is something you really don't want to do on a long bike ride. Any extra mileage when you're already pushing yourself can really wreck your head –not to mention how encountering fairies probably can too.

Anyway, unsurprisingly over 90% of the people of Dingle objected to this new place-name directive because the town relies very much on tourism. Having countless visitors wasting time and petrol looking for a place that was never going to be on a signpost (at least not in English) was too much for local people, so they took the law into their own hands. I was delighted to see now on Casltemaine's signs that next to the Irish name 'An Dangain', the locals had spray painted the anglicised name 'Dingle' – thereby solving the problem. In fact they've re-done the signs all over the peninsula and who would blame them?

The image of perfectly respectable people spray painting road signs is something that lingers happily in my mind. You have to wonder, did these activists wear hoodies as a disguise? Did they contemplate funky colours like pink or purple? Was a stencil used? Was there a temptation to tag their name underneath the work? And where did they get the paint – local sheep farmers?

Of course it could all have been a conspiracy. Dingle's chamber of commerce may well have taken out an underhand contract on the signs with a local youth gang – a sort of 'do a bit of paint work for us and we'll let you into shopping centres' type deal...

Whatever the circumstances, this blatantly rebellious act tells a lot about Irish people. It's evidence of one of our national characteristics – a healthy disregard for authority. Luckily, I knew what road to take for Dingle at Castlemaine this time, but it felt good to know that the people of Dingle didn't mind breaking the law to ensure safe passage to their town.

Just outside Castlemaine I passed the first Ghost Estate of my trip. These empty housing parks are an all too common phenomenon in Ireland, left-overs from the party of the boom years. The one I passed represented some property developer's naïve 'build it and they'll come' philosophy. Fourteen houses were built in this park in Castlemaine, but nobody came. Why? Well probably because the village is in the middle of nowhere and offers nothing for would-be residents. It's an example of mind boggling economics that ignores the basic principle of supply and demand, as well as demonstrating raw greed. I wasn't to know it then, but only a few days prior to my passing through, this 'eyesore' of 3 and 4 bedroomed houses sold at auction for just over €200,000. That's 17K per house. Ireland's 'healthy' disregard for authority (in this case probably the financial regulator) might not always be healthy.

I couldn't help but imagine a conversation with any one of the many 'property developers' that have now gone bust as I rode on:

'So Paddy, I see you decided to build a few houses here in this auld field.'

'That's right, I did.'

'And why did you decide to build a few houses in a field Paddy? A field, I might add, that's just left of the back arse of nowhere.'

'Ah well I owned the auld field, so I decided I might as well do something with it…ya know…'

'Right… I suppose you couldn't have just grown vegetables in it or something… no?'

'Ah sure stop. I probably should've, but you know the bank said there's a million, would ya not go and build a few houses and sure I did.'

'I see… You're a bit fucked now though aren't ya Paddy?'

'Ah sure layve it so…'

I had more interesting and pressing things to worry about however, which soon arrived in the form of a strong headwind.

As I struggled on I saw a sign which read *'Last Petrol Station before Dingle'*. When I got closer however, in tiny writing just at the top of the sign was the word *'Second'*. In reality this was the *'Second last petrol station before Dingle'*, but of course nobody would have been able to read the word *'Second'* if driving past at any reasonable speed. No doubt panic buying of sorts would have resulted from this almost misinformation, netting the owner some extra business. This is another example of the sometimes colourful entrepreneurial skills I mentioned that are peculiar to this part of the world. I'd seen it in Kenmare and here it was again in front of me, reassurance that cute chancer-ism was alive and well and living in Kerry, a genuine source of amusement.

Outside Boolteens I straightened up and prepared for the long linear road that would take me for 20 kilometres, all the way to Inch; that's 20k without really turning my handlebars. I figured this was going to be a bit tedious, even though I did have glimpses of the sea in between breaks in the ditches. I could smell it too but I could hear the wind. This was a perfect opportunity to get in some tunes. I took out *Black Grape* and battered the pedals in time with the beats, all along the road to Inch.

> *'I don't do what you do,*
> *And you don't do what I do but you should do....You'*
>
> Shaun Ryder

After nearly an hour of straight riding, I was spent. The wind had picked up from the morning and there was no place to hide on the unswerving road. I had to resort to my one pedal stroke at a time philosophy (one stretch of road was clearly too much). My knees were starting to feel pain and I began crawling along at a heartless pace. I tried to concentrate on nature and employ the meditation technique – I was riding under the Slieve Mish Mountains too – but it was hard. Eventually, when on the point of almost seeing desert-like mirages of Inch Strand's pub, I arrived there – broken and breathless.

Inch Beach is a kite surfers' playground and it took me a few seconds to figure out what all the people were doing when I saw them 'flying' around the strand. Indeed there looked to be parachutists going in the wrong direction which confused me somewhat in my semi-delirious state, but it was all good when the penny dropped. This huge beach is over three miles long and the 'parachutists' were at it for as far as I could see. My interest lay more in tea and further slices of cake however and I went straight for Sammy's café.

Evidently the café owners here had factored in the 'air show' entertainment from the kite surfers when determining their prices. Either that or they were just taking the piss. In any case, I took my overpriced scone and tea outside to the benches where the wind blew sand particles into my face and food. The wind was really testing me now. Back inside, where I felt slightly safer, I was treated to photographs on the walls of actors who have starred in movies that were shot on this beach. Under the smiling eyes of Robert Mitchum, on the set of *Ryan's Daughter*, I carefully picked the sand out of my scone.

'How far is Dingle?' I asked the young woman behind the counter.

'Yes' she smiled, but this wasn't the answer I was looking for.

'Dingle, how far is it?' I tried again.

'Yes', came her repeated reply, this time accompanied by beaming enthusiastic eyes and an even broader smile.

Only then did I realise that she was Italian and was clearly not up to the task of answering my question.

'It's nearly twenty miles from here' announced a more qualified local woman.

'Thanks.'

I began eating and thought about the next 20 miles. *That's over 30 kilometres.* I'd ridden this road before and knew that there'd be a few little hairpin bends as the road follows the cliffs upwards. It was going to be painful. I thought back to that morning when I left Allihies. It was hard to believe that the hills all the way back in Beara were part of the same day. It felt like a really different part of the country too.

'Are there always kite surfers here?' I asked the local lady who'd helped out our Italian friend.
'Yeah, they're a pain in the hole,' she said.
'Why?'
'Well they take over the beach, when it's windy anyway. You can't really swim without fearing a board coming down on top of you.'
'I see.'
'So what do you do?'
'Tell them to feck off'
'Okay'.
Good answer...
It was hard throwing my bag over my back again and remounting my bike for the final time. But before going, I read the wonderful piece of poetry that's written on the side wall of Inch Strand's pub. It always makes me smile when I read it:

> *'Dear Inch must I leave you*
> *I have promises to keep*
> *Perhaps miles to go*
> *To my last sleep'*

And I did have miles to go (20 at least) and a promise to myself to keep. As I got ready to move off, I took one last look out to sea and thought it wouldn't be a bad idea if publicans all around the country took Inch's lead and had poetry painted on the outer walls of their pubs. If not, maybe the spray painting gang of Dingle could do it. In any case, it brightened me up before the final hills and I was out of the saddle and climbing before my wheels had turned a single prayer.

◊

In the same way that mechanics and physics are a theme of West Cork, exploring and adventure seems to be a theme of the Dingle Peninsula. Not only was St. Brendan-the-navigator from just north of the peninsula, but Antarctic Explorer Tom Crean was from Anascaul on its south side. My progress was slow along the high cliffs, but before too long I joined the N86 road just outside the village of Anascaul.

It's remarkable really, but Tom Crean's feats made even St. Brendan's voyage to the Land of Promise seem like a walk on the beach. After enlisting in the Royal Navy before Ireland won independence, he became a highly regarded member of both Scott and Shackleton's expedition teams and he was involved in three of the four major British explorations of the Antarctic at the beginning of the twentieth century. His crazy treks and voyages for hundreds of miles with little food, in the coldest conditions on earth and with ridiculously backward equipment (by today's standards) were truly great. In fact, if what was happening that day at the Tour de France was dwarfing my big day on the bike, the things

Tom Crean did would in turn dwarf any Queen stage of any bike race, or indeed any endurance event of any sport anywhere, ever...

On one expedition for example, he did a 1600 mile trek across glaciers and mountains and on another made a sea crossing in a sailboat for 800 miles in a hurricane and in temperatures of –40°C. Nicknamed 'The Irish Giant', Crean won three Polar medals and the Albert medal (later The George Cross) for saving the life of one of his fellow explorers. In short he was a hero. He retired to Anascaul where he opened a pub, The South Pole Inn, which is still open and forms a major attraction in the village.

This kind of person really puts things in perspective. I had no hardship whatsoever to deal with on my bike ride, certainly by Crean's standards, but I wasn't really thinking about Tom Crean when I was riding off towards Dingle. No. I was thinking about my sore knees and why the world was so unfair – how dumping down showers and headwinds could be considered reasonable and what I'd do if there was no bath in whatever B&B I was going to end up in that night... This was hard and there were still more hills and kilometres to get through before I'd know my fate. Every kilometre seemed to drag and drag, almost like an ice sledge on a polar slope. Well, sort of anyway.

At Lispole I passed *the* last petrol station before Dingle and eventually the town came into view. I pedalled in feeling relieved but beaten and went straight to the back of the town where I knew there were plenty of B&Bs. There I found a busy looking one resting on a quiet hill.

'You're after riding a few miles,' I was told by the smiling woman of the house who'd introduced herself as Bridget.

'I am.'

And so started another Kerry conversation; this time it was clear that the colourful locals have an ingenious ability to extract information from you without asking a single question. They do it by making statements, statements which you either agree or disagree with and have no choice but to add further information to, thereby keeping everything about you in the public domain.

'A hundred miles actually, from Allihies in West Cork', I said proudly.

'And you're tired and starving with the hunger –Lord bless us and save us. You're only wrecked from it', announced Bridget.

'He's wrecked from it Pat,' she said to her husband who'd also appeared and who decided that my ride 'wasn't a bad old spin'.

Not bad? *'Ulyssian' I think you'll find is the word. God these people are hard to please.*

'Come in now 'til I show you your room.'

The house was beautiful and was really more like a smiley boutique hotel than a guest house. Considering I was 'wrecked', 'tired' and 'starving with the hunger' and was being shown a room before knowing the price, I had already decided to stay. Further cycling at this stage was clearly out of the question and it was almost 7.30 in the evening.

Fifty euro, as it turned out, was a good price for the hospitality alone. I needed it. I was pretty much alone all day and needed more than just a bed and breakfast.

My hosts were a dream of Irish friendliness and the room itself was a treat. I felt lucky as I sprawled out on the huge bed. For a half hour I lay motionless before showering and doing what I had to do with the Lemsip; it was hard to come down off a long bike ride.

When I walked into town an hour or so later, the rhythm of walking seemed somehow linked to the days' pedalling and I found it difficult to stop. My body was not allowing itself to relax – like it was 'locked in' to motion and needed to move. I must have done three rounds of the town before I could decide where to eat. An ordinary diner where I had ordinary food was my choice but I was happy with that. Really, I didn't feel like I had the energy to enjoy a big meal in a more thoughtful restaurant.

Afterwards I strolled around again, but it was quiet in Dingle and I began to feel sleepy. In the dying light of summer I moved slowly along the harbour and headed for home, but there was time for one last treat before bed. Outside Murphy's bar by the water and under warming street lights, a heavy black man from the Deep South, far across the sea was asking a local busker if he could play his guitar. The man obliged and what came out was the sweetest blues I've ever heard. A Robert Wilkins tune from long ago, was sung with a big blue voice and lyrics that were mine for just that moment:

> 'Said "I believe I'll ride
> Believe I'll go back home
> Believe I'll ride, believe I'll go back home
> Or down the road as far as I can go"
> And that'll be the way to get along'

The man's wife took out a harmonica and joined him and for those several minutes of playing I was taken into my imagination. When they finished, I thanked them; they'd rounded off my day in unexpected style, creating an impromptu blues gig on a quiet Dingle street.

'That's my pleasure,' beamed the man in his husky southern patter.

I would have liked to chat more but my brain felt like it was doing that freezing pause thing again that I'd experienced back in Castletown. So with a warm glow and a head full of blues, I wandered off to the outskirts of Nod – happy.

I believed I'd ride the next day, I believed I'd ride but I would not... Well not much anyway...

CHAPTER 5

'Everybody, soon or late, sits down to a banquet of consequences'
Robert Louis Stevenson

Something was different when I woke. I felt deeply tired and I knew that I couldn't ride far that day. Still, I got up and walked a few hundred metres to the shops before breakfast. The streets were empty and I feared that nothing would be open, but traders at least were up. My legs were stiff and my arms heavy, but they carried me – slowly.

I love Dingle. For me it's a spiritual home. I've come to the town regularly since I was a teenager. Something draws me –a magnetic pull. The town's location, far out on the peninsula, offers the feeling of being cut off from the world – reality even. It can almost feel like being on an island. The sea is ever present. Dingle's pubs too can help with the surreal atmosphere. When you've got hardware stores and shoe shops that double as pint producing pubs, it makes you wonder if the priest has ever thought of installing a beer tap outside the church confessional – so as to loosen up the tongues of his confessors. Drink too is ever present, if not the will for all to have it.

There are actually around fifty pubs in Dingle. I tried counting once but when bars are disguised as shoe stores, it gets tricky. A more accurate statement on the number of pubs in Dingle might well be – 'there are 100 business premises in Dingle, any number of which might well be a pub'. In any case, for a small town of two thousand people, that's quite a lot of pubs. But if drinking is a part of the routine, then as true as day follows night, hangovers are the penance.

'Jaysis, I'm fuckin dying'.

This alarming announcement was made by an unsteady young man who was holding his head in a half collapsed pose over the shop counter when I walked in. I'm not sure he knew the store was already open, but he went on unaware of my presence offering an insightful commentary on –what I gradually learned to be – was the sore price he was paying for last night's indulgence.

'I can't even remember getting home.'

'Me jaysis head feels like's it's been stuck in a feckin vice. Some craic though, wha…? Mighty.'

Now if I was a real foreigner, I might have had some concern for this lad. He was 'dying', suffering from amnesia and his head was in so much pain that he felt like it was being crushed – indeed in a vice of all things. A concerned tourist might have considered calling a doctor or panicking. Never do that. That would be a terrible overreaction which would cause only alarming confusion – and that really wouldn't do.

Indulgence is routine, as is the pain of counterbalance.

I bought the paper and headed back. If the fog was a quilt on Beara, the lime green hills were propped pillows on Dingle's bed. The curtain clouds too were drawn back and a flood of morning sunlight hit, waking the snoozing town as I returned. At last rain was a watery memory but I knew that my body or my mind wasn't up to a long ride that day.

My vague plan was to do the Slea Head loop, a thirty kilometre scenic 'drive' around the end of the Peninsula, then return to Dingle, pick up my rucksack and continue to at least Tralee via the challenging Conor Pass climb. By the time I'd gotten back to the B&B however, I'd resolved to stay in Dingle again that night. I would do the Slea Head loop only, try to recover for the rest of the day and then take in the Conor Pass climb the following day. It was a good compromise I thought.

Breakfast was a great feast of porridge, fruit and cold meats. My hostess Bridget was adamant that I was going to need plenty of toast too for my big bike ride.

'Where in god's name are you off to today?' she asked.

'Nowhere, if that's okay with you. I was thinking of staying another night.'

'Oh god, I don't know if I have any room. I might be booked out. Wait til I check '.

I didn't need to hear this and I waited anxiously for her to return hoping that I wouldn't have to move home again.

'I suppose I could squeeze you in alright,' she said as she came back clutching a plan of her rooms. I felt relief and grateful indeed for the opportunity to give Bridget another night's business.

'That's great'.

I told her my plan to do the Slea Head spin. Her husband Pat was now interested and he sat down to give me some counsel on how to handle this much trodden tourist route.

'Now, there are beehive huts by the road, but don't give anyone any money; they'll rob you. And if you go to Gallarus Oratory, go up the side way and don't be paying to go there either. They have some cheek to be charging people at all.'

The Slea Head loop is a treasure trail of historical and archaeological sites including these Beehive huts that Pat was talking about. It's beautifully scenic too with views of the Blasket Islands and Mount Brandon. I had in fact ridden this route before, but now that I had lots of time, I decided to actually visit some of the attractions. Any advice from the locals was welcomed.

'What do you mean Pat?' I asked.

Pat kindly explained that though the Beehive huts and Oratory were on private lands, they were also national heritage sites that were owned by the people of Ireland. He felt that it was unfair to charge anyone to access these sites and explained that there were actually folk charging tourists to enter. It wasn't illegal (they provided some information or facilities on the sites which 'justified' the price) but Pat certainly felt it was unfair. I sort of agreed and resolved not to spend any money seeing what clearly already belonged to me –famous last words.

Before I changed and set off, I had a leisurely coffee in my room and caught up on the news from the Tour. The Queen stage of the day before was won by Thomas Voeckler. The powerful Frenchman was the first to crest all of the mammoth Pyrenean climbs and in so doing he took all the points for the King of the Mountains competition, earning him the polka dot jersey that he'd not relinquish. The two Britons finished together, 'Froomie' continuing his loyalty to leader 'Wiggo'.

One of Ireland's two Tour riders, Dan Martin also had a good day on this stage, finishing 7th. He was writing a 'Tour Diary' in the newspaper and it was good to get an insight into his world. I lay on my bed and read that one of the 'tricks' his team used on really hot days, was to fill women's tights with ice and put them on their backs so as to reduce sweating and cool the body. I'd not heard of this unusual behaviour before but I knew, for various reasons, that it wasn't something I was going to be trying any time soon. It was a beautiful morning in Dingle, but it was unlikely to be a day for ice and tights.

Before long I was changed and back on my bike. I rolled out and immediately began pedalling up a short steep hill. But I couldn't. I just couldn't turn the pedals. My knees were in real pain when I pushed. In fact it was sort of like they'd been crushed in a vice. Yes, that was it. I was dying and I couldn't remember ever feeling pain like it. Of course there was no need to panic or call a doctor. I pulled up at a shop, bought an ice-cream and got stuck in – the treat counterbalancing the pains in my knees. When I'd finished, I changed to an easier gear and pedalled up the hill. *It's a miracle,* I thought, a feeling compounded by the notion that the hand of the Virgin Mary herself (reaching out from Ballinspittle no doubt) had appeared to give my arse a little nudge over the steep part. For a second I thought of asking her for a loan of a pair of tights for my back, but the ice cream had cooled me. The strange thing was that this all sort of happened on a stretch of road that's actually called 'Lady's Cross'. I knew Dingle was surreal and so it was proving.

In reality my knees were quite painful. Those hills in Beara and the rolling first days were the cause. They were certainly getting the blame anyway, specifically that 'Wall' climb. I reckoned they just needed to warm up and the weather would help so I spun on towards Ventry, skirting the bay by Ballymore. Everywhere in Ireland seems to have a good story and Ventry Bay, Ballymore in particular, is certainly not lacking.

◊

In 1939 a German U-Boat (U-35) sailed into Ventry Bay and delivered 28 Greek seamen to the shore. The Germans had torpedoed their ship *Diamantes* near

Cornwall the day before. They suspected it of carrying war materials but still rescued the Greek crew as it sank. As Ireland is a neutral country and was so during the Second World War, the commander of the U-Boat, Werner Lott, chose to deliver the seamen to Irish shores. In fact, the German's fed the Greeks well, dried their clothes and offered cigarettes and hot tea during the trip. The Greeks were so impressed, they kissed the wedding ring of Lott when they landed and thanked him for his kindness. I mean he only blew up their ship and sort of kidnapped them.

In truth, this was a commendable act of humanity in wartime; the Germans could have left the Greeks to fend for themselves in lifeboats on rough seas. And the good karma was to come back to Lott. Two months later a British Destroyer, under the command of Earl Louis Mountbatten, sank Lott's German submarine off the Norwegian coast. This time Mountbatten rescued the crew of the U-Boat and over the next decades actually became mates with Lott. They were sort of pen pals. This is all very bizarre but my favourite part of this story is what happened after the Greeks had landed.

It was rumoured that before leaving Ventry Harbour, Commander Lott asked these Greek sailors to give his 'best wishes to Mickey Long'. A theory put forward explaining this was that the German had holidayed in Dingle before the war and had become friendly with a certain Mr Long (seriously with a name like Mickey Long, it could well have been Mike Rotch or Ben Dover). In any case, at this time the British Government was paranoid that Ireland's people were colluding with German U-Boat Commanders. They weren't. In fact Ireland's premier Eamon de Valera announced that he wanted to help Britain within the confines of neutrality. Of course he also helped crossroad dancing flourish within the confines of having it banned. Anyway, the *Daily Mail* sent a reporter to Dingle to investigate. He visited certain pubs, fishing for information. The locals, on noting that he was spending money in these pubs, decided to keep him there drinking for as long as they could. They filled him with enough beer and bullshit to fertilize a farm and gave him what he wanted including tales of U-Boats surfacing in bog holes!

The gullible hack was delighted but the colourful entrepreneurial skills of these Kerry folk could actually have caused real damage. Winston Churchill wanted to secure Irish ports for Britain during the war and these types of stories further fuelled Britain's paranoia. A move to secure ports would not have gone down well in America and could even have had major consequences for American involvement in the war. It's amazing what a load of bullshit in a Kerry pub can lead to – the butterfly effect in action.

After a couple of kilometres I was riding through Ventry imagining U-Boats and Greek seamen. Thankfully that's all a distant memory but things still felt foreign to me in Ventry. Dingle is a bilingual town, though more English than Gaelic is probably spoken because of the number of outsiders living there. All places west of Dingle however, including Ventry, are fully Irish speaking. My Irish is rubbish. I spent many years at school 'learning' it and though I love language,

I'm just not good at this one – a respectful abstainer. If I had to however, I'd mumble a few words and I decided I would today if I could.

Orange Montbretia wildflowers or 'Coppertips' splashed the roadsides after Ventry and led me again toward the edge of Ireland. The sun was smiling, evidence finally that this was a holiday in summer. I felt great – save for my knackered knees.

Before long I came upon a sign near a small farmhouse indicating that there were beehive huts in the vicinity. This was to be my first stop. Another sign suggested that I should follow a narrow path beyond a rusty gate.

Beehive huts or 'clocháns' are corbelled roofed dry stone structures dating from at least as far back as the 8th Century. They were used by monks and most overlook the sea, which provides a stunning backdrop for meditation. In fact the site at Drogdzen Beara, the place I didn't get to due to the fog, is really just a modern version of these huts – a place of meditation overlooking the sea. There was no sign of any life when I strolled through the farmyard except a dog sleeping lazily in the shade. A small empty kiosk stood by the open gate that I had to pass through, but I figured there'd be no charge as there was nobody around. As I passed through, a hand appeared out of nowhere (actually out of the 'empty' kiosk). I could see no face in the darkness inside but heard a voice which declared that it was – 'three euro to see the beehive huts'.

Bollocks. I've been done.

The hand was also clutching a small leaflet which I accepted in return for €3. I'd been warned by Pat not to pay any money but it was too late and I was about to find out why he'd warned me. The leaflet told me nothing I hadn't already known; the amateurish printing merely informed that I was about to see a beehive hut. *No shit...*

'Thanks very much', I said to the kiosk phantom with as much sarcasm as I could squeeze into three words.

I followed the path up to where the 'hut' was but there wasn't even a hut. There was half a hut. Another sign offered an apology for the fact that 'reconstruction work' was taking place. I essentially found myself standing alone in a messy field of sheep and sheep shit, with ancient stones strewn around it, wondering how I had just allowed myself to be, well, fleeced. It wasn't even possible to go into the hut. I was standing in a building site and had just paid for the privilege. The only consolation was that there was a decent view of the sea, but there was equally as good a view from the roadside. In short, there was nothing attractive about this 'attraction'. *Pat was right. Move on.*

And I did, along the high coast road to the area of Slea and Dunmore Head where I stopped at the white stone cross and shrine near Ireland's most westerly point. I let the beehive incident go. It was funny really, but I do like to avail of bargains and that wasn't one. Here by the roadside I had more company in the form of two yellow beaked seagulls who took in the views of the Blasket Islands with me. The air felt fresh, my skin warm and the islands looked like an exhibit in the sun.

◊

Dunquin was to be my next stopping point. I decided to have a coffee there and plug in to the views some more. This place is the most westerly parish in Europe, so it was as good a place as any to have a coffee and in a way to celebrate having already reached Ireland's, indeed Europe's closest point to the new world. I rolled on above the surf and some old beached shipwrecks until I reached a cluster of stone cottages and saw an unofficial looking sign that read 'Dunquin'.

A makeshift summer café in one of these cottages was advertising homemade apple tart. Some tourists occupied the benches outside and looked happy with their coffees and the scenery. I decided to join them, parked up and followed the smell of pastry into the cottage. A woman in her thirties greeted me and took my order. There was no menu; I could have homemade apple tart or homemade apple tart.

'Yeah... I'll have some apple tart please... and a coffee'.

'No problem.'

'Can I ask – is there anything else to Dunquin aside from these few cottages?'

'Well', the woman paused. I noticed her ears turning a little red and her gaze turned to the floor. Seeming reluctant at first, sheepishly she spat out a confession.

'Dunquin is actually a little further down the road, like a couple of kilometres further down.'

'Oh, so this isn't actually Dunquin?'

'No.'

'But...'

I was about to point out the sign that read 'Dunquin', but I let it go. The moment felt awkward and I sensed the woman's embarrassment about the fact that the sign was only a few yards before her cottage. In fact she had a look of schoolgirl guilt and I reasoned she may have had a hand in putting it there. Actually the more I think of it, she had 'IT WAS ME' written all over her face. Okay, I was entertained by Kerry's colourful entrepreneurial skills before – maybe even a little impressed – but this was taking the piss. Someone had effectively faked a village out of a cluster of cottages and stuck a name to it, tricking unsuspecting tourists (me) into believing they were in a place that they weren't in. I sat down on a bench somewhat confused and waited for my food. I guess I could have gotten annoyed by this, but the views of the vast Atlantic and the islands just seemed to distract or calm me. The fact that the apple tart was delicious helped. In any case, it was still good to have a coffee in *not* 'the most westerly parish in Europe' – or wherever the hell I was.

Of course Dunquin is only the most westerly parish in Europe if you're not from Portugal, the Azores or Iceland but we won't go into that...

After my break I rose and fell with the road for a short while and guess what? I soon came to a little parish called Dunquin. There was no need to stop now but the real Dunquin does have plenty to offer the traveller. Near the village there's the Blasket Island Heritage Centre which gives a good insight into the lives of the islanders who lived on the Blaskets until the 1950s. The Centre also celebrates literature and art which comes from or is inspired by the islands. I had been before so instead I rode through Dunquin eyeing the scenery that attracted two major Hollywood film directors to the place. David Lean's *Ryan's Daughter* and Ron Howard's *Far and Away* were both shot in the area. Both were also huge box office successes, though critics weren't so convinced. Indeed Tom Cruise's Irish accent would have made even Fred Astaire cringe (they were as bad as each other) and Robert Mitchum's was, in a word – shite. Nonetheless, in true Hollywood style, a village was actually purpose built by the film makers of *Ryan's Daughter* to be used as the set. It was given the fictional name Kirrary and it was actually demolished after the film was completed. Making villages out of thin air was clearly a theme around Slea Head.

After Dunquin my knees were keen on continuing to take it easy so I resolved to have another little rest when I came upon the bigger village of Ballyferriter a little further on. As a kid I remember once visiting the shop there when on holiday and using my freshly acquired school Gaelic to conduct the transaction. We went in as a family and my parents encouraged us kids to buy sweets in our 'native tongue'. The old woman behind the counter was very accommodating, patient and complimentary, and I remember feeling proud that I had managed to sort of pull it off. In a way I wanted to relive this moment, find a welcoming guide in the form of someone's grandmother and feel proud of my 'bilingual' skills.

I pulled up outside the only shop I could find – in the place where I remembered the old one was – but I quickly realised that re-living the past was not going to be easy. The Celtic Tiger had clearly visited this place. Instead of being a small sole trading mishmash type country shop –the type that is almost always painted brown and stacked with sacks of dusty potatoes – I found a modern MACE minimarket, adorned with neon, deli counters, shiny glass, shinier chrome, carefully arranged isles and electronic Lotto machines. The faint smell of ham played second fiddle to the smell of window cleaner. I'd just entered modern Ireland and I hated it.

The Irish language did hang in the air, but the team of workers were young i-phone wearing trendies. No old grandmother could be found. I grabbed a packet of discount biscuits and waited to be served behind a French couple whose English seemed as bad as my Gaelic. The girl behind the counter patiently counted out their euro coins in English and I ran over in my head what I was going to say in Irish.

'*Cé Mhéad?*' *(How much?)*

The price was plastered across the front of the packet but it was a start.

Níl aon scamall sa speir. (There are no clouds in the sky)

This would be my attempt at more general conversation and would demonstrate general confidence, thereby showing that I was indeed 'bilingual'. From then on, I figured it would be a case of anything goes.

When the French tourists had finished and moved on, it was my turn.

I hesitantly placed the biscuit packet on the clean counter and said: 'mmhhm.... Eh....mmmhhm'
This utterance, belonging to no language whatsoever, forced the young woman to make a call on what language to conduct this transaction in, and her reasoning probably went something like this.
The guy who thinks he's in the Tour de France is probably not from around here so I'll speak English.
'One Euro please', she said.
'Oh.....eh, yes.........eh merci!'
'Merci', I mean like *'merci'* – you couldn't really make it up. It even came out with a perfectly pronounced French 'r' sound. What was I doing? I mean that's just not an appropriate language for this situation. *What in god's name was I doing?* I don't think I'll ever know but with that I smiled, picked up my biscuits and took my hot blushing face back out to the safety of my bike. One thing was certain; I wouldn't be speaking any more 'Irish' on this trip.

◊

Near Ballyferriter is Smerick Harbour which in 1580 was the scene of a very bloody episode in Irish history. It was as much about religion and England's wars with Spain as it was about Irish freedom, but a Papal force of six hundred Spanish and Italian soldiers, sent by the 'Holy' Pope Gregory himself –(you couldn't make that up either) joined the Desmond rebellion against the English Crown. It was of course a Kinsale-like disaster for the rebels but this time all the rules were broken.

Arthur Grey, who led the Crown with a strong force, promised to spare the lives of the Irish and Europeans if they surrendered. They did, but he massacred them, all six hundred, sparing only the leaders, and it took two days to do it, burying their heads only in what is now known as 'Gort na gCeann' (the field of the heads). The Irish proverb 'Grey's faith' comes from this incident and the belief that Grey went back on his word. A monument to those killed can be found at Dun an Oir (Fort of Gold) near the harbour.

I thought about riding out to the area when I was leaving Ballyferriter but all that stuff seemed a bit depressing so I decided instead to visit a different kind of burial site – Reask Monastic site, which was only a couple of kilometres away.

The Reask site, located up a narrow side road off the main Slea Head loop, is little known as it was only excavated in the last couple of decades. It too dates from the 5th or 6th century and it's like a little village of low ruins which once housed a monastery, beehive huts and all the usual ancient stones. I was the only person around when I arrived, probably the only person for miles. As the sky was now cloudless and with that holiday feeling secured, I finally did what people on holiday do. After a mini picnic of clearly priced discount biscuits and some water from my bottle (not the most exciting picnic I know), I lay out on the warm grass of the Kingdom of Kerry and closed my eyes, feeling damn glad that I was above ground and still had a head –albeit one that mumbled inappropriate languages. I slept, uninterrupted for a good half hour. This was another little miracle, as I usually can't nap. Life was good in the afternoon sun.

When I woke there were no tourists looking at the strangely dressed homeless guy on the grass, and my bike was thankfully still by the wall where I'd left it. The country silence was only interrupted by the odd birdcall and as I sat up in the warm air on the cool ground, I decided to do one last tourist thing before returning to Dingle. Gallarus Oratory was to be my destination and this time I was determined not to let those 'robbers' take my money.

Again riding there didn't take long. The towering Mount Brandon could be seen far off in the north and the treeless fields offered wide views for miles around. The Oratory is near Wine Strand in Smerick Harbour and Pat back at the guest house had told me to cycle up the side road and to enter the site from there. He warned me not to enter through the visitor centre as I'd be charged for doing so.

Gallarus Oratory is an architectural and historical gem of Ireland. It's a small chapel which could be over 1200 years old and it has never been touched in terms of restoration. It's a waterproof dry stone structure with a corbelled roof and sloping walls. In fact, it looks like an upside down boat, so it's easy to see how it could have survived the Atlantic weather for so long. No mortar holds the stone in place; the workmanship and precision that went into its construction is remarkable.

I arrived at the visitor's centre and watched some tourists head towards the Oratory from there. These people would have been charged 'a few euro' and were clearly unaware that paying for access was not necessary. I felt great that my superior knowledge was going to see me beat the charge. So with a springy step and the cockiness of a local, I walked my bike up the side road and looked for the entrance. Cockiness of a local is one thing but knowledge of a local is something else entirely. I found a gate which led onto a grass path. *Was this the entrance that Pat was talking about?* I decided to chance it. I opened the gate and went through, but I seemed to be walking for quite a while and there were now trees around which blocked my view of any church. Suddenly a farmer appeared. I asked him if he could direct me to the Oratory.

'I'll bring you there', he said.

'Even better, thanks'.

This was clearly the right way to treat tourists.

'Nice day', I said.

'Tis.'

In silence we walked on. I knew I was probably on his land and he knew I was probably trying to avoid the charge, but I was delighted that he was bringing me to the church – as it were; this annulled any fears of getting lost or having to pay.

But the path led back to the visitor centre. Before I knew what was happening, the farmer opened the back door and shouted in to the ticket seller:

'Sean, I have a fella here who wants to buy a ticket '.

'Send him in', said Sean.

No I don't you fucker. I don't want to buy any fucking ticket.
Before I could even think of asking how much it cost, I had produced my wallet and handed over the cash. It was €4. I was told I could see a short video about the Oratory in the 'audio visual room'. *At least I get something for my money.*

I took my ticket and now walked the more civilised gravel path up to the chapel where I was greeted by two people from the Office of Public Works who were standing at the side gate handing out *free* tickets. It had now become apparent that I hadn't gone far enough up the side road and had taken the wrong 'entrance'. *There was only one word for this - 'done'. Pat was right. Move on......Again.*

It was pleasant to hang around the Oratory for a while. Inside I could see how meditation and peacefulness could come so easily. The silence of West Kerry was ever present.

After a while I decided to get my money's worth and returned for the film. It wasn't a Hollywood blockbuster, but it was something to do –something forgettable that is. Four euro and three euro was never going to break the bank; it wasn't the money that I was concerned about, but it was a little annoying that some people were cashing in on something that didn't belong to them. They provided a nominal 'service', but it was cheeky. It certainly felt wrong. You don't see people being charged to enter Notre Dame Cathedral or St. Pauls. The whole point of the Oratory is to provide a tranquil place that encourages prayer or meditation, not to extract money from people by providing gift shops and audio visual rooms. Incidentally Gallarus means 'Church of the Place of the Foreigners' so, ironically it is supposed to be for foreigners. It's not called 'Church of the place of the foreigners for €4 with a dodgy dated short history film thrown in for box ticking purposes '. No. In any case, the more important thing for me to note from this experience and the more worrying, was that I'd been warned by my host Pat not to pay to access any of these sites. Sadly however, I made a total balls of it – twice. *Idiot!*

There's another church close to Gallarus Oratory that dates from the 12th Century. Kilamalkedar's original 6th century monastery is thought to have been associated with St. Brendan before the more modern Romanesque Church replaced it. It's also a big attraction in the area and its grounds are strewn with ancient Ogham stones. I'd had enough of being a tourist by now though. There was a small matter of the last mountain stage of the Tour de France going on and I figured if I got back to the B&B I'd be able to watch the final half hour on the Irish language channel TG4 – (I said watch – not understand). Anyway, that's what I opted to do. I headed for Dingle, taking a last look over to Mount Brandon as I was riding off. There is a beehive hut at its top too. The mountain of course is named after St. Brendan and it's said that from its top he claimed to be able to see his 'Land of Promise' hundreds of miles away. This is a remarkable claim when you think about it. Clearly he was either bullshitting or hallucinating when he said this. Or he may have been just bored out of his mind and imagined he saw it. Either way, it doesn't say much for where he was if he was looking westward into the vast empty Atlantic and thought – *'this looks promising*. Maybe he was disillusioned about being charged to go into his own church or something and felt emigration was a good option.

The Slea Head loop is a magnificent bike spin and was definitely the highlight of my trip so far in terms of scenery. My knees were improving too, so I was in a good mood when I returned to the Guest House.

'How did you get on?' asked Pat who was sitting outside catching some rays when I pulled in.

'Great Pat – thanks for that advice. You saved me seven quid,' I said.

'Good man. I wouldn't be giving them any money.'

'God no, I'd never do that. I saw the beehive huts and the Oratory and I went up the side road as you said, but I didn't give them any money'.

Let's be frank, I already looked like a plonker. Middle aged country folk like Pat wouldn't be too enamoured with a man walking around the front of his house wearing tight figure-hugging shorts that had a padded arse as well as a revealing front. I wasn't going to let him think I was a total plonker...

'I need a shower – see you later Pat'.

◊

Stage 17 of the Tour appeared on my room's TV screen soon after. I panned out on the bed and watched Chris Froome wait for Bradley Wiggins on the last major climb of the race. Froome should and could have won at least the stage that day but he remained loyal to his teammate, nursing him up the hill. I was perplexed. It was dramatic for all the wrong reasons. I couldn't get away from the fact that the two riders should both have been trying to outdo each other in the true spirit of competition, where they could let nature decide the better man; this was after all a physical contest.

Or was it? I wondered what else it could have been – a race of truth, loyalty, honour and friendship? If so, how was Wiggins faring in those areas? He was getting help but was he giving it? Would he give it back in the future, in another Tour? And what were the consequences of all this – for both men? This is where trust comes in. And why was I so sceptical?

It didn't help that an ex-doper who had recently served a ban did win the stage – Alejandro Valverde. But was I impressed with Chris Froome for waiting for Wiggins and for being steadfast in his loyalty? No. I can't say that I was and I couldn't get away from the fact that cycling history repeatedly showed that loyalty doesn't always pay off. This was a bike race after all, not a Tesco Club-card competition. I liked Wiggins but I didn't like what I saw. Either it was weird or I was weird.

The whole thing nearly drove me to Lemsip. In fact it did. I couldn't resist the sachet that was staring at me from my little wash-bag. My knees provided the excuse this time. After I downed it (I even considered a double dose), I decided to make the most of the good weather and opted for an early evening stroll around Dingle.

'You're off again,' said Pat as I left his house.

Of course this was a question and really meant 'where are you going?' 'I am. I'll take a walk around and maybe I'll eat dinner some place'. Cue some more of Pat's counsel.

'Right, you'll be going for a nice dinner.' This was also a question. 'I hope so. Would you have any recommendations Pat?'

'I suppose I do'.

Remarkably I was now the one in need of information. Pat had orchestrated things so that it appeared he was doing me a service by providing it. In reality I wasn't too bothered where I ate; this wasn't a culinary expedition but he was clearly eager to recommend a few places, for fear no doubt that I'd be unnecessarily relieved of money, so I indulged him –after all, his previous advice was good – if not acted upon. I wasn't however prepared for what followed. For the next twenty minutes I got a detailed run down of the inner workings of most of the decent restaurants of Dingle. I was given costings, profit margins, food sources, prices, opinions on value, opinions on freshness, opinions on service and finally a list of what constituted 'seasonal produce'. This was interesting if unexpected. The end result was a recommendation to visit one restaurant and one restaurant only – *The Canteen*.

I was impressed – if a little unnerved that someone could have so much knowledge. Nevertheless, I felt confident now that I couldn't make a balls of this task. I mean all I had to do was not go to a different place.

I took the back road into town and passed the old Dingle Hospital. The building, perched on the hills above the town used to be a Victorian Workhouse. These days it looks more like the set of a horror movie as it falls into disrepair. I wondered if Pat had a review for that place too – *'Exceptional views of the harbour, but let down by the thin consistency of the cheap foreign gruel'*.

Soon it was time to eat. I found *The Canteen* and did manage to make it in. It was quiet there, not a good start but it was early too. By the time I'd ordered the place had filled up and most customers were returnee tourists who thanked the Maître d' for the fabulous experience on their last visit. *Clearly they too had been talking to Pat.*

In truth, everything about this restaurant was great. I had a rack of Kerry lamb and a salad that was decorated with some kind of purple edible flower. Eating flowers is something I find difficult to do –albeit not for any love of the flower, more my stomach.

'This is edible', I said to the waitress – noting that I had now mastered the Kerry habit of asking questions with statements.

'Oh it is yes, you can eat them'.

'What are they called?' I asked.

'Flowers', she reasoned earnestly.

But I couldn't do it. Conditioning is a terrible thing.

While drinking coffee, I spotted a poster advertising a play that was on that evening in Dingle. Kerry writer John B. Keane's *Moll* was being produced by The Beehive Theatre Company and it was on in half an hour. I figured this could be a good way to spend an evening so I decided to go and when I'd finished dinner,

I skipped off to the edge of town to the community centre where the play was to be held. I wasn't really expecting much; this wasn't exactly the West End but it seemed cosy. I spent the time before curtain-call watching young people taking kayaks out into the harbour in the soft evening light. There was a magic in the Kerry evening, which summer often conjures and I felt my soul was smiling down on the world. Either that or the Lemsip had kicked in.

About sixty punters finally gathered for the performance and when it started, I was lost in laughter as the lines of the play danced a jig around the room. Set in a Church house, Moll, the main character uses her cunning to manipulate the priests she looks after into lining their own pockets. At the same time, she secures for herself a more than adequate salary and pension. In fact, she manages to almost reverse roles and becomes more the employer than the employee. The play is an examination of ambition —some might call it greed. It becomes a contest of manipulation, where the mentally strong flourish, reminding me that cycling too, on holiday or in the greatest bike race of them all, is also a case of mind over matter. Wiggins was the Moll of the Tour, cunning, vulnerable, yet master of his own rise. '*All the world's a stage.....*'

The silver apple moon fed grey light to the plum coloured rocks on the shore when I came out. It lit too the giant wedges of lime asleep above the town. Going to the play had been a great idea. I swallowed in the cool air and took another walk by the fishing boats before deciding to finish off my stay with a night cap.

No visit to Dingle would be complete without a call to Foxy John's pub. I went to Main Street, passing plenty of drinkers who were spilling out of other pubs until I found Foxy's. Inside it was surprisingly quiet but not so much as to deter some locals from sowing the seeds of their imminent 'deaths', bouts of amnesia and vice-crushed sore heads that might well have visited them next morning.

'You're on holiday'.

'I am'.

So began another Kerry 'chat', a line of questioning really, where all information about me was extracted as a dentist might start a busy morning. I was hopelessly in love with this town and I swore – as I slipped onto a barstool in the hardware store cum pub – that I'd be back again soon, returning like I've done so many times before.

CHAPTER 6

'In a sport where 'love' means nothing, it's not surprising that etiquette means everything'
                                                                Mike Tyson

I felt fresh next morning. The previous night's visit to Foxy John's was more of a courtesy call than a night out. There I had no choice but to reveal to the locals that I was cycling around Ireland and rather than be asked why, it was just accepted with a few generous nods – as if it was a perfectly normal thing to do. *This is generally the more macho response.* Having felt accepted by the men, I was confident that unlike Jacques Anquetil, nobody was going to call me a 'girl', despite wearing skin-tight shorts.

I was also advised by a few of the lads on where to go and what to do in the various towns and villages that I might encounter on my journey.

'Stay away from Milltown Malbay,' said one man.

'They're all stone mad there.'

But I had no intention of staying away from Milltown Malbay. In fact I was heading straight for the place. Depending on tone of course, an instruction from an Irishman to do something like 'stay away from Milltown Malbay', followed by a reason like – 'they're all stone mad there' – actually might really mean – 'you have to go to Milltown Malbay, it's great craic, everyone is nuts.' This is what I decided was being communicated anyway. It's no wonder tourists are often baffled.

Now I was awake and ready to hit the road again. There were quite a few kilometres between Dingle and Miltown in County Clare but I was up for it.

'You're not staying again are you?' asked Bridget when I arrived for breakfast.

'No', I said, wondering what I'd done to deserve this kind of a welcome.

'Thank god', she said.

A bit of a pause followed which I was keen to end.

'Why?' I asked.

'Oh, I'm totally booked out now for tonight.'

'Where are you off to today?' she asked.

'Milltown Malbay maybe.'

'My god, you're half mad' – but her smile informed me that she was nonetheless impressed. *This is the less macho response.* I was glad to note too that a few days earlier I needed my 'head examined' but now I was only 'half mad' – *Progress.*

'I have your clothes ready for you, they're washed and dried.'

This was sweet. Bridget had kindly washed some of my stuff. This is not normal practice in Irish B&Bs and I was warned by Bridget not to tell anyone –'they'll think it's a feckin laundrette'. Still, the Kerry entrepreneurial skills can work both ways. When I decided to stay for a second night, I told Bridget what a wonderful place she had and that it would be an awful shame if I had to go out now in search of a laundrette, instead of having the opportunity to go to Gallarus Oratory and the Beehive huts (Pat was nodding in agreement). And of course, I said that 'considering I was now staying two nights, sure wasn't I almost a lodger at this stage? And wouldn't it be a capital treat if I could get a few small things flung in the washing machine for ten minutes, until I got them freshened up only. Sure I'm not going to get the chance to do it again – aren't you great and hospitable and you'd be saving my life as well!'

This is called plámás. It's a Gaelic and Hiberno-English word. There really is no English translation; the best example might be *'flatter for what advantage you may glean'*, a quote from *Hamlet* no less. It's essentially a mix of bullshitting and flattery – for the purpose of achieving a goal. The goal is often to extract information, but in my case it was to get Bridget to do my washing. It's no coincidence that I was in an Irish speaking area and I was using a bit of plámás. This is where the act of plámásing is more common. I have no doubt Bridget recognised it for what it was and for that very reason consented to wash my stuff. If god loves a trier – Kerry folk absolutely adore one. She smiled at my cheek but happily accepted my damp sweaty threads and now I was getting them back freshly laundered. I'd promised not to tell anyone, not because there would realistically be a queue of tourists lining up to have their washing done, but it was said so as to give me the feeling that I was special and different – a bit of reverse-plámásing if you will.

For that of course I owed her one. In fact I owed her one hundred and as I took out two crisp €50 notes to pay for my two nights' stay, I reflected again on the wonderful ability that Kerry people seem to have to instil guilt in the customer for bothering the trader into accepting some business. I was grateful and did feel slightly guilty for having asked to have my washing done, but that feeling didn't last. Fresh clothes in hand, I knew this was going to be a good day.

I bid farewell to my hosts. They were ideal: charming, helpful and very entertaining. Of course I was given a little more advice from Pat before I left. He mentioned a beautiful lake that could be accessed when descending the Conor Pass climb. I thanked him but knew that I'd be tearing down that climb at 60 kph heading for County Clare and for today at least, I wouldn't be stopping for a hike to a lake. I was intent on going full gas until I came to Tralee. It was almost 10am and I was late – again.

'Good luck on your trip', said Bridget.

'Thanks for doing my washing', I whispered discreetly.

'Will you be stopping in Tralee for lunch?' asked Pat.

I sensed another comprehensive and encyclopaedic evaluation of Tralee's restaurants, but I didn't have an hour to spare.

'No – not Tralee, I won't be going near the place. Thanks Pat.'

A slow silence filled the hallway.

'See ya, yeah? '

'See ya', said Pat, a little disappointed.

I was a little sad myself to be leaving Dingle, but I had 'promises to keep', and maybe 'miles to go'. The morning sun was a little shy but I rolled out confident that the clouds at least wouldn't be too tearful. I was less confident that my knees would hold up; they felt stiff and sore again as soon as I started pedalling.

I left town on the narrow road by the little bridge on Main Street and as soon as it was flanked by fields and hedgerows, it began to rise. I was already on the Conor Pass climb.

◊

The Conor Pass is the highest mountain pass in Ireland –except of course that it isn't. It's especially not if you're from Wicklow or Donegal or even if you know how to google stuff. One thing is certain; it's a big climb. The average gradient is about 6% and it's about 7km long when approaching from its south side. I had a way of finding out what passes were higher and it didn't even involve doing any calculations. Luckily my bike computer could tell me how high I'd ridden. I was probably going to be doing some big climbs in at least Wicklow over the next week, so figured I could certainly establish if one or other climb was higher. But I wasn't going to be uploading that information until I got home. In any case, the Conor Pass was certainly the highest mountain pass I'd encountered so far.

The road kept rising and I kept a steady rhythm going up. My knees warmed up quickly and this eased the pain somewhat. It was quiet out on the ascent too; a few tourists passed in cars but it was just me and the sheep again. In less than an hour I reached the windy top. The views of Tralee Bay and back to Dingle Bay were sublime. I stopped for a minute to eat a little and to drink in the scene. As I did, I noticed two other cyclists coming up the far side of the pass. These were the only riders I'd seen in the past few days. I reckoned the poor weather and the fact that I was riding during work hours made it unlikely to see many around, but Britain and Ireland's roads are filling up fast with cyclists. There really is a two wheeled revolution going on.

The first fellow up approached me. He was a pot-belied man in his late forties and he was breathing heavily.

'Hi'.

'Hi'.

'Jesus that's some hill', he said.

'It is'.

'Have you just ridden from Dingle?'

'Yes, it's a long climb.'

'Ah yeah, we're only amateurs,' he admitted as his bearded friend let out a roar of 'ahh you bollocks, you beat me', which not only revealed his frustration but also managed to scare away most of the sheep.

'Hello', I said to the second man as he caught up.

'This fella's after beating me twice now,' he declared pointing to his beaming buddy.

'Where did you cycle from?' I asked.

'Castlegregory, but we'll just drop down into Dingle now and then get the missus to come and collect us in the car. We might have a beer or some lunch – take it easy for a bit. We're only amateurs.'

We're only amateurs?

'Wiggins will win,' said the first man. This of course was a question and referred to the Tour.

'He will,' I said.

I don't know who they thought they were talking to. It wasn't like I was some kind of pro. I had a bag on my back, was about to put on a dirty old rain jacket and had a mouth full of chocolate. I was as much an amateur as they were, but somehow their self-deprecating 'we're only amateurs' just had to be shared. I wondered why, but I also grinned at their enthusiasm.

'It's a good feeling when you get up it,' said the first man up.

We all nodded and smiled.

It's true that cyclists can be a little intimidating for some. There can be a lot of talk of equipment, gear ratios and complex jargon which can sound alien to the newcomer. There can be machismo too – think Jacques Anquetil the 'girl' or Lance Armstrong the alpha male. But maybe these lads were just trying to say – 'don't talk jargon to us or go on about gear ratios – we're only amateurs and we won't know what you're on about'. I wasn't sure but I had to work it out.

Was this an Irish thing? Did these men not feel entitled to get on their bikes and enjoy a spin in the countryside? Did they have self-esteem issues? Did they lack confidence? Why the self-deprecation? – 'We're only amateurs!'

These guys were cycling fans – purists really; they were lovers of the act of getting on the bike with a mate and racing up a hill. They enjoyed the scenery, the companionship and probably getting out of the house for a few hours. They were also fans of the sport and they were unaffected by bullshit and machismo. Though they called themselves 'amateurs', I thought: *aren't we all amateurs?* But I couldn't help thinking that these guys were kind of heroes as well. They were doing what every star and water carrier of the sport of cycling had done in their youth; they were just getting on a bike and riding. They loved it. The joy of it was evident – and the purity of it. And who'd be a professional anyway? It's a hard life.

This is what it's all about I thought. *Two friends doing a bit of exercise; it was competitive without being serious and it was all rounded off with a spot of lunch in a Dingle pub – what could be more perfect?*

This was the point when my attitude towards Chris Froome changed. As I bid my friends good-day and pushed off down the mountain, I realised that maybe 'Froomie' was right not to attack Wiggins. His job was to protect Wiggo, not beat him, and though it must have been frustrating for him to know that he may well have been the best rider in the Tour (certainly in the mountains), at least he wasn't corrupted by the need to win. He was loyal, unaffected by greed, he didn't need to cheat or dope and he was doing his job to perfection. *There must be some serious satisfaction in that.* I felt now that he was the purest, most unaffected rider in the peloton. It seemed like he was one of us: doing it for fun, a winner but not wearing yellow. There really was no need.

This encounter with fellow cyclists was great for my morale. It was short but I understood their joy in riding a bike. I knew I had about ten days of riding left and I knew now that I would enjoy it, that I was enjoying it and that I had enjoyed it. Tralee Bay was in front of me and napping mountains were all around. I dropped down from nearly 1300 feet, wearing my glasses and jacket now, crouching low holding the drops and glided through the air with most of Ireland still in front of me. It was blissful – even for an amateur.

By the time I'd landed on the flat roads, the sun's heat lightly caressed the air. I skirted Brandon and Tralee Bays under Beenoskee Mountain until I arrived at Camp village. At Camp it was time for coffee.

◊

The village of Camp and the area around it is actually the birthplace of Ireland as we know it. Irish mythology has it that around 1400 BC the Milesians came to conquer the land. They came originally from Scythia (Iran), via Spain, and when they landed the local kings (the Tuath de Danann) complained that they weren't quite ready for a battle. They sent the Milesians back to sea for a while until they had time to prepare; it was only fair, they argued.

When the Milesians did eventually attack, they still won and this battle happened around the area of Camp. These folk were Gaels (from Galicia) and modern genetic analysis has shown that people from around Galicia and Asturias in Spain are closely related to the Irish. When they settled, they divided Ireland into the four provinces of which it is still made up of today. At this time, each of the three goddesses of Ireland, Eriu, Banba and Fódla asked that their names be given to the Country. The Milesians agreed and Eriu or Eire's name became the most used – hence Ireland became Eire's land or Ireland.

It felt good to be in Ireland's birthplace but to be honest – it's not the most exciting place in the world. Apart from Tralee Bay to the north, there really isn't much to Camp except a pub – and an empty pub at that. I was the only person there when I walked in. I mean *the* only person; there was no landlord or publican or any staff – nobody. I waited.

I was reasonably confident while waiting that somebody would eventually turn up but I also feared that they'd probably be a little annoyed to see me and might complain that they weren't quite ready. I thought maybe they'd ask me to go outside and come back in again when they were ready – just to make things fair of course. Luckily that didn't quite happen, but it nearly did. After about

ten minutes sitting at the bar imagining what would happen if I made my own coffee, the middle aged woman-of-the-house appeared.
'Hi – Just a coffee please.'
'Have you been there long?' she asked.
'A few minutes.'
'I'm not open.'
'Oh, really? I'm sorry. The door was open,' I said.
'Yes the door was open, but it wasn't open-open, it was just open.'
'Okay.'
'What time will you be open at?'
'I could open now I suppose.'
'Right…'
'Can I have a coffee then please?'
'Just one coffee is it?'
I looked around the bar as if to say, 'there's nobody else here', but my gesture fell on deaf eyes.
'Yes, just one – thanks.'
'Give me a minute.'
'Of course, take your time.'
I really didn't want to be unfair, but it was agreed that the pub was now open and that was a relief. I needed coffee and there probably wasn't another place for miles, but again I was amused at how Kerry people effortlessly can do that trick of making us feel ever so grateful for their services.

If it's true that the Milesians did wait for the Irish Kings to prepare for battle, then it says a lot about how fair minded these people were. Either that or they were just supremely confident. If Irish people are descendants of the Milesians, then it's reasonable to assume that we would take on their traits, but considering the two 'amateur' cycling mates whom I'd just met, I'll conclude that we in Ireland are more fair minded than confident.

Indeed Earl Louis Mountbatten and Werner Lott also seemed to have this fair-mindedness when they were saving the people whose boats they blew up in 1939. Fair play to them, but as I sat waiting for my coffee, my thoughts turned again to the sport of cycling. *How fair-minded are people in that world?*

In the 2010 Tour de France Andy Schleck's chain slipped just when he'd started attacking Alberto Contador on a climb. Contador ignored his rival's mishap and decided to launch his own attack which resulted in Schleck losing time to Contador. Some complained that this was unfair and that the gentlemanly thing to do was to wait for Schleck to sort out his mechanical problem. Others thought that was ridiculous and that Contador had every right to attack. A few days earlier, in the present Tour, Bradley Wiggins was being a true 'gent' and ordered the peloton to wait for Cadel Evans after the saboteurs littered the road with tacks and caused him to puncture. This was the act that was responsible for the French media warming to Wiggins and is why they dubbed him '*Le Gentleman*'. The French like fair play but they are also mindful that this is a particularly British sporting trait. In British eyes, I've no doubt that it would have been seen as unfair, or at least not the gentlemanly thing to do, if Froome had attacked Wiggins. There may have been consequences too, so it's easy to see how Froome would remain loyal in this regard.

So maybe Froome, who was becoming a very interesting character for me, was bound by a bit by etiquette. Or, I wondered, maybe he was actually freed by etiquette – that etiquette had freed him from the possibility and the burden of winning the race? The very strange thing about all this cycling etiquette is that it is upheld by almost all riders and by so many dopers too. The baffling contradiction of the sport is that some riders will happily break the law and the rules by doping, yet they'll refuse to break etiquette and will wait for a hapless adversary should they encounter trouble. These are some of the quirks of European bike racing. Anyway, it was good to know that fair play was as alive in this Tour as it was in Camp over 3000 years ago.

After I'd finished my coffee, I skipped on towards Tralee on the busy N86 which was furnished with a decent hard shoulder freshly laid with new tarmac. I hammered the pedals on what looked like a long line of liquorice, passing Blennerville windmill on the outskirts of town before crossing the Lee River.

Tralee is Kerry's largest town. It's colourful and lively but it was not a place I intended exploring. While passing through, I came to a set of traffic lights. I unclipped from the pedals and leaned over the crossbar waiting for the lights to change. It dawned on me that these were the first traffic lights I'd encountered on the whole journey so far. Actually, in stopping, it was also the first time that I *had* to do something on the road. There were no choices here. The freedom I was feeling really was reinforced at these lights.

I knew that I was moving into a new stage – my mind and body had become relaxed and free. Thoughts of routine and London life were far away. Geographically too I was moving, from the Southwest to the West. From now on the landscape and the people would be different and I felt instinctively that I would be too.

◊

A smaller road out of Tralee led me to the village of Abbeydorney. I was headed for Listowel but chose this quieter route. Abbeydorney itself is probably most famous for being the place from which Heavyweight Boxing Champion John L. Sullivan's family originated. Sullivan was a 19th century Irish-American boxing animal. Nicknamed 'The Boston Strongboy', he was the last bare knuckle Heavyweight Champion of the World and the first gloved Heavyweight Champion of the World. While gearing up to enter the priesthood, John L. decided that he loved drink, women and messing with people's heads. He therefore knew that becoming a priest was the perfect profession for him. For various unknown reasons however, it never happened. Instead, boxing came a-calling and by 1880 he was a pro, earning a great living from throwing punches.

As was common at that time, he liked to keep a massive moustache (no doubt to reinforce his manliness) and his great thick bristle would make even

Tom Sellick's effort look like a bit of bum fluff. Nonetheless, like has befallen many alpha male sportsmen, some people were calling Sullivan a bit of a girl (not to his face I'd imagine), but it was claimed he'd become afraid of bare knuckle fighting and had gone a bit soft. Rising to the bait, in the sweltering Mississippi heat of July 1889, he took on Jake Kilrain to settle the 'the big girl's blouse' issue and to silence his critics. This was the last bare knuckle heavyweight title fight in history and it took a whopping 75 rounds for Sullivan to win. Like wrestling, these bouts could go on for hours before rules and regulations made them more watchable (or less watchable depending on how civilised you are). By 1890 Sullivan was a millionaire and he was the first ever American sports celebrity. Everyone knew who he was. Everyone feared him too except for one man – Jim Corbett.

In 1892 in New Orleans, under Queensbury rules, Sullivan agreed to fight the college educated Corbett, but he would lose his title. In taking it, Corbett also became known as '*Gentleman Jim*' (presumably because he was educated). In any case, he was the first sporting '*Gentleman*' to be dubbed by the press, well over a hundred years before Bradley Wiggins became his namesake – '*le Gentleman*'.

At Abbeydorney I turned right and headed towards the village of Lixnaw. The road was pancake flat now, more like Holland than anywhere else, but the distinct smell of peat rising from the low bogs was unmistakeably Irish. I imagined that turf cutters would be out that evening, their backs bent 'footing' the turf until the half-light sent them home. In the distance to my left I could see for miles over empty fields to the coast. There was little traffic on this route and I was getting through the kilometres quietly and quickly. I skimmed past Lixnaw and continued to the village of Finuge where I crossed the River Feale and pushed on for a final few kilometres to the town of Listowel.

Lunch was a huge salad roll from a café in the town square. I'd never been to Listowel before. This part of Kerry and indeed most of Clare were new to me, but it still felt familiar. This town actually calls itself the 'Literary Capital of Ireland' which is a remarkable claim really, and as I sat in a post lunch haze, my mind drifted into careful consideration of how this could be.

Dublin, that big brute of a place on the other coast is regarded by many as the Literary Capital of the World and is a UNESCO World Literature City. How therefore can a small town of four thousand people in North County Kerry arrive at the conclusion that it is the 'Literary Capital of Ireland'? Is Dublin not in Ireland? If Dublin is at least one of the 'literary capitals of the world' and it is in Ireland, then surely it's also the literary capital of Ireland? If Listowel really is the true literary capital of Ireland and beats Dublin to that accolade, and if Dublin is one of the literary capitals of the World, then by that reasoning, can we not conclude then that Listowel is actually the literary capital of the world?

I wasn't sure if I was amused or concerned by Listowel's delusions of grandeur, but thankfully there is some evidence to back the idea that it is at least a literary hotspot. Every year the town hosts '*Listowel Writers' Week*', an international festival for bards and wordsmiths from every place imaginable. The forty year old festival has had Nobel Laureates and all kinds of award winning scribblers participate in the workshops and lectures that it hosts. It's also the home town of many writers including the late John B. Keane whose play I had seen the previous night in Dingle. As I rose to head further north, I could only reason that through its festival, the concept of 'hyperbole' is well learned in 'Ireland's Literary Capital'.

In the warm afternoon I grabbed my bike and walked it through majestic pun-filled streets, past poet's pubs wherein no doubt Ireland's future laureates were carefully crafting their next epics. The smell of fresh ink lingered surely on every doorstep and words it seemed were being plucked expectantly out of the air, like apples for summer cider by all the people of Listowel. This is Ireland at its best.

'Look at the gay in the cycling shorts', were the very words, freshly plucked, that interrupted my day dream. I came to and saw an angry teenaged 'corner boy' eyeing me with furrowed brow and heaps of suspicion. At this point I decided I'd be better off coming back another time to discover Listowel's lyrical genius. So swifter than was maybe necessary, I remounted my bike and took off with all the grace of a scrummaging tight-head prop.

◊

The silent road I took out of Listowel led me over the Galey River towards Ballylongford. This village, resting on Ballylongford Bay by the banks of the River Shannon is the birth place of Horatio and later Lord Kitchener. He's the guy who famously points on war poster ads from WWI and who claims to 'Want You'. His fearsome moustache would give even John L's a run for its money, but it is Kitchener's death rather than his birth that has had tongues wagging through history.

Kitchener, who was Britain's Field Marshal during the Great War, died after his vessel hit a mine which was laid by a German U-Boat near the Orkney Islands. More conspiracy theories than kilometres on my clock came about soon after his death however. Many felt that he was more of a hindrance to Britain's war effort than a help, so theories of foul play surfaced. His body did not. It was never found which gave further fuel to the conspiracy fires.

I worked straight through the village of Ballylongford and edged along the banks of the Shannon until I came to Tarbert. Here I would get a ferry across the Shannon Estuary and land finally in County Clare. The car ferry takes twenty minutes and is not expensive. It's perfect for cyclists travelling the west coast. Without it, there'd be a lot more cycling through Limerick or Ennis. I didn't have to wait long and for a short time at least I made progress on my journey without having to turn the pedals.

The River Shannon itself is the longest river in Ireland and flows for 360 plus kilometres from its source all the way up in County Cavan. County Clare however was waiting on the other side, the county where according to my Dingle friends at least, everyone is 'stone mad'. Immediately I would understand their concerns.

I'd read up on a few of the places I knew I would visit before my trip and as the ferry docked at Killimer, I remembered a slightly worrying tale from there from a long time ago. Even this tiny village has its own saint. Sixth Century Saint Imor is supposed to have had a girlfriend who, annoyingly for him, was also fancied by some other bloke. When he went to marry her, the other dude intervened and in the melee the unfortunate young lady was killed. After that, poor old Imor (possibly a murderer now) became a meditating recluse. He probably felt it was a reasonably good option to 'go underground', but as it turned out, he was never actually an official holy person in the first place, as he never took holy orders. Having proper papers didn't seem to bother people though, and he remained a 'saint' in the eyes of most. So my introduction to Clare was to land in a place that's named after a murdering and woman fancying 'saint' (and not even a qualified saint) who spent his days on his arse sulking and staring into a field. If this behaviour was considered appropriate, indeed even saintly in Clare, I feared what bad behaviour, even mere poor etiquette might entail. Now I was worried and knew the men in Foxy John's were right. *I hope I get through this.*

The N67 road rolled on a bit to Kilrush where I stopped at a quaint old pub to fill up my water bottles.

'How far is Miltown Malbay?'

'Tis a fair auld clip,' answered the old man stationed at the bar sipping a pint.

'How far is that?'

'It's about twenty miles, or... around... fifty kilometres.'

Most of the older people in the south of Ireland still think in miles and that's fine, but like me this man was clearly not a numbers man. If it was twenty miles, it'd be just over thirty kilometres, but fifty kilometres is not twenty miles and riding that much at this stage in the day would have been painful. I was tired and wanted my destination to appear as quickly as possible.

Kilrush looked to be a beautiful old town in the evening sunlight. The stone buildings give it a timeless quality that I would have liked to enjoy more. But instead I cut across the county and headed directly into the wilds of West Clare towards Milltown – hoping the old man's first suggestion (of 20 miles) wasn't as bonkers as his second.

Kilkee, a town I decided I'd visit another time is further down the N67. It is a small Victorian resort town. Every year it hosts a Ché Guevara festival. This gathering celebrates all things Latin American as well as the fact that the Cuban revolutionary paid an unofficial visit there in the 1960s. A young artist, Jim Fitzpatrick, claims to have served Ché while working in a hotel bar during his stay. He was probably inspired by this chance meeting and later went on to create the iconic image that we all know of Ché Guevara today. It's the one that's plastered on posters, t-shirts and mugs and sold at every music festival and t-shirt shop in the world – yeah that one. I'm not sure the commercialisation that has accompanied this image is what Guevara had in mind for himself when he was being a bit of a Marxist revolutionary. It all sort of awkwardly misses the point. But what is quite coincidental is that two of the most iconic war/revolution posters in the world (Kitchener's and Guevara's) have had connections at least to the same part of Ireland.

My legs felt weary as I battled on towards Miltown. I crossed the Doonbeg River at Cooracare and rode until I eventually arrived at Spanish Point. There was a quiet evening light on the roads and I felt triumphant when I heard the ocean.

Spanish Point is more of a southern extension of the town of Miltown Malbay. It's another busy spot for surfers and I was confident of finding a cosy B&B with a good view. After a short spin up the beach road, I came to a large guest house.

'Hi. I'm looking for a room for the night', I said to a much older lady who was doing some gardening at the front.

'Is it just yourself?' she asked.
'It is.'
'Right'
'But we have only double rooms.'
'Okay.'

There was a long pause where the woman seemed to be doing some figuring in her head.

'You'd have to be a couple you see.'
'But you do have vacancies?'
'We have rooms, yes.'
'It's couples only. Sorry.'

So if I go for a wander and come back with a new girlfriend, I can stay?

Without quite saying it, the woman was communicating that she would get more for the room if I was part of a couple and that she wasn't willing to charge me €70. It was good to know that she didn't want to rip me off, but it was also frustrating. My computer showed that I had ridden 146 kilometres and it was getting close to 7pm. I needed a shower and my body was sick of moving.

'How much is a room?

Why don't you go into town? There's a hostel there and it's cheap. It's only up the road.'

I agreed and took off without thanking her. It was annoying that this woman, like the woman in Schull, was holding out for more cash and wasn't willing to hedge her bets. I hoped her next tax bill would be frightening, as I pushed off again. I was getting cranky now.

◊

In the town's main street I found an old hotel, the rooms of which were above a pub. The pub itself looked like it had seen better days and when I was eventually met at reception by a young man who failed miserably at suffering the inconvenience of making me feel welcome, I just knew that to stay there would be a mistake. I figured the place used to be a hotel but was now regarded as a 'hostel' because it would have been too delusional to call it a hotel. Anyway, I asked to see the room before handing over the €45 that the man wanted up front. I was given the key and climbed a few flights of stairs to a musty old chamber that looked like it hadn't been refurbished since the 70s – the 1870s. It was wrong, just plain wrong. When I returned, this 'receptionist' was nowhere to be seen, so I chucked the keys on the desk and hopped back on the bike not knowing where to go. *This is shite!*

Miltown Malbay consists of one street. There really was nowhere else to go so I retreated back to Spanish Point. After a few knocks on a few doors, I eventually found a B&B. The woman of the house was a cheery country woman who was full of energy and heart.

'You're welcome. You can throw that auld bike in the shed'.

That's no auld bike and I won't be throwing it anywhere, but thanks.

'You're very good. Thank you. I will.'

'You know I was up in the town there and the fella in the hostel was a right gobshite. He didn't seem interested in renting a room at all. He was rude and he wanted the money up front. And the place looked like it hadn't been touched in years. And I've been cycling all day and the other B&B people sent me away and I'm really sick of that and I don't know… I just…'

'Where have you come from?'

'Dingle.'

'Right,' she said.

'You're head's gone mad with all that cycling. You need to sit down now and then stick your head in a sink of water. You're gone all wound up like an auld mongrel dog.'

'Am I?'

'You are.'

'Come in and I'll show you the room.'

With that this woman, who had a better understanding of me than I had of myself, showed me to an interesting double room which, while perfectly adequate and clean, also had infinitely more modern décor than the last place –more 1970s than 1870s. *Maybe retro is a theme of Milltown.* But it was cool.

I thanked her and asked if it was normal policy in County Clare to ask for money up front.

'No. The fella in the hostel was probably just worried that you would refuse to pay at the end… Although sometimes the young fellas when they stay here do give me the money before they go out on the town. They say – "take it off me now because I won't know what condition I'll get into and I'll only spend it if I have it". And I would, sure that'd be normal.'

It was good to know that the young generation of Irish were sensible, fully in control and liked to plan ahead…

The woman-of-the-house, Mary, was all drama and chat, and in her strong Clare accent continued to reveal how fortunate I was to have made it to her B&B.

'But you did well to come out of it now; you did well to come out of that hostel. He does have the lock-in for the town, so when the pubs close they all go there for the after hours' drinking. Sure you wouldn't get a wink of sleep and if you did you'd be tormented dreaming about tin whistles and fiddles all night. Sure he lets them play music until the cock would be crowing. You did well to come out of it altogether. That's right. You did... that's right...'

After stretching and doing my usual post-ride ritual, I was back on the road –walking this time – with dinner on my mind. The straight and narrow country boreen, flanked by reed-filled flat fields led me again to the main street where I had a good meal in what looked like Milltown's only restaurant. There were probably more, but this town is famous for its music. Culinary delights are generally not the focus.

Music in fact really was the very reason that led me to Milltown in the first place. It's the traditional Irish music capital of Ireland, maybe even the world and it holds that claim without any delusions of grandeur. Every year the Willie Clancy Festival and Summer School is held here. It's a celebration of the late musician's famous pipe playing as well as all things 'trad'. I wanted to hear some music and after dinner I slipped into one of the many bars that were hosting sessions.

It was Friday night now and I was excited by the prospect of an aural treat. There were a couple of young Irish women readying their instruments in the corner of Cleary's bar when I walked in. I sat up at the counter, ordered a drink and waited. One of my favourite Irish songs is actually a modern one from musician Andy Irvine called *'My heart's tonight in Ireland'*. I'd heard it for the first time only a couple of years earlier at a gig in London. It's a song about missing Ireland from afar, Milltown Malbay in particular and I guess it struck a chord with me, so to speak. Somewhere deep inside, my exiled slumber was disturbed by this song and I felt a longing to explore this part of the country. I wanted this place to be part of my odyssey, my journey home. Incidentally, it's also a song about being bought drink by the Garda Sergeant in a pub until at least four in the morning. *Of course it would be better to have the cops at the lock-ins in case someone broke the law or something...*

> *'My heart tonight is far away across the rolling sea*
> *In the sweet Milltown Malbay*
> *It's there I'd love to be'*

And I was there. It was no longer a dream or a longing. The women began playing tunes and in ones and twos people followed the sounds inside.

'What kind of banjo do you play?' a middle aged American man asked one of the musicians when there was a break. It turned out that he and his wife were both 'trad' musicians and had come over from Florida. They were ordered by the Irish girl to get their own banjo and fiddle out and to join in the session. They did. We now had four playing and there was an international flavour to it.

A couple of tunes later, a darkly dressed funeral party arrived. One or two also clutched fiddle and flute cases. After some soft words from the publican, it appeared that melancholic mourning was not on the agenda for them, but the more common practice of celebrating the life of the deceased. All-out chatter and musical notes filled the air now and the pints began to flow. Steadily the bar filled too. By ten o'clock a young Frenchman and a German teenager had joined the musicians with another fiddle and a guitar. I was a bit puzzled, but they played as well as anyone. In fact Pierre and Patrick sort of took over. They were gifted musicians.

'Lash away lads, we're gonna take a break,' said one of the Irish girls as both of them laid down their instruments and joined some friends at the bar for a drink. We now had four people playing reels and none of them were Irish. It dawned on me how truly international this music is. I later found out that there are Irish traditional music festivals all over the world now – from Denmark to Dorset and from Meath to Milwaukee. I understood too that the music I had longed for could have been found anywhere and through anyone, but I was still glad I was here.

The four 'foreigners' continued playing jig after reel and the Irish girls continued hanging out at the bar. Others later joined the playing. Both the drinking and music session went up another gear now, but I started to fade and managed to escape before I could be tempted by the craic of any potential lock-in. By the time I'd left, the local girls were still at the bar and had not returned to the music. I contemplated how skilfully the two had managed to get bailed out of their night's work by a German and Frenchman. Nobody seemed in the least bit bothered and it all felt a bit familiar. *Maybe they could run the country...*

CHAPTER 7

'God has given you one face and you make yourselves another'
From *Hamlet*, William Shakespeare

Next morning I had no idea where I was going to end up that evening and I was quite excited by that. I sat looking out the window of another dining room, feeling grateful that the sun was lighting the world outside again. It was Saturday and it was my seventh day on the road.

'How was last night?' asked Mary my hostess.

'Good; I went to a session in Cleary's but I wasn't out too late.'

'No, you couldn't be out late if you're doing all that cycling. Five or six pints would be the limit I'd say.'

If I'd had five or six pints I'd be dying and doing that head-in-a-vice amnesia thing. Thoughts of cycling a bike would remain just thoughts.

'No Mary. I couldn't be out late.'

'But you had a few anyway.'

From this I concluded that Mary was just making sure I was enjoying myself and for her that meant having 'a few anyway'. I felt that confessing to not drinking and being more interested in cycling was too complicated, so I lied.

'Oh yeah, I had a few anyway Mary.'

She smiled, relieved no doubt that I wasn't too much of a weirdo.

I tucked into sticky toast that I'd smeared with honey and kept myself entertained by the museum that was Mary's dining room. Ancient maps covered the retro wallpaper and all sorts of objects from every corner of the world rested on busy shelves and in cabinets. As I sipped my coffee, I noticed on one of the maps that we were quite close to the Aran Islands. I'd had a vague notion that I might visit an island on my trip if the opportunity arose, so I figured it would be good to at least explore the idea.

'How do you get onto the Aran islands Mary?'

This was a simple enough question and I really wasn't prepared for the answer.

'Well what you'll do now is this: you go on up to Doolin and you can stop off at the Cliffs of Moher on the way. Then you get the ferry at Doolin onto Inishmore, but you'll probably have to stop in Inisheer first. You'll stay on Inishmore for the night. There'll be rakes of places to stay on the island and you can have your few pints. Then the next day you can get a different ferry off the island to Rossaveel in Connemara. The ferry is only a few euro and sure isn't Connemara only beautiful?'

Wow! Mary may well have just turned into my PA and I wasn't ruling out the possibility that she was up half the night planning my day. She then produced some flyers and brochures for the Aran Island ferry companies and pointed out on the map where I could arrive back on the mainland. I was tempted. I told her I'd think about it and I did. Two things had to be considered. Firstly, I wanted to visit The Burren. This is a truly unique place covering 250 square kilometres of karst limestone plateau formed 350 million years ago when it was the bed of a tropical sea. It's also home to around ninety monuments and tombs, some of which are thousands of years old – older even than the Pyramids of Egypt. I'd never been and this is one of Ireland's great treasures. If I followed Mary's itinerary it would mean skipping The Burren which was not ideal.

The second consideration was that I felt I'd be cheating if I went to the island and then continued on to Connemara on another ferry. By doing that I would cut out around a hundred kilometres of road, which I would have had to cycle. It was probably cheating in the context of riding a bike around Ireland, but it wasn't in the context of 'life is so unfair, my knees might get sore again and why do I have to do all this cycling crap anyway?' So in fact, the proposition of going island hopping appealed hugely to my sense of *laisser faire* as well as my sense of laziness and fairness. But could I still claim to have cycled around Ireland if I had cut out 100 kilometres? To be honest, I didn't really give a shit.

'I was thinking of heading to The Burren, it's not too far from here.'

'That's right', said Mary in what had now become a comically rural Clare accent.

'Tis not far, that's right, but Doolin isn't far ayder.'

I pondered this for a minute.

'Ok, I have it. I'll go to the Cliffs of Moher on the way to Doolin.'

Mary then cut in excitedly.

'And you can have lunch then in Doolin and you can decide what to do then. Sure you can always come into The Burren through Kilfenora if you don't go to the Islands.'

'Exactly', I said. We triumphantly agreed that this was the perfect plan and it was good to know that I had a destination settled on for the morning at least. After I'd changed and packed up, I gave Mary my well spent forty euro and thanked her for her hospitality. Before leaving however, I decided to plámás her a bit. Though I had no real motive for doing so, I felt I needed the practice.

'You're a great hostess Mary'.

'Go on away out of that and don't be talkin shite.'

'No really, thanks a lot and I'm gonna do your idea. I'm gonna go to the Aran Islands. I just wanted you to know. It's a great idea.'

'And sure why wouldn't you go? They don't even close the pubs there at all.'

'Of course, I don't know why I didn't think of this before.'

'Now feck off and don't be embarrassing me. I have to make up the beds.'

Mary wasn't able to handle praise it seemed. Either that or she was wise to my plámás. She did what she felt was right and in many ways it was right. I was on holiday after all and her plan was really beginning to tempt me. It would be a nice jaunt up the coast in the morning sun, followed by a spot of lunch in Doolin and then a ferry ride to the Aran Islands where I'd have the whole night to sample the delights of the pubs that never close. I saddled up, waved goodbye to Mary, who had now come out to see me off, and began to turn the pedals. *Just one stretch of road at a time......*

◊

I was through old Milltown almost immediately and soft pedalled out the road on its northwestern side where I came to Mal Bay (from which the town gets its name). Here I reflected on the fact that Mary had advised me not to 'be talkin shite'. This was unfair I thought and Mal Bay was a reminder of why I felt this sense of injustice. Really, most of the west of Ireland exists in the midst of an awful lot of bullshit, which adds hugely to the lure of the place and for me, it started here.

Legend has it that an old hag named Mal fell in love with Cú Chulainn in these parts. Her love was not returned however, so instead of giving up gracefully, she stalked him. In fact she chased the lad around Ireland. He was of unimaginable strength of course and managed to jump off the mainland to an island in an effort to escape. She used her magic to follow, but when he jumped back, she was dashed on the cliffs; her jump fell marginally short. This was where it all supposedly happened. The faint smell of the sea greeted me when I arrived but I allowed time only to glance around the bay before continuing.

Cú Chulainn himself is a well-known figure in Irish mythology. When he was only seventeen he single-handedly defended Ulster against the army of Connaught. Not bad for a young fella. And he was popular with the girls too. In fact I suspect so many conflicting stories were told about his unmatched physical appearance that eventually, all of them were agreed to be true. His hair for example was not only brown, but blood-red *and* golden yellow. Also, he had not one but four dimples in each cheek. If this wasn't enough, he had seven bright pupils in each eye and his superiority is further demonstrated in the reports that he had seven fingers on each hand. Luckily he had a similar number of toes on each foot; I mean nobody wanted him to look weird or anything...

I was back on the N67 road now and the flat route delivered me in time to Lahinch. I cut through the pretty town and skirted the rough of the old links golf course (the Irish St. Andrews), where morning golfers were playing their rounds. The long sandy grasses of the dunes slow-danced in the breeze and I pushed through feeling truly alive.

I came quickly to the coastal village of Liscannor. This is one of the places where the Tuath de Danann, the fair-minded original Irish settled. Fearing St. Patrick and his Christian teaching, one story has it that these pagans turned themselves into horses and hid in a nearby cave. In my youth I'd heard of some ingenious efforts and excuses designed to avoid having to go to mass. Indeed I've come up with a few myself including – 'I'm allergic to incense' and the rather less successful – 'but it's a bit shit' excuse. This excuse however (turning into a horse and hiding in a cave) was definitely up there with the best of them. Unfortunately the horses met a similar fate to the witch Mal. When they did emerge from the cave years later, the light was so blinding that it scared the bejaysus out of them before they galloped off the Cliffs of Moher at a place that has become known as 'Leap of the foals'. If only they'd taken the leap of faith instead – ah well.

Liscannor's legends are plentiful. There are also stories of lost underwater cities, massive Tsunamis and giant eel slaying saints. But it's not hard to see how the cliffs would have a major impact on the imagination of the people. I was close now to the famous and spectacular Cliffs of Moher and I was looking forward to some quiet contemplation in their breath-taking splendour.

If the cliffs can provide inspiration to the people of Liscannor then it's fairly reasonable to assume that the sea would fire imaginations too – and it has. In the late nineteenth century one local man, John Philip Holland, used the sea (and possibly also the mythological story of the underwater city) as inspiration to invent none other than the submarine. After teaching for short time with the Christian Brothers, Holland sailed to America where his designs were eventually accepted by the US Navy. The company that was set up to make his inventions was known as the Electric Boat Company/ General Dynamics and it still makes vessels for the US Navy today. Who'd have thought – '*Liscannor man invents submarine*'.

That's all very well, but of course the problem is that he didn't. He especially didn't invent it if you're Dutch, English, American, German, French, Polish or even Ecuadorian, because in reality, people from all these countries had at least a hand in 'inventing' what we know today as the submarine. To be fair to Mr Holland, I don't think he was guilty of making such a claim himself – the fertile imagination of others being probably less innocent.

Dutchman Cornelius Drebbel invented the first navigable submarine back in 1620 but Mr Holland did advance the development of underwater travel greatly. His designs for the first time allowed use of both an internal combustion engine and electric power. Without this, subs today wouldn't be very effective. *Never let any facts…*

Tall silver birch trees lined parts of the road as it rose up closer to the sun and the sounds of the cliff birds, if only in the 'heart's core', seemed to welcome me to what felt like home.

'Oh my Gad they're so beautiful. I just can't believe it.'
'Oh my Gad I know. Where are the rest rooms? I gotta go again'
'Oh my Gad you just went already'.
'Let me take a picture'.
'Oh my, this is like a wonder of the world right?'
'I really need to pee'.
'Alright already.'

If only it was breath-taking for all.
These were the very audible utterances that cut through the air like spears when I pulled up. Some British tourists and I had found our meditative bubbles burst as we tried to take in the scene. We glanced at each other and gave a knowing smile. But silence returned as our friends waddled off to the loo. I managed to plug in once more to the dramatic beauty of the cliffs and I really did feel glad to be alive.

The Cliffs of Moher is one of Ireland's most visited tourist sites. Close to a million people each year come to the area which forms part of The Burren Geopark – a member of the European and UNESCO assisted Global Geopark Network. The inexpensive visitor centre, which has been carefully built into the hillside, provides virtual tours of the caves and all sorts of information about the birds and wildlife in the area. I was tempted, but I don't think I'd quite gotten over the Gallarus Oratory fiasco yet. Almost a million Americans visit Ireland each year too and it's easy to think that they are the more common tourist. They're not. Three times as many Britons come to Ireland and they are by far the most common visitor.

At this point I still wasn't sure where my ultimate destination was and I felt a little uneasy about this. So after another few minutes by the cliffs, I jumped back on my bike and headed for Doolin. *Would I end up island hopping? What to do…*

◊

Cyclists everywhere have somewhat of an affiliation. Like it's a rule, we will always acknowledge another cyclist on the road. Friendliness exists amongst us, but also maybe an understanding of the loneliness and challenges that a long ride can sometimes bring. This rule is part of the unofficial cycling code.

The acknowledgement can come in many forms, from the simple raising of a few fingers that are resting on the hoods, to a more discreet upward turn of the head. Some will vocalise the acknowledgement and opt for the all out 'hello', and if you meet someone on the road who is headed in the same direction, a full-on conversation is not out of the question (though not advised around the London or Dublin areas – or indeed in any city for that matter, as you are liable to be receive weird looks, especially at traffic lights, like I found…)

On leaving the Cliffs, I finally encountered what turned out to be a peloton of riders headed in the opposite direction. Actually there were many groups and the riders were of all ages on all types of bikes. They were clearly involved in some fun-run type cycling event and I felt it my duty to mouth a few hellos. Also I felt a little less vilified in what I had been doing for the past week; I wasn't the only 'eejit' out there pedalling. At first it was pleasant: Hi. Hello. How are ya? Hi. How's it going? Nice day. Hi. Form? Alright? Hello.

And then it got a bit tedious

Hi. Hello. What's going on? Morning. Oh it's afternoon is it? Afternoon then. Hello. Where's your helmet? *Muppet*. Hi. How's it going? Morning.'

It's easy to notice that in Ireland farmers and rural folk often try to get in on these friendly acts as well, by raising a single finger from the top of their steering wheels when passing cyclists. In fact, they do it when passing anything, maybe even their own dogs. They have their own code, borne out of friendliness, loneliness and maybe even nosiness. It's the code of the country and it's all very charming. I've found myself waving to many a stranger whose mucky index finger has commanded a response from the grip of a wheel. My wave back is never accompanied by total confidence or a lack of confusion however. *Do I know you? Have we met? I think you're mistaking me for someone else? Are you really waving to me? Okay why are you waving to me? This is making me uncomfortable. I'm shy, you know...*

Eight pleasant kilometres later and I was veering off the main road and dropping into the village of Doolin. Immediately I got a sense that this place and its people work in a completely different time frame – one of slowing motion, something in fact that may be even a little limiting, perhaps even zombie-like. Everyone seemed sleepy or maybe stoned. Some, I guessed, were nursing hangovers and others were in some kind of monk-like meditative trance –probably happier shadows of what they might have been.

My mission was to find out about getting a ferry to the Aran Islands where some of these people had probably just come from. I pretty much had decided to go. Maybe I too, after several days on the bike, wanted to tap into this somewhat handicapped state.

There are a few ferry companies that make the trip to the Islands and all their bureaus were open in the village.

'Hi, I'd like to go to Inishmore,' I said to the more spritely college girl behind a desk in one office.

'No problem, there's a ferry leaving in about an hour, though it might be two hours.'

'Okay. I'll only need a one-way ticket though as I've been told that I can get another ferry to take me off and bring me to Rossaveel in Connemara tomorrow. That's a different company isn't it?'

'Oh yes. They're a different company.'

'Oh and obviously I'm cycling so there isn't a problem taking my bike on the ferry?'

'No that's fine. We have space for bikes.'

'Great, thanks.'

Just as I was about to hand over my card to pay, the girl paused and said – 'Oh wait, there might be a problem.'

'What's that?'

'Well, the other company, the one you want to take you off the Island; they don't actually allow bikes.'

'What? What do you mean they don't allow bikes?'

'It's a new rule. They only brought it in last week. They don't bring bikes anymore.'

This sounded ridiculous. I felt that my bike had become almost an extension of myself by now. I was sort of welded to it and I was baffled as to why this would be.

'Do you want a return ticket instead? Maybe you can come back again through Doolin.'

'No, I can't do that. I'd lose a day's cycling if I did that. I have to be able to come off in Connemara.'

'I can give you their number if you'd like to call them to check,' she said.

And I did – with all the rage of what turned out to be a really polite person inquiring softly as to why my bike wasn't allowed on their ferry. I understood that the ferries were not car ferries but smaller passenger boats and therefore less spacious. *Surely they can still take a bike though?*

The woman on the other end promised to call me back with an explanation: 'My boss is at lunch, so I'll let you know what the situation is in a few minutes.'

'That would be great', I said, deciding that lunch was a good idea for me too.

Hot homemade beetroot soup was ordered in a restaurant down a little backstreet. I sat reading about Doolin and discovering that it's quite an interesting little place in its own right. The sport of caving (or potholing as it's sometimes called) is a popular pursuit in County Clare. The Doolin Cave boasts the largest stalactite in the Northern Hemisphere and attracts many visitors who marvel at it under the 'cathedral-like dome'. The village is also a hotbed of traditional Irish music and it seems that musicians and the ancient Irish are not the only ones whose imaginations have been fired by the landscape and stories of this part of the world. Japanese games writer Hidehisha Miyashita was inspired by the place so much that his 2007 PS3 computer game *Folklore* is actually set in Doolin. The objective of the game is to tap into the memories of dead people who exist in the spirit or fairy world (Netherworld). One of the important locations in the game is The Cliff of Sidhe (Fairy Cliff) from which characters jump (sound familiar?) and one of the characters, 'The Hag' (probably inspired by the witch Mal) proves problematic in the plot. Interestingly, it seems that Miyashita noticed too that the people here weren't quite there, if you know what I mean, and clearly thought it a believable location to set a cast of ghosts.

I'd never been to Doolin before and it was certainly a place that I was glad to have discovered, but as I sat waiting for the call-back from the ferry company, I tried to imagine what to expect from the Aran Islands. The little obstacle of not being allowed to take my bike on the ferry had made me more determined to go – demonstrating clear and typical self-defeating stubbornness. The joys of being a bloke... Anyway, thoughts of the Islands filled my head and I was reminded of at least one Irish writer associated with the place.

John Millington Synge was encouraged by W.B. Yeats to use the islands as a setting in his work. Synge spent many summers there perfecting his Irish language skills (the islands are Irish speaking) and learning about the islanders' way of life. He wrote a couple of plays that were based on stories he collected there, but it wasn't until 1907 that Synge's work had a real impact on Irish society. Major disturbances accompanied the first production of his masterpiece

A Cyling Fan's Ride Around Ireland

–*The Playboy of the Western World*. Set in the west (though not on the Islands), the comedy tells the story of a man who kills his father, is full of shit, does no work and has a warped sense of his own abilities. This man is celebrated by the other characters and Synge, it was felt, makes these characters out to be unholy and a bit stupid. But what really riled the audience was the inaccurate portrayal of ordinary Irish people as being not only unholy, but downright violent. This was clearly wrong and unfair in their opinion – so their solution, believe it or not, was to start a riot. You couldn't make it up.

To be fair to Synge, the riots which did mark the play's opening performance really were a rather extreme reaction to the play. I sat thinking about St. Imor of Killimer – the murder suspect, fake priest guy who did no work but was still regarded as a saint – and wondered what all the fuss was about. Maybe the play had touched a nerve for the rioters. Was there some truth to Synge's portrayals?

In any case, after a while I resigned myself to the belief that I wasn't going to get an explanation from the woman in the ferry office, so I packed up knowing that Island hopping would have to wait. I wasn't sure how bothered I was because I now had The Burren to look forward to for the afternoon. Still, without an explanation, I concluded that not allowing bikes on the ferry was just plain ridiculous. I slipped my phone into my jersey pocket (in case it rang) and cycled up to the junction at Roadford just outside Doolin. There and then, surprisingly, it did ring.

'Hello'.

'Hi, you were inquiring about bringing a bike on the ferry?'

'Yes that's me. Thanks so much for calling back.'

'No problem', said a more authoritative sounding woman.

'I hear you've changed the rules', I said.

'Yes. Well a Health and Safety Officer was here last week and he said that lifting bikes onto the top deck was dangerous, so we've had to stop taking them.'

'Okay. Why can't you keep them on the lower deck then?' I asked.

'He said that they'd get in the way there. If the boat sank then people would have to get past the bikes when they are....'

'Jumping into the sea? '

'Well. That's what he said anyway.'

'Okay. Thanks for phoning me back. You're only following rules but that is a shame. '

'I understand and we're going to lose business because of this.'

'I'm sure you are.'

'Anyway, I'm sorry about that.'

'Don't worry about it. Bye... bye bye bye bye... bye....'

And that was it. I finished the call with a worrying number of 'byes' – at least seven, which is now a common feature of Irish phone etiquette (don't ask me why). More worryingly however was that I was now faced with the fact that some jobsworth decided to piss the Touring around Ireland by bike world off (just me probably), by making up some stupid health and safety rule that has no function in reality. What actually annoyed me was that my bike was so light that anyone could easily have lifted it onto a top deck. After some pointless cursing of the Irish Civil Service, I reasoned that fate was sending me the other way, so I took out a map and found that a narrow cross-country road would lead me to Kilfenora and into the heart of The Burren. Mary would have been disappointed, but I really wasn't.

◊

There was some potholing of a different kind on this poorly surfaced route that brought me into Kilfenora village. It was a bit of an obstacle course, but once there, I decided to pop into The Burren Visitor Centre to ask for directions. Inside, spotlights, chrome and glass lit the place up and I was invited to 'take the journey through time' where I could learn about the Burren by looking at large photographs of it. I opted however to take the actually journey through The Burren and look at the actual Burren, so I just asked for directions to one of its highlights, the famous Poulnabrone Dolmen. Before leaving I did pop into Kilfenora's 12th century cathedral which is right next door.

Originally a sixth century monastic settlement and like Rosscarbery's, the cathedral was part of this very important European 'city'. Kilfenora was actually known as 'the City of the Crosses' and some of these important carvings and crosses are to be found in this church. They were impressive, but what I learned later impressed me more.

Though only a tiny place with a population of two hundred, Kilfenora still claims its right to be a bishopric and has appointed none other than the Pope himself to be its default bishop. Imagine that, the Pope, whose titles are: Leader of the Catholic Church, Sovereign of the State of Vatican City, Bishop of Rome, Successor of St. Peter the Apostle, Primate of Italy, Vicar of Jesus Christ (like Jesus needs a vicar) but also, and far more importantly for those around here – *Bishop of Kilfenora*. I wonder what Pope Francis said to the Cardinals after they saw white smoke – 'Cheers lads, thanks for the start. I hear the craic is only mighty up in KIlfenora'. *Possible, but, you know – he speaks Spanish so... unlikely...*

After a while I came to Carron. This place, which lies above a sort of valley, has an ambience all of its own. Temple Cronan, its ruined church offered a lonely and ghoulish atmosphere. I left my bike at its perimeter wall and crossed a field to explore. This silence unnerved me and I had a strange feeling that I wasn't alone or that I had been there before. It was like déjà vu, but scarier. I felt like I was in the country scene of the novel or the movie version of Orwell's *Nineteen Eighty Four*. It just felt very supernatural. The carved Romanesque heads on the outside of the church didn't help, nor did the gravestones all around and when I realised that I was also near the site of one of the world's largest Turloughs or 'disappearing lakes', I was totally freaked out.

The science explanation of how these lakes disappear is quite simple; gaps in the karstified limestone under the soil allow the lakes to fill with water and empty quickly and some of them can be affected by the tides. This was all very well, but now I wondered if there had been any instances of disappearing cyclists too. I was definitely the only person around, but the eerie feeling that I wasn't alone wouldn't go away and it was confirmed when I stepped back outside the ruin. I felt an urgent desire to return to the safety of my bike, but it wasn't so straightforward. A dopey but dangerous looking donkey type animal appeared and stood staring at me – probably with viscous intent. I didn't know what to do. *Had I stepped into another world? Is this some kind of midsummer afternoon dream? Am I in Netherland, the world of the computer game or some kind of fairy land? Am I even alive? What is this beast and what is he trying to communicate?*

I tried to scare the animal by shouting 'boo' to it, but he just stood there looking at me, doped off his face from eating weird plants. Then I realised that he was probably just as freaked out as I was. Here was a guy dressed in skin-tight clothes, with a mushroom shaped helmet on his head and dark sunglasses covering his eyes – and alien of some kind. This gave me the confidence to just walk past where I regained my bike and was soon turning its cranks.

Almost immediately I was off the bike again at the site of the famous Poulnabrone Dolmen. Busloads of Italians were filling the air with their chatter as I parked up and crunched my way on foot up a gravel path to the site. Though the dolmen is a fairly simple looking tomb of portal stones that hold up a tabular capstone, I spent a few minutes among the other tourists admiring it. There was something quite refreshing about its simplicity and it was hard to believe that what was in front of me was up to six thousand years old. The twenty five or so people who were buried there were buried with quartz crystals, weapons and pottery, so clearly some belief in an afterlife existed for these folk. There was more to discover however and I still didn't know where I was going to end up that evening.

The lunar landscape of The Burren unfolded in front of me over the next kilometres. It is a magical and beautiful place. The temperate climate and the crevices in the rocks provide conditions that allow all sorts of unusual Arctic, Mediterranean and Alpine flowers and plants to grow side by side – including the purple spring gentian. The month of May is the best time to view the floral offering but it was all very impressive and the humble feeling I'd had from the Lakes of Killarney returned. I felt lucky.

Brightly painted signs tried to lure me into the Ailwee Caves. '*Aill Bhuí*' meaning 'yellow cliff' is another attraction where rivers and waterfalls underneath the karst landscape combine with stalagmites and stalactites to provide a no doubt horrifying experience if you have a touch of claustrophobia – which clearly I have. Holing myself up in a cave for an hour would have been the very antithesis of what I was doing anyway – cycling a bike around the open countryside of Ireland. It wasn't for me. The knowledge that the cave is one of the last known bear dens in Ireland didn't appeal either. I could barely cope with a donkey type animal (which I later found out was a Connemara pony), never mind a bear den (even without the bears) and there were rumours of suicidal wild horses too in other nearby caves. *No thanks.*

Ireland's oldest perfumery didn't appeal either – though I could probably have done with something to mask the stale smell of sweat that was growing on my body.

At this stage I decided to get to Ballyvaughan, a small village in the north of the county. This place too was postcard perfect. White cottages tucked into the beached hills as boats slept lightly on the rocking chair sea.

From there I skirted Galway Bay on the N67 road until I came to Kinvarra. I'd done quite a bit of cycling by now and visited my fair share tourist attractions. I took stock over tea and a sandwich. It was well into Saturday afternoon and I felt that getting a room around this area would be difficult; tourists were everywhere. Though I had a general plan to stay away from cities, I reasoned that Galway would be my best bet for accommodation. I'd also be well placed to head to Connemara next morning. Onwards.

◊

From Kinvarra I powered on towards Galway city linking up with the horribly busy roads. It seemed a whole world away from Carron churchyard but I wasn't alone this time either. Guiding me into the metropolis, I had the Sultans of Ping FC in my ears.

> *Put on your flipflops and let's go shopping dear*
> *You can buy crisps and I can buy jam*
> *You push the trolley*
> *I'll push the pram*
>
> Niall O'Flaherty

When I arrived, I walked my bike down 'Shop Street' but the crowds of shoppers were too much, so I bailed out of town to Salt Hill where I knew there were B&Bs. I rolled up to a few places but they were all full. It was now Saturday evening and everyone was hitting the town. After a few more knocks, I started to encounter what I'd feared. B&B owners were holding out for couples and ultimately more cash again. One man actually answered the door and stood looking at me for a full minute and in a very uncomfortable silence. I could see him totting up figures in his head too as I waited.

'Your sign says vacancies,' I eventually said.

'Yes. Is it just yourself?' he asked.

'Yes'

'Right….. Eh…No. We're full. I just rented the last room,' he explained.

This was bullshit. He wouldn't have asked me if I was alone if he had rented his last room and his sign wouldn't have read 'vacancies' either. I walked away with the hump; I knew what he was doing but there was no need to lie about it.

After a while, a much more accommodating woman directed me to a B&B which was located down a dimly lit back street.

'She always has vacancies,' I was told.

I wasn't sure if this was a good thing, but I didn't have much of a choice. When I arrived, I knew straight away that I was in luck.

'You're welcome', said Valerie, a slightly frail yet over-occupied middle aged woman.

'And you've a good bike there but we'll have to put that in the shed. I'd be a bit worried about it though.'

'Why is that?' I asked.

'With burglaries and things.'

'Well can you lock the shed?'

'Of course, but you never know.'

This is great. This woman is really looking out for my bike.

'Tell you what, I can show you the shed and you can decide if it will be safe, but I must warn you that if the bike goes missing, I wouldn't be able to take responsibility for it.'

'Okay.'

Valerie led me around the back of her large house to a concrete shed that had small windows (small enough not to be able to fit a bike through) and a heavy wooden door that could be locked with a key and a Yale lock. As far as sheds go it was Fort Knox; I couldn't see what the problem was. There was no obvious hole in the roof either. Okay, I was in a 'city', but this wasn't Hackney and I'd left my bike in unlocked sheds already on this trip. I wasn't too concerned but Valerie was shitting herself.

'If you think this will be secure, but I'm not sure'.

'Well if the door locks properly, then I think it'll be fine.'

'Yes it does.'

'Have you got any locks of your own?' she asked.

'I do actually, yes.'

'Great. I have an idea,' her face lighting up.

'Why don't you lock the bike to the lawnmower so that if they try to steal it, they'd have to steal the lawnmower too and that would be awkward for them.'

I kept wondering who 'they' were, but this was great. The woman was more concerned over the safety of my bike (and ultimately my wellbeing) than I was myself, and I'd be cautious enough.

'Good idea,' I announced, though not without some confusion.

'And then', she continued, 'what we'll do is we'll put old coats over the handlebars and the seat, so that it doesn't look like a bike.'

By now Valerie was rooting out old clothing from a dusty black sack in the corner of the shed. She hung a couple of coats over the bike and though it was July, even put a scarf around one of them as I was locking it to the lawnmower. When we had finished, we had what looked like a scarecrow – in fact two scarecrows – in fact two dwarf scarecrows. Any potential thieves who might have shone a torch in the window, would have done a runner immediately on seeing the pair of leprechauns inside. My new hostess even decided that it would be a good idea to put hats on them too. This is where I stopped her.

'No need now – let you go in and have a nice cup of tea. I'll have a shower.'

'Grand so', said Valerie and she thanked me for inviting her into her own house to make herself a cup of her own tea. I liked Valerie.

Before long I was back on the busy promenade of Salt Hill. It was now a cloudy evening and the quiet of The Burren seemed a world away. The smell of fish and chips and the sight of ice-cream was all I needed to decide to have a good old traditional seaside 'tea', but first I was eager to find out who'd won the day's stage at the Tour.

I learned that unsurprisingly Bradley Wiggins had won the traditional Saturday time trial. The Tour was now over bar the cheering, but I was surprised to see that Chris Froome was second. This confirmed my suspicions that he had the beating of Wiggins. Time trialling was not Froome's best discipline, yet he was able to come second in a TT at the Tour. It was a great performance, but it was going to be Wiggins' Tour and *le Gentleman* deserved it. Whatever the outcome, things were looking pretty good for British cycling.

After vinegary paper-wrapped fish and chips, I bought a 99 ice-cream cone and sat near the water listening to it slap and plop against the sea-wall. I'd had a damn good day. The city was close and there'd be thousands of people filling the bars and restaurants at this time, but I had no desire whatsoever to join them. I was enjoying the quietude of being on the road and crowds for now seemed so unappealing.

Before long I was back in my room at Valerie's house. It was spacious and I was the only guest, but its space only reinforced the fact that I was alone. I lay on my bed feeling nevertheless content, and turned on the TV for some 'company'. After a few minutes of half-watching, something very strange happened.

We all know that people on these shores have an extremely important relationship with the weather. It's an integral part of everyday interaction. We're obsessed with it really, probably because we have no control over it. Still, I couldn't quite believe what I was seeing. RTÉ's Saturday night talk-show was pushing our relationship with the weather to a whole new level. The weather, it seemed, had now become a celebrity in Ireland, or at least those who forecast it had. Not one, but three weather forecasters who feature regularly on Irish TV were sat on celebrity couches being interviewed by the excited hostess. I was gobsmacked. It was like something out of Father Ted and the interview went something like this:

'So how did you get into the weather in the first place Susan? '

'Well Miriam, you know I've always loved the old weather you know, ever since I first felt rain, as a child you know running around in puddles and sitting in them, I remember thinking – what's this wet stuff making my arse so cold'.

'Yes, I see'.

'And did you have any training in weather forecasting?'

'Of course I was good at geography at school, but I never really had any ambition to become a forecaster. I suppose one day I just applied for the job and got it. The rest is history as they say.'

'Wow.... I see.'

To me this was hilarious. Of course no self-respecting interviewer would let this interview pass without seizing on the opportunity to get the actual weather forecast for the coming days. There were no flies on Miriam, and she duly asked the guy who is famous for winking, when saying goodnight to his viewers (you really couldn't make this up either), what the forecast was for the rest of the weekend.

'Rain' he said, and with that he wiped the smile clean off my face. *Prick.*

Then Miriam asked him to do the 'wink' and he did. It was like – here you are now, it's going to piss down on you for the rest of the week and you're all going to regret the fact that you live in this scuttery bog-hole of a country, but here's a little wink for you, just to brighten up all your miserable feckin faces.

Thanks wink man.

After a while I lay reflecting on the fact that I'd grown up. Only a few years ago the thought of spending a Saturday night in a bed and breakfast in Salt Hill/Galway, alone, watching winking weather forecasters being interviewed on TV, with a landlady downstairs who was waiting for 'them' – the intruders that existed only in her head, would have appalled me. But this was the reality of my life, and though my face might not have shown it, I was fine with that. *Dick...*

CHAPTER 8

'Think you're escaping and run into yourself. Longest way round is the shortest way home'
James Joyce

I brought my own wrinkled map to the breakfast table early next morning. Valerie had encouraged me to rise early. I suspected that she might have wanted to go to mass and I was right. A cooked breakfast was waiting when I got down but it suited me to leave by nine. I was eager to make progress again and though it wasn't raining yet, it was only a matter of time.

'What's Joyce country like?' I asked Valerie as she poured coffee.

'Oh. Let me see... Lovely but that's up in Sligo. Isn't it?'

I reckon Valerie was thinking of Yeats' country. Joyce country is an area northeast of Connemara. It has nothing to do with James Joyce; it's just where the Welsh-Norman Joyce clan settled in the fourteenth century. This family were one of the fourteen tribes that controlled the city of Galway from the thirteenth century and it's from this that Galway is named 'City of the Tribes'.

Most Irish people called Joyce are probably descendants of this clan, including James Joyce, but Yeats' Country in Sligo is so named because it greatly inspired W.B.Yeats. I wasn't too up on the history either, but I could see how Valerie could get mixed up and not really know much about local history. Clearly she never left the house, for fear of course that it would be burgled – except to go to mass – where she would probably spend her time praying that no burglary would actually take place while she was out. Life was complicated enough for Valerie, without having to worry about Joyce Country.

'You're cycling around Ireland is it?'

'Yes'.

'And where are you going to today?'

'Maybe Westport', I said as I looked at the map and tried to figure out how far it might be.

'And would you not get lonely when you're out on the roads?'

Valerie asked this question with an odd tone. It would have sounded the same had she prefaced it with – 'you're a bit of an oddball aren't you?'

To be fair this was a good question, and I hadn't really thought much about it. *Did I get lonely?* I wasn't sure. I had music to distract me on busy roads and there was also of course the beautiful countryside to admire too. Every new stretch of road brought something different and the days were passing quickly. Maybe at night when I stopped pedalling it was less than ideal to mostly eat alone, but I didn't feel lonely. In some ways, I probably felt I wanted to get away from the rat race a bit and that's why I hid from the crowds of Galway City out in Salt Hill. Also, when we are silent, we share the silence with millions of people, but when we talk, we often talk rubbish that doesn't really matter anyway. I was finding that I liked being silent more and more. This was something I hadn't known about myself before. Maybe I really was learning to meditate. I thought about Amit back in Allihies. He seemed enthusiastic for a bit of silence. Something was sinking in I felt –slowly. And it felt good.

'Oh I could never do that. I'd need some company,' said Valerie.

That's all in your head – like the burglars. Company is nice, but silence is golden.

'And there was me thinking you were going to grab one of those old bikes from the shed and join me. No?'

'God no', she said with a look of real horror.

'I haven't ridden a bike in years.'

I let the silence hang for a while before she disappeared and reappeared wearing her coat and apologising for having to leave.

'You won't mind letting yourself out?'

'Not at all', I said.

Leaving a stranger alone in a house wasn't consistent with a penchant for worry about burglary, but I had a suspicion that her husband was lurking somewhere.

'Thanks for your hospitality,' I said as I paid my hostess. It was a pleasant stay, but her house was devoid of other guests and its silence was an uneasy one, a different silence to the welcome silence of the road.

'Any time and good luck', she replied.

With that Valerie eagerly skipped off to mass.

I'd pretty much resolved to get to Westport in County Mayo, but I wasn't sure about whether to take the longer and more scenic route around Connemara, or the more direct route through Joyce country. A decision would have to be made at Maam Cross, which was my morning destination. One thing was certain; it was going to rain and I was afraid of it as much as Valerie was afraid of the burglars.

◊

I cycled back towards the centre of Galway along the waterfront and came to Claddagh before finding the main N58 road heading northwest. Claddagh, which is now part of Galway city, used to be a place all of its own. In fact the fifth century dwelling is about seven hundred years older than Galway city. Though the old city walls are only a short walk away, Claddagh had up until the twentieth century kept its own identity and culture. The Anglo-Normans of the city and the Gaelic Irish of Claddagh did not generally mix. Claddagh even had its own 'king' and was identified culturally as being particularly Celtic.

As you might have guessed, this one-time fishing village is famous for giving the world (in a roundabout way) the Claddagh ring. Legend has it that Richard Joyce of Galway designed the ring while in exile in Algiers. The goldsmith master of William III was so impressed by Joyce's work, that he offered him half his own fortune and his daughter's hand in marriage if he would become a partner and work with him when they returned from exile. Joyce refused the offer stating that he had already promised to marry a Galway girl (possibly a girl from Claddagh). When he did return, he gave her a ring which he'd designed and made for her. This became known as the 'Claddagh' ring. The design features two hands (friendship), a heart (love) and a crown (loyalty). These rings are now popular with the Irish diaspora all over the globe and are commonly passed down from generations.

Richard Joyce was only one of many Joyce characters of Galway who made names for themselves in one way or another. Hateful to both the British and Irish from the 1920s was William Joyce – aka Lord Haw Haw. Though born in Brooklyn, his parents returned to Galway when William was young. Unusually for Catholics, his family were Unionists and William is known to have helped the Black and Tans during the Irish War of Independence. He became an IRA target and later fled to England. There, he became a fascist and developed a distaste for Jews and Communists. At the outbreak of the World War II he moved to Nazi Germany, where he got a job as a broadcaster on German radio's English service. People all over Europe, including Britain, listened to him feed listeners German propaganda and he often exaggerated Britain's losses in various battles. Information about the war was limited in Britain through the BBC and Joyce became a well-known radio figure. He often mocked Britain's war effort and he even encouraged Britons to surrender. The name 'Haw-Haw' came about due to broadcasters' accents which were haughty and posh. After the war Joyce was hanged for treason. He'd held a valid British passport and it was for this reason that he was deemed to be a traitor to the King. Ironically, owing to his Irish nationality and American birth, he should never have had a British passport in the first place. Little did he know that by getting one, he would be signing his own death warrant. Ah well…

James Joyce of course is the most famous of all Joyces, but it is Nora, his loyal wife and muse, who is actually from Galway. Ireland's smallest museum in the centre of town is 'Nora Barnacle's House', a tiny two roomed cubbyhole where she grew up. Joyce's father, John Joyce, who didn't really approve of Nora, once famously said, 'Barnacle by name, barnacle by nature, she'll stick to him'. And she did. Her loyalty deserved many a Claddagh ring and more, but this attitude was curious coming from a man who drank his own family into the gutter. Indeed his son wasn't very different. James developed a penchant for whoring from the age of fourteen and also drank heavily. Nora and James' love proved very resilient however, and their love letters are considered (even by today's standards) as obscene – even pornographic. Some have fetched vast sums at auction.

Surprisingly all was quiet on the N58 road when I found it. I put my head down and got my legs moving and as I skirted Lough Corrib outside the city, I realised that I'd been lucky to have found a place to stay in Galway. Had I arrived a week later, there'd have been no chance, as the Galway Horseracing Festival would have been on. This attracts huge numbers to the city. Accommodation is booked up for months in advance as every kind of person from pauper to prince descends on the city in the name of fun and good fortune. A certain kind of working woman is also known to arrive. These women dress unusually and tend to stay indoors during the evenings. They do not attend the races and the authorities are known to keep a very close eye on them during their visit. Unfortunately it's not thought that Claddagh rings are given to these guests by those who might be interested in their friendship, love or indeed loyalty. I don't know if James Joyce ever visited Galway for the festival, but if he did, I'm sure he'd have loved it.

I was now glad to be away from the city and I was at ease in the serenity of Sunday morning. After I'd cleaned my chain and had a quick watery coffee in a station forecourt in Moycullen, I found myself riding into the naturally wild west of the county. Still mountains and lakes began to appear. At Maam Cross I stopped and looked at the sky. Turning left or going straight on would take me into the calm of Connemara but the clouds were grey. I turned right and headed for Joyce Country and the Maumturk Mountains and I was pleased I did. Within minutes I was dropping into the parish of Maum in a haze of drizzle but the grey of the beautiful Leckavrea Mountain and the lakes, were all that I needed. Suddenly it was perfect and the fear of rain seemed unnecessary. There were still no sounds, just the peace of the empty road.

I opted to stop and have another coffee in the only pub I could see. Fifty kilometres were in my legs now and not much was in my stomach so I parked up and wiped the wet off my face.

'Hi. Just a coffee and do you have some cake or chocolate?' I asked the chirpy publican who was probably the far side of forty.

'No problem. Only chocolate I'm afraid. Do you want cream in the coffee?' he asked.

This was old school. I certainly hadn't been asked that question for a long time. Ireland to me seems to have gotten carried away with its skinny, decaf, latté , single shot, soya milk and just a little cinnamon requests that are heard nowadays in coffee bars and pubs. This was back to the eighties, where you could have coffee with or without cream – simple as that – and it sounded perfect.

'Yes please, cream. I haven't had cream in coffee for a while.'

The man checked to try to understand if I'd made that comment with enthusiasm or sarcasm.

'Sounds lovely', I added just to be clear.

Soon he returned with a mug of hot coffee topped with a dollop of melting cream and a bar of plain chocolate. I'm not sure I could have been happier.

A cheerless man sat at a table by the window reading the paper with a glass of red wine stationed next to it. It wasn't too long past midday and the radio station was rounding out its news bulletin with the weather forecast.

'*Rain this evening in parts of Connaught will follow bright spells this morning*'. There was a short pause.

'Tommy is that rain I see outside?' the publican sarcastically asked the man by the window, as he stood looking at it drift across the road.

'It is'.

'Well I've been up since six o'clock this morning and it hasn't stopped feckin raining. I mean all they had to do was phone up'.

"Howaya? Are you in Connaught?"

"Yeah"

"Is it raining?"

"Yeah"

"Grand, thanks."

'What in the name of Jaysis are these forecasters doing? I mean don't tell me it's supposed to rain this evening after bright spells when I can see with me own two eyes that it's already raining now. What sort of technology are they using? A phone is all ya need, ne'er ne mind a satellite. Look at it – they haven't a feckin clue.'

I felt his frustration and he did have a point. To imply that it wasn't raining now in Connaught when it clearly was – was a bit annoying. It was probably more annoying for me, but I was getting used to it.

'Feckin eejits', he said with a shake of the head.

I can only assume that the bar owner didn't see the prime-time Saturday night show that featured Ireland's more celebrated weather forecasters the previous night. There were no 'feckin eejits' on that show. These were ambitious people who did geography at school and who winked and to be fair, they did say that it might rain. Although on reflection, they said that it might be sunny, windy, bright, fairly cloudy, very cloudy and warm as well. In fact the wink man was rather noncommittal the more I thought about it.

As I got stuck into my coffee, an elderly gentleman emerged from the lounge area walking slowly while counting out a handful of coins.

'Paddy, how are ya?' shouted the barman loudly, a call which seemed to annoy both customers.

'A pint is it?'

'Go on,' said Paddy, in a grudging tone that suggested he didn't really want one but had now been persuaded. Having the exact change already counted out and placed on the counter would have indicated otherwise however. This man seemed to prefer his own company to that of the barman's, so it was without enthusiasm that he answered his questions.

'Were ya out dancing last night Paddy?'

Paddy was at least eighty years old.

'I was not'

'Why not?'

Here I was in the heart of Joyce Country, a place that was very remote and I sat wondering where the hell Paddy would have been dancing even if he had been out throwing some shapes: *in a barn?, at a crossroads? Strictly? The thought of it...*
Or maybe it was a rave? Paddy could well have been a product of the late 80s club scene, someone who was really only sixty but who'd aged badly due to years of consuming an ambitious numbers of Es.
'My dancing days are nearly over,' he said resignedly.
Only 'nearly', this man still had ambition!
'Ah now Paddy you've plenty of moves in you yet'.
I was impressed and the barman did well to lighten the mood, but peace soon regained the room and the outside air went on spitting dots of drizzle on the glass.

◊

Sugared up, I left the pub in Maum and sliced my way through the lime green valley that splits the Maumturk Mountains and Bennacunneen. The wet poured more colour into the hills and onto the road. Soon, in the half-mist, I emerged above a damp graveyard that overlooks Killary Harbour at Leenane. Heavier rain drifted across the harbour deep in the distance and for a moment I was torn between the beauty of the scene and the disappointment of the rain.

Killary is one of Ireland's only fjords and when I stopped to admire it, the weather slowly became unimportant. I was completely taken by the rawness and almost spooky, mystical quality of the scene. It was here, near Leenane, where in 1948 famous Austrian Philosopher Ludwig Wittgenstein lived and worked. When you have breath-taking scenes like this, it's really not hard to understand why a thinker would opt to stay here.

Wittgenstein was a remarkable character. Apart from being a celebrated Philosopher, he hailed from one of the richest families in Europe. His Father was an Austrian steel tycoon and when he died, he left millions to his family, but Ludwig gave all of his inheritance away. He never bought a house and never married, choosing instead to live a freer life without constraints.

During his life he had many jobs. Apart from being a philosopher and professor of philosophy at Cambridge, he was a gardener, a primary school teacher, a hospital porter, an architect, an engineer and a soldier. During World War I he is said to have written parts of his first major work *The Tractatus*, while fighting for Austria in the trenches. Other men might have been more concerned with the rats, lack of food and the probability of getting shot, but Wittgenstein was forming his hypotheses on 'language and reality', seemingly unconcerned by the shells being fired around him. *Who said men couldn't multitask?*

When the war ended, he became a primary school teacher and worked in rural parts of Austria. His family thought he was mad. Maybe he was, or maybe their obsession with wealth was the truer madness. In any case, he didn't really get on well with any of the country folk who he described as 'one-quarter animal and three-quarters human'!

Wittgenstein visited Ireland many times from the mid-1930s and settled in a holiday cottage in Killary harbour in 1947, where he worked on his second major work – *Philosophical Investigations*. One of his beliefs was that the answer to the riddle of life lay in the disappearance of the question –'*not what life is, but that it is*'. He was a mystic of the everyday and believed that common life is all there is, a sort of religion in itself. He once said, 'silence tells no lies, silence does not deceive'. That's certainly something that Wittgenstein would have had an abundance of in this part of the world. The humble holiday cottage where he stayed, right out on the western end of the fjord, is still there and is so remote, that to this day it's inaccessible by road.

As I watched the scene, I wondered again what the silence of the road was doing for me. I was on a journey. I felt I was looking for something, but I wasn't sure what it was. So far I'd spent a week riding mostly through soundless countryside. I was feeling relaxed and at ease. I'd left behind the rush of city living and here I was in the peaceful surroundings of Leenane, thinking about a philosopher who lived here in the silence many decades ago. What did it all mean?

I still wasn't sure, but I was sure that I was going to get soaked if I didn't get a move on. That drift of rain further down the fjord was closing in and I still had a good chunk of riding to do. Remarkably, and it had really just occurred to me, that it was actually raining twice – at the same time. The omniscient drizzle was punctuated in almost all directions by heavier showers that could be made out from afar. To be fair, it was shite. And for now, my answer to the riddle of shiteness lay in the disappearance of the rain. I rode on.

The fjord at Killary Harbour marks a natural border between counties Galway and Mayo and I was soon crossing it. Already I was on the last leg of my day's ride as Westport is only thirty or so kilometres north of Leenane. So what had I to look forward to on this stretch of road? Well, County Mayo is famous for emigration and bogs, so not much I assumed. The younger version of me might have been concerned to find myself in this situation, but I was learning to lower my expectations.

To be truthful, the natural beauty of Galway continued right into south Mayo. The Partry Mountains to the east and the many rivers and lakes that I encountered en route provided more easy quiet on the road. On the N59, I soon reached Carrowkennedy and then twisted my way into the handsome town of Westport. Already I was done for the day.

◊

After a few rounds of town, I found myself stood in the slate porch of The Castle Court Hotel. Cigarette smoke clung to the air and I clung to wondering what to do. I had no idea where all the B&Bs were or which ones might be recommended. There was a Tourist Office up the street and I thought about asking about accommodation but the shower I was now hiding from prevented any such venture. I waited – listening to Sunday drinkers chat about some GAA game that was being played. It suddenly occurred to me that staying at this hotel could be an option and before I had time to weigh up the pros and cons, I was inside at the desk waiting for a receptionist.

'Hi'

'Hello, I'm just wondering if you have a room and what price it would be. It's just me – for bed and breakfast'.

'Yeah sure – we definitely have ze room', said an enthusiastic French woman as she checked her computer screen.

'Actually, we are doing a deal tonight. Ze bed and ze breakfast is just fifty five uuro.'

Holy shit – that must be a mistake. Take the room quickly. Grab the bike and get to it before they realise.

'Right. Okay. Yes. Yeah.... I'll take it,' I said as I tried to make it look like I felt this was a normal price and that nothing unusual was happening. I didn't. I thought it was too cheap. It seemed a well-designed and decorated four star hotel. The staff were friendly, it was busy and from the pictures by the desk, there looked to be a stylish leisure centre there too. Really it was only five or ten euro more than what I was expecting to pay in a B&B. It felt like I'd struck gold.

'It's okay to bring my bike to the room isn't it?' I asked with squinting eyes and half raised cheeks in a sort of pleading expression.

'If you don't mind, we don't mind.'

'Wow.'

In hotels I'd much rather my bike was in my room. With so many people around it feels safer if I can see it, but I always imagine the staff would never be too happy about this. In reality they don't really care where it goes. In fact, they'd probably prefer not to have the responsibility of looking after it.

When I found the room I couldn't contain my excitement. It was comparatively palatial and anyone would have thought I'd never stayed in a hotel before. I parked my bike by the window, jumped on the bed and sprawled out like a starfish. The relief was massive and of course charging fifty five euro wasn't a mistake. I'd just let my imagination decide that staying in hotels for two weeks would be very expensive, so generally ruled them out. But now I considered how easy it all was. Only a few minutes before, I was stood at the porch glancing inside and stressing about where I was going to stay, when all along the answer was right in front of me and it was far better than any B&B that I could have imagined. I felt that maybe this was a metaphor too; that often what we want is in front of us.

When you're on the road and pushing your body, the luxury of a hotel like this is really appreciated. How many times have we stayed in hotels before where we dump our bags, go out, return very late, sleep through breakfast and get turfed out next day without experiencing the hotel itself? That certainly wouldn't be happening this time. I was going to use and appreciate this place and I had the rest of day in which to do so. There was also the town too, but first up would be the leisure centre.

I arrived wearing my cycling shorts. I had nothing suitable for the pool so they'd just have to do but I was pretty much the only person around except for Johnny, a skinny fair-haired man who I'd guessed was in his late forties. I was about to learn quite a lot about Johnny – more probably than he knew about himself.

I went for a steam first and within thirty seconds Johnny, who had been lurking by the shower area, joined me.

'Hi,' he said in his gentle drawn-out Donegal accent.

'Hello.'

'Aw it's a dirty auld day', he moaned in what sounded like a polished impression of Daniel O'Donnell – the best I've heard, but it was no impression.

'You're cycling I see'.

No shit Sherlock but you'd have only known this if you were actually looking at my cushioned arse or crotch.

'Yeah– doing a bit.'

'I'm Johnny' he said, as he offered me his hand.

'Nice to meet you', I said uncertainly as I shook it.

'I love cycling. I don't do it but I like watching the races on the tele. Did you see the Rás? I love the Rás. It's so colourful. It was up in Donegal this year.'

'No I wasn't around for it'.

'Aw that's a shame'.

After a bit, I sensed that Johnny was bored but I really didn't feel like that was my problem. I just wanted to sit in silence and sweat.

'It's so hot and steamy in here' he said as he let out a sigh.

It's a feckin steam room you gobshite. What did you expect?'

'Yeah, it is hot alright', I agreed.

After a few minutes, I got up, said my goodbyes and took my sweating skin into the cool water of the pool. I did a couple of lengths to loosen out my leg muscles but I'd ridden around a hundred kilometres so I wasn't really inclined to do more. Johnny, I noticed, was back hanging out by the shower area, so I felt it was an ideal opportunity to have the Jacuzzi all to myself. I got out, stepped up to the bubbling water and eased myself in. Within a minute Johnny had joined me.

'Oh, I love the Jacuzzi' he said with enthusiasm.

By now I'd have taken back the silence of the road in exchange for this.

'It's so bubbly.'

No feckin shit. This guy is a genius.

'Yeah – it's bubbly.'

'Hmmm, that's nice,' he moaned.

I tried to encourage the silence and it worked for a bit but before long Johnny broke it again:

'I like giving massages,' he announced without warning and when I looked at him his eyes were fixed on me.

Oh shit.

'Really? Well, why don't you become a masseur then?' I said, feeling a little uneasy.

'Oh I am – part-time'.

It may have been my imagination (I had already thought I saw the Virgin Mary wink at me on this trip), but for a split second I was sure that Johnny had offered me a little wink of his own – a gesture (real or imagined) that had me out of the water in –well, the blink of an eye – with my towel firmly wrapped around me.

'Have a good evening. Nice to meet you,' I said as I tried walking casually to the relative safety of the changing rooms. There I grabbed my stuff and did one, opting to wash off the smell of chlorine back in my room. Luckily Johnny stayed put and after another shower, I decided a little housekeeping was needed; hand-washing my cycling kit using ordinary soap was a chore that just had to be done.

◊

Later from the ITV news I learned that Brad Wiggins had unsurprisingly just become the first Briton to win the greatest bike race in the world –the Tour de France. *Chapeau to him,* I thought as I saw him unselfishly lead Cavendish out for the last sprint of the race. Again there was no surprise that Cav won the final stage on the Champs Elysees. Our man Froome was second overall and the place part of my each-way bet was landed. This was good news and my stay in the Castle Court hotel at least was covered. It was a profitable Tour for this fan at least.

It was now time to 'celebrate' and I did with a fine roast dinner in the hotel's carvery restaurant which I washed down with a lemon sorbet –a modest celebration. The evening showers had finally stopped so exploring the town was on.

Westport was new to me and I was impressed by its Georgian architecture as well as its tree-lined streets and riverbanks. Folks from the town are known as 'Coveys' and at one time they had their own 'impossible-to-understand' dialect. I suppose they're sort of Connaught's answer to Cockneys but without the singing or dustman lineage. Some words of this dialect actually remain in use including 'doner', which means woman. I'm not sure where this comes from but it's unlikely to be related to Turkish kebabs. Any proposal to 'sink a few light ales and murder a doner' is ill-advised should you ever find yourself in Westport of an evening. Similarly the word 'lay' means a drink and indeed it's probably best not to be too alarmed should you hear of any locals going out for a 'lay' with the hope of 'chatting up a few doners'.

During a saunter I wandered into Matt Molloys pub for a 'lay'. It was busy. Half the town were out laying and though music is what the pub is most famous for, the session hadn't started yet. The owner of this bar is none other than Matt Molloy of *The Chieftains,* one of Ireland's best known traditional groups – the

Take That of trad. There was no sign of him when I planted myself at the bar counter, but the atmosphere more than made up for the lack of celebrity.

'Where in the name of Jaysis was that referee from?' asked a Meath man who was obviously sore about the fact that his team had just lost to Dublin in a Gaelic football match. GAA sport isn't really my thing but the banter of the fans made for interesting listening.

'The fuckin blind association of Ireland,' answered a fellow Meath fan, a comment that was generally well received.

'Ya know', he continued, 'I read in the paper they're gonna get him to referee the All-Ireland final with a golden Labrador leading him around the pitch.... and a big white stick.'

'Feck off, that was never a penalty,' argued a man wearing a Dublin jersey, but this only strengthened the Meath men's protestations.

'Don't be giving me that – sure even a dog with a hammer up its hole would have given a penalty.'

This comment, rather than elicit some sort of laughter in the name of good craic, did the opposite. An uneasy silence punctuated the group as everyone, myself included, stopped to imagine how a dog would have managed to get such an object stuck up its arse. The man who said it, took a slow sip of his pint and peered around over the top of the glass in search of some kind of approval. It was slow to come but eventually it did.

'Yeah... and a whistle in its mouth, blowing for a fuckin penalty – I'm tellin ya – that was the game changer, shouldda been a peno. It's shockin.'

This comment also appeared to nail the Dub's argument to the cross and everyone just let it go. There were also Donegal fans in the bar. Their team too had won earlier in the day and this served to create a jovial sing-song atmosphere with the locals. Maybe the Coveys are like Cockneys after all. It was all very good humoured and I was enjoying the craic.

Then surprisingly Johnny walked in, with, would you believe, his wife. The article I was half reading in the newspaper suddenly became very interesting as I tried to avoid his gaze. When I eventually looked up, I saw that my friend from the pool had settled at the back of the pub. For a while I stayed at the bar imagining Johnny turning himself into a one-man Daniel O'Donnell tribute act. I had visions of the whole place swaying from side to side in unison – a frenzied riot of country music and GAA excess. It didn't happen. Not while I was there at least, but I left soon after. The idea of eating pizza had also planted itself in my head and it wouldn't go away.

Another stroll led me at last to a pretty bad Neopolitan pizza, the base of which was more like a child's Liga biscuit. Still, I managed to put it away and not long after decided to call it a night. Despite the rain, the day had been a good start to my second week of touring and I went to my king sized bed happy, hoping that four star hotels would become a bit of a theme. And they would.

CHAPTER 9

'Science and art belong to the whole world, and before them vanish the barriers of nationality'
Johann Wolfgang von Goethe

When Paul Kimmage signed with the RMO cycling team for the 1986 season, he was surprised to learn that riders were required to hand-wash their own kit. This meant that in July at the Tour, after daily tortuous rides of around 200k in the Alps and Pyrenees, he spent his evenings scrubbing oil and road debris from his jersey and shorts. He was only given five sets of kit for the whole three week Tour. This is a chore that some riders have continued to do until very recently in the sport. It's not all glamour. Even twelve year olds who play football get their kits washed by the coach or his wife!

Kimmage's salary for that season was £700 per month. In today's money that wouldn't be much more than €2,000, or €24,000 per year, which is considerably lower than the new minimum wage for top teams' riders of around €37,000 per annum. These figures are really quite shocking considering the hardship that riders endure. A lot of top level European footballers earn this sort of money in a week and when they have to play two games in that week, they whinge and moan. The less grateful tweet things like:

'seriously getting pissed off... do I wanna go Hull City No do I wanna go Stoke No do I wanna go Sunderland Yes so stop f****** around'

This was a message from Darren Bent to Tottenham Hotspur chairman Daniel Levy from a few years ago. I mean the grammar alone... The tweet was actually sent before Spurs did finally offload him to Sunderland where he earned €3.6 million a year. Poor Darren – life is so unfair.

In relative terms, *domestiques* or team riders earn a pittance in pro cycling. Only the stars earn salaries approaching those of top footballers'. Most of the rest are water carriers, but to even finish a race like the Tour de France is a huge achievement. I know I couldn't do it. You have to wonder if these pros are sort of artists too. They replace the potential of better money and security in other jobs with a kind of 'risk' – all for the love of what they do. Surely there are easier jobs too. I suppose if the love is there, there's no choice. This applies even more so for amateurs. There are easier ways to spend an afternoon. I didn't have the answers, but I can't help but have admiration, especially for the 'water carriers'.

In some ways, though I know I wasn't racing, as a fan of the sport I also wanted to know what it would be like on a practical level to ride for a couple of weeks around a country. I've ridden many a sportif and raced briefly as a kid, but these excursions are over in a few hours. Riding my own little tour, albeit solo, was also giving me even more of an appreciation of what real cyclists do for a living.

I remembered Paul Kimmage's displeasure at having to hand wash his kit, which I'd read about years ago, when I stretched up to check if my own kit was dry. It wasn't, but I didn't care. Morning mist and rain haunted the world outside. The winking weatherman had said it would clear by midday, which was also chucking out time from the hotel, so it wasn't hard to choose this as a departure time. My destination? Who knows?

Waistcoat wearing waiters flitted around the buzzy dining room when I walked in. I was offered a choice of newspaper and brought to a table where I was informed of the special options, which included pan-fried rainbow trout. There was also a huge traditional breakfast buffet but the trout sounded great so I ordered it.

'Help yourself to the buffet anyway,' the waiter said.

'Really?'

'Of course... for your first course.'

'Of course – my first course.'

So I did. In fact, I helped myself to breakfast and lunch at the buffet anyway. Lunch came in the form of French pastries, Irish cheese and Jamaican bananas, which I discreetly shoved into a napkin and kept for the road. Okay maybe not that discreetly. I started off with thick porridge and fruit yogurt. When the fish arrived I knew immediately it was going to be good and I couldn't quite get over the fact that everything was the price that it was. Savouring every bite, I must have taken two hours over breakfast and lingering in the aroma of coffee, pretty much read the whole paper.

The back pages were all about Wiggo and Team Sky. The British team and British riders generally had just had their most successful Tour de France ever. Sky dominated with the top two places in the General Classification. Wiggo took two stages, Froome one and sprinter Mark Cavendish had taken three. The team also finished second in the team classification. But there was another British rider, David Millar, who took a stage for the American Garmin team. That's Britons winning a third of the stages, the overall and the runner up spot. Road cycling is traditionally not a British sport and it's easy to miss the enormity of this achievement. To put it into perspective, what British riders did at the 2012 Tour, would probably be akin to France winning the Cricket World Cup.

You only have to go back to 1955 to discover the pioneers who really brought the UK into the consciousness of Europe as a cycling nation. The Hercules team (so named after the bicycle company which later merged with Raleigh) were the first British trade team to ride the Tour de France. Unlike Sky's outfit, all ten starters were actually British, but only two finished the race. Tony Hoar finished last but Brian Robinson came in an eye-catching 29th overall. This didn't quite start an influx of UK riders or teams. Hercules never returned and British involvement for the next fifty years was limited to individuals and small also-ran teams that were few and far between. Nevertheless, Robinson did a lot more for British cycling in riding the 1955 Tour than the result sheets show. He was the seed sower who led the way for others. Tom Simpson and Barry Hoban soon followed and all of these riders would in turn influence the riders of the 80s through to those of today.

When David Millar won stage twelve of this Tour to Annonay on 13th of July, he did it deliberately on the forty fifth anniversary of Tom Simpson's death. For me, as Millar is a vocal anti-doping ex-doper and Simpson died riding the Tour on Mont Ventoux with amphetamines in his system, this was the true blossoming of British cycling. And it was good to watch. *No more roping off the Brits as also-rans.*

After a silky hot bath, I used the hair dryer to finish off drying my shorts, but there was really no point. At midday the rain was very real. It looked like it was here to stay too. When I pulled out of Westport, the backwash from my rear wheel made a mockery of my efforts to dry my shorts. I might as well have ridden off with someone aiming a fully charged garden hose at my arse. The roads were disgustingly wet and though I felt rejuvenated by the whole hotel experience, it was hard to feel good. Also again I sensed St. Swithin's smug smile from above.

◊

Before I had left town, I noticed a flyer in the hotel foyer. It read: 'Westport – The Outdoors Capital of Ireland'. I gave this a little thought as I met the open road. We've already seen how brazen the marketing in Ireland can be. Listowel as 'Literary Capital' being the prime example so far, but I couldn't really let this one go either. In reality this is an example of how to turn absolutely nothing into, well, a flyer at least. Can Westport really be the 'Outdoors Capital of Ireland'? Is there really more outdoors in Westport than anywhere else? Or are there just less doors in Westport? If there are less doors, then there's just less stuff. Less stuff generally means less to do, but not in Westport, because clearly less is more – outside at least...

Yes there are things to do in the area like fish, hike, sail, run and cycle ('Covey Wheelers' being the cycling club) and most of these things are done outside, but really, people can do those things anywhere. Anywhere there's an outside in fact. It's not necessary to go to the 'Outdoor Capital of Ireland' for this and if you do, it won't necessarily be better than anywhere else. I knew this because for the previous week at least, I'd been outdoors and there's a lot of it. Though it is a fine spot, there isn't really more of it in Westport. If you want a real good helping of the 'outdoors', get on a boat and row it far out into the Atlantic – plenty of nothing there I'd imagine.

Of course the marketing doesn't stop there either. In 2014 the Irish tourist board launched 'The Wild Atlantic Way'. This is a route covering the Atlantic

Coast from Cork to Donegal. As you can imagine, it's very outdoorsy. But what has changed? Well nothing. Previously known as *The West Coast of Ireland*, it's a coast that has been there for millennia but that's a name we're not really allowed to use anymore. It's the *Wild Atlantic Way* now and there are blue squiggly signs all over the place to prove it. Nobody needed these signs before 2014 of course. Intuition and luck was used to get you to places then. I love too how they've cleverly added the word 'wild' to the new name so as to suggest that they already know the weather is going to be shite, but that it's still worth visiting: 'What, you didn't bring your waterproofs? On the *Wild* Atlantic *Way*? Sure ya didn't think you were in feckin Magaluf did ya? Gobshite…'

As it happens, one of the best known outdoorsy people in Irish history was from Westport. *Oh no – maybe there is a bit of truth in the claim after all.* Her name was Grace O'Malley – aka Granuaile. She was really the first person to tap into the earning potential of the outdoorsy qualities of Mayo – a pioneer in her own right, and she was active in the mid to late sixteenth century.

Attracted by the sea from an early age, Grace became a very good sailor and it's on the sea where she made most of her fortune. In short, she was a pirate. Ships that passed her lands in Clew bay or at Clare Island were boarded and the cargo was taxed. Maybe it was a first outdoorsy tax? Who knows? Anyway, she was very successful and much feared. Anyone who didn't cough up was likely to end up sleeping with the fishes. Whatever her true nature, I couldn't help think she's set the example of making something out of nothing in Ireland's west.

I found myself on the N5 road out of Westport heading northeast. It really wasn't a day for leisurely cycles up the coast. Without really thinking about it, I knew that I was headed for Sligo. This would be a diagonal cut straight across Mayo County. There was nothing more I could do.

Shortly I arrived in Castlebar, where the rain ravaged the road. I was soaked. Imagining St Swithin smiling smugly, gave way to actually seeing real people laughing and pointing at me from their cars. A few were nice enough to blow horns and shout encouragement out their windows too.

'Go on ya mad hoor,' was one particular holler.

'Would ya look at the state of yer man?' being another.

'What a bollix', was a more concerning one.

Their 'encouragement' did make me realise that riding in this was a bit excessive but, I knew the rain would clear soon. It didn't.

Castlebar is the actual capital of Mayo – the indoor capital. There are certainly more doors in Castlebar than anywhere else in the county. I made no attempt to pass through any however. I didn't even pass through the town, just rounded its outskirts. One crowd who did manage to make it into the town back in 1798 were the United Irishmen. Soldiering being an outdoorsy pursuit generally, it was only natural that they'd arrive in Mayo and they were accompanied by around eleven hundred French soldiers under General Humbert. Contrary to Wolfe Tone's disaster back in Bantry two years earlier, their invasion was initially successful and they took the town of Castlebar from British Crown forces. In fact, they took it quite well, prompting many redcoats to flee rather rapidly. This episode became known as the 'Castlebar Races' – on account of the speed at which the British fled. But it didn't last long.

A 'Republic of Connaught' was quickly declared by the Irish and French. This however was just another early example of hopeful marketing (there's a definite pattern here). Unfortunately for the rebels, the British saw through it. Within days they were captured in Longford. The French were sent back to France, a happy fate really. The Irish were less fortunate and were sent to their maker.

Rain has a habit of making you go faster, especially on a bicycle. It's sort of like a conditioned response. When you feel wet, you move quickly. It just happens. After Castlebar I reckoned Sligo was about eighty kilometres away and I pretty much decided to aim to arrive without stopping. The route I was now going to take helped with this decision, primarily because there was actually nowhere to stop anyway. Certainly there was nothing to see (except of course the outdoors). In short, I decided to time-trial my way to Sligo. I had food in my back pockets, courtesy of the 'breakfast' buffet, my water bottles were still full (you tend to drink less when it's raining) and I felt I had the fitness now to just ride on without needing much of a rest. Also, it was pretty flat and if there was a breeze, it was at my back. Maybe it wasn't much of a decision after all. There was really nothing else to do but ride.

Not far from Ballavary I peeled off the N5 and found myself on the N58. This was quieter and a much more pleasant road to be on, though it too was awash with grey rain. I pushed along, crossing the hissing Moy River until it brought me close to the shores of Lough Conn and Lough Cullin. But before long, I was off it again and onto some fairly narrow pattering country lanes.

Some major attractions of the west of Ireland are the beautiful lakes and I was looking forward to seeing a couple of them at least over the next few days. Mayo's Lough Conn is one of the bigger and more beautiful ones. An island on the southern shore is known as Illannaglashy, which means 'Glass Island'. It's so named because for four hundred years it was used for the illegal distillation and bottling of poitín (poteen). This alcoholic spirit is a made from malted barley, maize and potatoes and can be up to 90% proof (ABV). It was outlawed in the 1600s, probably because if it didn't make you violently sick or mad, it would at least have turned you into a mumbling gobshite. It's Ireland's 'moonshine', so named because its production and distribution was done covertly and often under moonlight. It could easily be called Ireland's face-shine for other reasons. Anyway, it was common practice to distil the spirit on lake islands, for the simple reason that the authorities could be spotted approaching and it was easy to dispose of the produce should a raid be made. If you ever want to know what poitín tastes like, or the effect that it might have on you, go into your shed and pour yourself a nice glass of paint stripper.

Remarkably, in 1997 the Irish authorities decided that, though banned for four centuries, poitín was no longer bad for you. Either that or they felt there weren't enough mumbling muck-savage gobshites knocking about. There are. In any case, this 'drink', which is sometimes used for rubbing into sore muscles and on livestock for all sorts of reasons, can now be consumed without the threat of prosecution. There's no guarantee that you won't be prosecuted after you go off your game from drinking the stuff however. Just some of the other side effects of drinking poitín include blindness and death.

None of this seemed to bother a Mayo man who'd recently appeared in court in Castlebar. He'd been arrested at A&E for being intoxicated and for 'threatening and abusive behaviour'. The court heard that the man had obtained poitín in order to treat his sick dog. He claimed that when he drank it, he didn't know he was drinking poitín as it was just a clear liquid in a clear bottle *(yeah and it tastes exactly like lemonade)*. When asked by the judge if it was to 'rub on' his dog, he remarked, much to the amusement of the court, 'the dog didn't drink it anyway... he doesn't drink'.

Unsurprisingly the man can't remember much else about what happened the night of his arrest. He was made to write a letter of apology to the hospital staff and pay some money to a charity – and you really couldn't make this up either – a charity for the blind no less! Poitín is still banned in the North of Ireland.

The road I was now on got narrower, grittier and quieter the further along it I went. After a while, though I knew that I was headed in the right direction, I decided that I was lost. Deep down I knew I wasn't, but the remoteness of the countryside in this part of Mayo was such that I felt I needed reassurance. I spotted someone walking the road in the distance and decided to ask if I was headed in the right direction. I knew from my map that if I got to a place called Aclare, I'd be able to figure things out from there.

'Hello, am I headed in the direction of Aclare?' I said to this older man when I came to him. He had the appearance of someone who probably worked on the land. He had an almost toothless head, rough red skin and his clothes didn't look too dissimilar to those which you might find on a rugby player after a hard match. In truth, and to be quite blunt about it, he was covered in shite.

'Aclare... Oh, but Aclare is in County Sligo'.

'Yes... but is it this way?'

'You're in Mayo now.'

'I know... but I want to find Aclare.'

'But I'm from Mayo'. I wouldn't know Sligo at all really.'

This fellow seemed to have some kind of mental block around the geography of another county, even though it was only ten or twenty kilometres up the road.

'Have you been to Aclare?' I asked.

'Ah... years ago maybe', he admitted.

'So do you know which direction it's in?'

'Keep going.'

'Thanks.'

It's known that people in Ireland are very proud of the counties they come from, but it appeared that this fellow didn't want to admit that he knew much about Sligo. It was almost as if he accepted reluctantly the fact that it was even there, and there was certainly pride in his voice when he said that he was 'from Mayo'.

'Keep going' I did. The smell of peat that I'd last encountered in north Kerry returned. The boggy land I was now riding through is not much use for farming and I got a real sense of how money might be scarce in this area. I could certainly see how emigration is common, loneliness probably too. As the rain kept falling, the earth kept swallowing and I kept pedalling.

◊

Loose and excitable dogs are the occasional curse of cyclists. We encounter them more so in rural areas. I have a friend Dale, who has a great way of dealing with them. 'Show no fear and look them in the eye' is his mantra. When I saw that a fox sized mongrel 'dog' which looked exactly like a fox (it was red, had a bushy tale and sharp teeth) had spotted me from afar, I thought about Dale's advice. When it ran towards me eyeing my ankle and barking madly however, I showed no guts instead. The fact that I'd never seen a 'dog' like this before didn't help. The belief that I was a goner strengthened, but I clicked the chain into the biggest gear and rode like a lunatic past it. The problem was that it took quite a while to get past. Sprinting and barking upsides me, this angry cur caused a final mad charge of adrenaline to course through me. One last burst of energy ensued. I'd have easily taken Mark Cavendish in a sprint had he been there, I thought (*I could barely take this fox-dog*), but unfortunately Mark was in Paris and I was in a bog in Mayo. This 'win' would have to remain in my head (like most things) for now.

When I eventually looked back, I saw the animal stood in the road and heard its triumphant howl. The time trialling at least was going well and I soon made it to Aclare, where luckily signposts, if nothing else, were in fashion. Here I felt I was back on track, though I was never really off it. I was in County Sligo now and had the Ox Mountains in the west to dwell on. It didn't really matter that I couldn't see them very well in the gloom; the knowledge that they were there was enough. It was time too for lunch and I ate as I rode.

After a while on these silent roads something quite significant happened. Near Cloonacool, I realised that the rain wasn't so bad after all. Okay I was wet, but my clothes were designed to keep the moisture off my skin. Even if it hadn't, skin is luckily designed to keep water off your insides. I had a rain jacket and I was warm. It really wasn't all that bad and I felt that in a strange way I was actually enjoying riding in the rain. I understood too that the fear I'd always had about these riding conditions was just that – fear. It was irrational, like the fear of being lost when I wasn't actually lost. I tried to think of negatives about it and really, I couldn't think of many. So what if I was wet? We don't jump into a pool and then get out complaining that we're soaked. It wasn't cold and if it was very hot I'd have been wet from sweat anyway. It was a penny dropping moment and I thought back to the fjord at Killary harbour (where it was raining twice) and understood that the rain was as dramatic and beautiful as a sunlit road. This was the moment when I killed the fair-weather cyclist that I'd always been. I swore that I'd never again complain about the wet. This probably lasted for five minutes, but I put that down to habit. The cold in winter might be a different matter, but for now at least, I was suddenly enjoying my watery day.

Before long I found myself riding just above and parallel to an old disused railway line near Coolaney. Ghosts moved in imaginary carriages from fifty years ago. The silence of the world, the empty roads and the vacant lands were a joy too. I rode on and on, over the Owenbeg River and finally linked up with the main route into Ballisodare from the west. The rain here was still on show and though I was happy on the bike, I was also looking forward to getting off it.

Ballisodare could well be the ghost estate capital of Connaught. The empty newly built buildings are the curse of greed – a monument to developers' dismal attempt to 'add the halfpence to the pence'. I was now moving into Yeats' country and his words still haunt the land.

Sligo actually means 'shelly place', on account of the shells that are found on its shores. Nowadays it could well describe the unfinished shells of buildings scattered around the county. In total, seventy seven ghost estates, the second highest number in an Irish county, are lying empty there – a frightful thought really in any society.

It didn't take long to get to Sligo town from Ballisodare and by the time I did, I felt I'd done enough riding for the day. Without hesitation, and on the back of my luxurious stay in Westport, I headed for the first decent looking hotel I saw, where I hoped that some similar midweek deal would be available. That hotel, right in the town centre, happened to be The Glass House.

As its name suggests, this modern and less disastrous relic of the Celtic Tiger economy, reflects a newer, more sophisticated Sligo. It certainly was all new to me. I hadn't been to the town since I was a child, but in the rain, Sligo really didn't stand out from any other Irish town.

'Out training in this weather?' asked a suited man at the hotel's entrance.

'Touring actually, I've just come from Westport'.

'My god, that's a good long spin and you must have gotten soaked.'

'Ah well. I love the rain really me.'

'Really?'

'Not really... No, though I'm learning not to get too pissed off about it.'

'Well you've no choice I suppose. I ride a bike myself. We're doing Alpe d'Huez next month.'

'Wow. That'll be tough. Hot too.'

'I know. I'm shitting it. I've only been cycling for a month.'

'Oh'.

'Well good luck with your touring.'

'Thanks'.

And off he went. I'd just met one of the new wave of cyclists. I was impressed that he'd be taking his bike to ride in the Alps, but if he was impressed by my 102 kilometre flat spin from Westport, he's right to be worried about his trip to Alpe d'Huez.

A Cyling Fan's Ride Around Ireland

◊

With its fourteen kilometres of uphill riding at an average gradient of 8%, Alpe d'Huez is the Mother of Alpine cycling climbs. It was first introduced to the Tour de France in 1952, when Faustino Coppi claimed the win at the famous ski station summit. It wasn't much liked however, certainly not by journalists and it took eighteen years before it was introduced again where this time, the perception of it was wholly different. The climb became legendary. It does not however feature in every Tour and I'm sure Wiggo, not being a climbing specialist, was glad it was missing from the 2012 edition.

Winning atop Alpe' d'Huez immortalises its conqueror because one of the twenty one punishing hairpin bends will be named after the stage winner. For riders, this Alpine stage is like a classic race within a race. It may not be the hardest climb, but it is the Queen of all Tour climbs, the one that attracts the most people and the most dedicated cycling fan. Up to half a million cycling pilgrims are known to go wild on the slopes as the Tour comes through. It has been described as 'The Glastonbury Festival' for Tour fans and it is the largest natural sports arena in the world.

Dutch fans are the most vocal and numerous on this Alp. Some camp out for weeks in advance at 'Dutch Corner' and come race time, the beer and house music set the scene, where they literally and metaphorically paint the hill…well, orange. There is even a Dutch sportive event that climbs the Alp not once, but six times! In the 2013 Tour, the race ascended it twice in one day for the first time ever. It became known as 'Double d'Huez. 'Irish Corner', also appeared on Alpe d'Huez for the first time that year. Being not one for roping off nationalities much, even within a nation, I wouldn't be the most enthusiastic about doing it on a mountain. But if singing football anthems and the Fields of Athenry with greenly-clad revellers is your thing –then you're in luck.

Thinking of Alpe d'Huez outside this hotel, I was really quite relieved that I didn't have to endure any of the kind suffering that my friend had ahead of him. Not yet anyway…

The Glass House, a tall angular glass structure which lies along the Garravogue River, was built to resemble a ship docked in port. Inside I was offered a room for a reasonable price and decided to stay. I clumsily lifted my bike into the lift and took it to where the 1970s IKEA-like showroom that is this hotel appeared before me. In my room everything was orange and brown. Management even had oranges placed in glass bowls just in case the curtains, carpets, lamps, bedding, pictures and fixtures weren't orange enough. It could well have been a tidier version of Dutch Corner at Alpe d'Huez. It was certainly different.

After a short rest I wandered off to check out the town and right opposite my shiny hotel, just across the river, I stumbled upon The Yeats Memorial Museum. This was a much more romantic redbrick building and it provided more than just situational contrast; it's a symbol of old Ireland.

Yeats, I don't think, would have been too enchanted by my hotel and all that it stood for. He had a 'spawning fury' of the modern world. In a way, he probably would have preferred if we all rode horses and carts around, spent our time picking daisies on fairy hills and writing poetry in yoga poses. He agreed that where the Saxon was often pragmatic, practical and scientific, the Celts were much more emotional, poetic and spiritually inclined. In fact, he saw the Irish as almost opposite to the English.

Was this too a roped off generalisation, or was there truth in it? I wasn't sure.

I was pleased and surprised that this museum was still open as it was well past 5pm. A couple of foreign tourists who were ahead of me led the way inside and I felt glad that my day would not after all, be solely a day of travelling.

The dark rooms within revealed an old musty handwritten world. Dull black and white photographs clung to its walls and dusty books lay opened in well used display cabinets. All this enabled us to delve into the world of the great poet. I, being more inclined towards sentiment and meditation, was just beginning to get excited when a panic stricken woman entered.

'Oh no, did I leave the door open? Eh, you can't come in I'm afraid. We're not open. We closed a while ago but I mustn't have closed the door properly. You'll have to come back tomorrow. We open at 10am sharp. Sorry.'

It was clearly beyond the bounds of the woman's imagination to allow anyone inside after closing time. Rules are rules. It was important to be practical and pragmatic, for fear of course that we might open the floodgates to other late-coming dreamy Yeats enthusiasts. There was clearly nothing to be gained from allowing us a few minutes to browse through the open letters and poems. Spontaneity was out, as well as emotion, spirituality and obviously poetry. The foreign tourists, who I think were Spanish, looked bemused and a little hurt that they too were shuffled on.

'Vale, Vale.'

At least it had stopped raining – kind of.

I decided to eat early. I wanted to visit Lough Gill next morning before I headed north again. Yeats was also the reason for this visit. The tiny Inishfree Island on Lough Gill was the inspiration for his most famous poem – *The Lake Isle of Inishfree*. The lake at least, where 'peace comes dropping slow', was something I wanted to see. Monday was likely to be quiet around Sligo, so with Lough Gill in mind, having an early night appealed.

While wandering, I discovered that Sligo is in fact a 'city'. The realisation that I had now broken my ambition to stay away from cities on this trip didn't bother me however. In reality, Sligo is a city in name only. It's really a pretty town – a town I was soon to discover, which has its own 'Italian Quarter' no less! My excitement at this discovery didn't last long unfortunately, as the 'Italian Quarter' is made up of just two Italian restaurants and one fairly lonely Italian flag. All are situated on a narrow pedestrianized street near the river. That's really it. There wasn't even a *Vespa* around that might have made the scene more convincing, but I couldn't help notice again our need to rope everything off when it comes to nationality. In any case, I had been fantasising about a giant bowl of pasta all day, so this area seemed perfect, if a bit delusional.

The kindly and very apologetic Irish hostess in one of the restaurants informed me that I'd have to wait 'a half hour at least' for a table. Unlike the empty street, I was surprised to find that the restaurant was full.

'I'll wait,' I said. This was a good sign after all.

'Are you sure? I'll try to get you a table quickly but I can't guarantee it'll be soon. It's just that we've had a coach load of Italian students booked in and they've just sat down.'

'Oh, okay, I'll wait anyway. I really fancy some pasta.'

'No problem'.

For a moment I felt she was disappointed that she hadn't talked me out of staying —but sooner than expected, amid the animated noise which resembled that of a school canteen, I got my table. It was nice to see that Italian teenagers were exporting the 'When in Rome' idiom to Sligo, and that they were enjoying their holiday in a new culture. I had an excuse – research. Also, pasta is the staple of the pedalling tourist and I hadn't had any since Killarney.

The food, which added to the school-dinner theme, was plentiful at least. I carbed up, but soon found myself back in my hotel room feeling frustrated. I sat eagerly awaiting the TV weather forecast from those stars of RTÉ and wondered if they were just making stuff up for the craic —if they were 'feeling' what the weather would bring based on their emotions, as the Irish might. They may as well have been, because the science approach definitely wasn't working. It was no surprise then, to see that they were again fairly noncommittal; every type of weather was mentioned bar snow.

Sleep soon came knocking and I lay my head down to dream of better pasta, fearing pasta might be dreaming of a better me.

CHAPTER 10

'Coincidences are spiritual puns'

G. K Chesterton

All Irish people have some relationship with W.B Yeats. His poems are pressed into us at school and it's no bad thing. After breakfast, I packed up and left the titanic hotel that is *The Glass House* and headed off in search of Yeats.

I'd been advised to find Cairn Hill, from where I would have a champion view of the lake. A short spin out of town heading south led me to the spot. It was radiant. Morning sunshine pushed through defeated clouds and the easeful silence filled me. Yeats wrote his poem *The Lake Isle of Inishfree* while living in London. Had it not been for a water fountain on display in a shop window, which produced the sound of running water, the poem may never have been written. It reminded him of the 'lake water lapping' and his much longed for Sligo. It begins with the line: 'I shall arise and go now, and go to Inishfree'. The 'pavements grey' of his urban existence was not appealing and in his mind, seeming almost possessed, Yeats travels back to Lough Gill where he creates a utopic natural environment. Nor was urban life appealing to me. As I stood reciting the poem in my head, I understood that my bike trip around Ireland was also a call from 'the deep heart's core'.

My minute meditation was interrupted by a slightly older man who was walking his dog down the hill.

'It's lovely isn't it,' he said calmly as he too stopped to appreciate the scene.

'Gorgeous, it's a great viewing spot.'

'Which island is Inishfree?' I asked as I raised my arm as if to point.

'You can't really see Inishfree from here but that one there is Beezie's Island', he revealed proudly as he pointed it out.

Also known as Cottage Island, this was the home of 'The Lady of the Lake' or Beezie Clerkin, who lived there alone until her death in 1949. Beezie was much loved by Sligo people. She was kind and hospitable and had a great rapport with the animals and wildlife whose home (the island) she shared. After her husband's death, Beezie refused to live anywhere else and often rowed the ten kilometre round trip into Sligo where she bought provisions. She was eighty when a small fire in the cottage finally took her life. In many ways this woman lived the dream that Yeats created and yearned for in his poem. Beezie however was real.

We stood in silent contemplation for a few seconds. It was an informed and informing silence. We knew that what we were looking at was special, the antithesis of stress. But it didn't last long.

'Those fuckin flies have me ett', declared this now half-tormented man in his brown, flat accent.

Small flies, treating his head as breakfast, had been swarming around it since he'd arrived. This drove him mad. He clapped his hands in front of him in an attempt to kill one and then scraped the tiny carcass into his sleeve.

'Bastardin midges... I'm destroyed' he said as he scratched his head furiously and bent low.

'I'm off. Good luck', he added abruptly as he moved away with his now barking dog.

While this man continued down the hill, I wondered how long he, or indeed any of us, would last living the hermetic life on a lake island like Inishfree. Harmony with nature? *Beezie was probably of a rare breed.*

Soon it was time for me to go too. I was heading north towards Donegal, but I had another Yeats related stop to make on the way. *I shall arise and go now, and go to Ben Bulben, and a small café built there, with tae and waffles made.* My second breakfast, which I was sort of getting used to having, would be had at the café at Drumcliff Churchyard, below the famous Ben Bulben Mountain where Yeats himself is buried.

◊

It didn't take long to get back to and beyond Sligo town where the wide N15 road zips through the open countryside. This led me up the soft incline towards the towering and impressive Ben Bulben. Just before it, is the old Drumcliff churchyard, a place where in the evening when the tourists have gone, peace there too 'comes dropping slow'. If the ninth Century Celtic high cross isn't attractive enough, the remains of the ancient round tower which was struck by lightning in 1396 might just do it for you. The dramatic location, below the fatherly rock that is Ben Bulben, which has its own quality of silence, delivers another utopia.

Of course, as I've already pointed out, no self-respecting Irish tourist trail would be complete without its saintly associations. Drumcliff has them too; it was at first a 6th century monastery founded by St. Columba (aka St. Colmcille).

Though born in Donegal and often more associated with Derry, St. Columba's actions at this very spot would greatly affect his life and to a lesser extent all our lives, including the life of the man most associated with the graveyard, W.B. Yeats. For here is where the seeds of the laws of copyright were sown. St. Columba was the original P2P (Peer to Peer) file sharing guru. He was the Napster of the sixth century and so forthright was he in his convictions, that it led to some old school litigation – a massive battle, with proper axes and blood and screaming and stuff.

St. Finnian, Columba's old teacher, had acquired in Rome the 'Vulgate', an ancient Latin translation of the bible. Columba felt that this text, along with other psalters and books, should be copied so as to spread the word of God easily to the people. This was after all his job, as well as his purpose in life. Finnian however was very protective of the texts and was not in favour of allowing others to own copies. His selfishness and reasoning was really akin to today's 'my ball no goal' shout spouted by domineering children. It was hypocritical too because Finnian himself benefitted from the practice of copying books. In any case, this was supposedly the word of God, not the word of Finnian and I'm not sure he had any real claim on the intellectual property. Ignoring the attitude of his old master, and not one for the 'lethargy of custom', Columba tried to secretly make a copy of the *Vulgate*. This copy became known as *The Cathach of St. Columba*.

Finnian was not impressed when he found out and he believed that he now owned the copy too. Columba unsurprisingly disagreed. Their dispute continued until the matter was sent to the High King Diarmuid at Tara for arbitration. Much to Columba's horror, the King ruled in favour of Finnian and famously said, 'to each cow (belongs) its calf, to each book its copy'. Though there were other triggers, this then led Columba to deal with the issue in the old fashioned way, which arrived in the form of an axe grinding mob. Enraged no doubt at not being allowed to carry out his purpose, he possibly employed that old saying – 'To each gobshite, his comeuppance' – before unleashing his soon to be victorious warriors onto Diarmuid's men. And it all happened right here at Ben Bulben.

Really, all of this was rather ironic and it's not hard to take Columba's side. Had he and his followers been allowed to have copies of the holy texts, they might have learned about the sixth commandment, or indeed the concept of sharing. Instead, three thousand men were slain that day in what became known as 'The Battle of the Book.' Diarmuid fled the battle (not cool in those days) and Columba was later banished to Scotland, but Diarmuid's decision is the first known judgement ever to have been made on copyright.

Thankfully things were a bit more peaceful as I walked my bike past the café and up to Yeats' grave in the church grounds. There were tourists from all over the world lolling about in the cool shade of the sycamore trees. Around the simple plot were clusters of Russian visitors. From what I could gather, their guide was explaining the epitaph on Yeats' gravestone. After they'd moved on, I strolled towards it and read it myself –

> *'Cast a cold eye*
> *On life on death,*
> *Horseman pass by'.*

These blunt and seemingly hopeless words stayed with me through my break at the café, where I ate no waffles after all but sipped the promised tea. I did join some in quiet cake-gobbling contemplation however and considered where I was. Really, was there any place in Ireland more befitting its description as 'the land of saints and scholars' than this? This place was special. I was in Ireland's heart and I could feel it pumping still.

◊

I was on the road again soon after and I couldn't help but bring this epitaph of Yeats with me. *Were these words really as hopeless as at first appeared?* The more I dwelt on them, the more my attitude changed. In fact they sort of taught me a bit about life – to take it a little less seriously. *We live, we die, we get buried – so what.* In a way, it became kind of comforting, suggesting there's no big deal or major secret to life. '*Not what life is but that it is*'.

Whatever it meant, for the moment at least, my eye, whether cold or not, was being cast towards life. This was my preferred state for now and I was hopeful of not seeing any horsemen or Grim Reaper types any time soon. That's why what was about to happen would scare the shit out of me and leave me plenty baffled for quite some time.

It didn't happen straight away. In fact I passed through a tiny corner of County Leitrim first, but somewhere at the heel of County Donegal, just north of Bundoran where I'd come off the N15, it appeared. I rounded a corner and in front of me, parked outside the long driveway of a modern house, was a horse drawn carriage with two horsemen on board. It was a black hearse carriage – the horses standing very attentively in the still air. With Yeats' wintry words not yet dried onto my mind, I could well have needed a hearse myself; for I nearly succumbed to shock when I saw it.

There are times in life when we say to ourselves, 'wouldn't it be mad if (such and such) happened'. Occasionally what we imagine happening does happen and we say 'oh I knew it' or (for the opportunists), 'I should have backed it'. There are other times, like when a magician does something baffling and we get genuinely freaked out. This was one of those times.

Because of the Yeats epitaph, I had actually imagined seeing a horseman on a horse drawn hearse when leaving Drumcliff, and very soon afterwards, my floored jaw might have hinted at astonishment because I was now really seeing one. If I'd imagined seeing a tractor and did, this wouldn't be an issue because tractors are commonplace in rural Ireland. But this was different. I have only ever seen a horse-drawn hearse a couple of times in my life and that was in East London, where the tradition is just about still alive. In Ireland, I have never seen one.

Still not quite believing that I had and the timing of it, I stopped just beyond where it was parked and looked back. *Was this real? Maybe they're ghosts? I can't talk to them because they could be, but I can take a picture.* And I did, but from a very safe distance.

I don't think I was scared but there was certainly something very odd happening. It was sort of chilling. Realists would call this a coincidence, but I wasn't so sure. Meeting someone who knows your cousins (like I'd already done on this trip) was a coincidence. There was something more happening here however – something spiritual or supernatural. That's what I told myself anyway.

I didn't stick around too long (just in case) and rode off half believing I had just seen a brace of grim reapers. I could only conclude that I was now, or soon at least, going to die – maybe. This wasn't great, especially when you're on a bike trip around the country and you have hopes of completing it. But what could I do? I did all I could think to do, what I was being programmed to do. I kept calm and carried on.

◊

W. B. Yeats believed in ghosts. He believed in fairies, symbolism, coincidence, superstition, mysticism, the supernatural, the Otherworld, black magic and all things otherworldly. He was actually hugely into the occult and even did séances in an effort to contact spirits. He claims to have seen a ghost too in his youth, at Lissadell House, a large estate in County Sligo – the original ghost estate.

As part of the Celtic Revival of literature, Yeats believed that in order to discover our roots, Irish people needed to rediscover a time when all these things were a real part of life. It was important for him to engage in it too. Visions, dreams and fairies are often found throughout his work. They don't tend to teach us this kind of stuff in schools; I'm not sure the religious authorities would approve, but there's also a risk of creating more teenage Goths and there's really no need for that. I wasn't sure what to believe in myself, but after this episode I felt that nothing was certain – not even the idea that we might already have an appropriate quota of Goths...Now that would be weird.

As well as Yeats, the North West has also given us *Westlife*. This boy band was one of the most successful in Europe, selling close to fifty million records. But for one member, that just wasn't enough. On top of the millions he had earned from prancing around in a vest, Shane Filan felt that more money was required. So, he decided to start up a property company with his brother Finbarr, which he cleverly named Shafin (just to remind people who the owners were it in case they forgot).

Shafin Developments quickly developed problems, and later a reality check, which was about the only things it did develop. Amid the property crash, in 2011 the 'heartthrob' reassured everyone (not that we gave a shit) that his 'empire will survive' – but his 'empire' didn't survive at all. In 2012, owing €23m, Shafin diversified and began developing excuses instead. It collapsed –gracelessly. Shane then moved to England, where bankruptcy laws are ten times more lenient, leaving his loans to be written off by the banks that we all bailed out. Classy... Westlife have split up now, but not before they cashed in on their 'Farewell Tour', which will surely precede their reunion tour. Anyway, I wonder what Yeats would make of the fact that Shafin has left some untidy modern reminders of the good old days around the northwest. After all, ghost estates were as much a part of the Celtic Twilight as they are the Celtic Tiger.

The road after Bundoran was wide and bright. I was now moving deeper into Donegal but my freaky encounter stayed with me for a time yet. I pushed on and was happy to arrive in the beautiful Ballyshannon – alive. This little place claims to be the first ever town in Ireland and the six thousand year old archaeological sites would add weight to this claim. For me however, the attraction is that the town is the birthplace of Ireland's first legend of Rock Music – Rory Gallagher. I wondered too what Yeats would have made of the symbolism of Rory being born in *The Rock Hospital* and christened in *The Rock Church* in Ballyshannon. Would this be considered a mere coincidence? *I'm not sure.*

While he was born in County Donegal, Rory is more associated with Cork (an anagram of Rock) where he grew up, and indeed Belfast where he became a true poet of music. He too was successful –selling thirty million records worldwide – but the music and his organic and original style always came first. He was a gentle soul, quiet, shy and generous. But when he graced a stage, he became a conduit for musical genius, raw energy, purity and power. Not many have been cited as major influences on the guitarists of bands such as U2, Queen, The Smiths and Guns N' Roses. Not many too would go off to tour Japan instead of joining *The Rolling Stones*. Rory did however, always remaining true to his art and himself. He has left behind, not ghost estates, but ghost blues and a legacy that has inspired much, including the creation of some beautiful sculptures around the country. These are dedicated to him and have been erected in some of the places that now bear his name: *Rory Gallagher Place* in Cork, *Rory Gallagher Corner* in Dublin, *Impasse Rory Gallagher* in Paris and – well it's close enough – *the Diamond* in Ballyshannon.

I climbed up the hill to the Diamond and took a gulp of water by Rory's life-sized bronze sculpture. It was impressive and it was refreshing to see the man acknowledged in this way. By now lunch was on the cards but I continued on to Donegal town, a favourite little haunt of mine, where I would eat and decide where I was going to end up for the night. I still had no idea.

It would be wrong not to bring Rory with me on this leg of my journey and just as the sun went in, my tunes came out.

> 'Well the rain ain't fussy about where it lands
> It'll find you hiding no matter where you stand'
>
> R. Gallagher

Very true Rory...

◊

I hadn't met many other cyclists on the road and hadn't ridden with any but that was all about to change – kinda. A couple of kilometres outside Ballyshannon, as I weaved in and out of the hard shoulders' broken lines, I felt a presence. Thankfully it wasn't like back in Ballinspittle or even Bundoran. After my encounter with the horsemen, I don't think I could have coped with a statue of the Virgin Mary winking or hovering behind me. This presence came in the form of another, somewhat older cyclist who rode up behind me and decided to benefit from my draft. He was clearly out on a training ride.

'How's it going?' I asked in a very friendly and enthusiastic manner.

I drifted closer to the edge of the road and encouraged my new friend to ride up alongside me so that we could maybe have a chat.

'Mhmm' was his grunted reply.

Maybe he's foreign.

This man stuck fast to my rear wheel and made no effort to join me. I decided to let him 'recover' for a minute. I reckoned he must have made an effort to catch me and so needed a little time now to catch his breath. I took Rory out of my ears and felt pleased that I now had a bit of interactive company on the road. After a bit, I looked behind again.

'Have you ridden far?'

'Hmmm,' was again his only response.

This situation was unusual. Normally in the countryside, if you meet another cyclist on the road who is going in the same direction, one of two things happen: you ride side by side and have a chat (usually about cycling, where you're headed, where you've come from etc.), or you both may decide to just 'ride'. In this scenario you will take turns riding on the front. Doing this means that you 'share the work', as the person behind will benefit from the draft and thereby use up to 30% less energy. This is cycling etiquette – something I soon realised was a bit alien to my new companion.

'Where are you off to?' I tried again.

'Hmmm'

I let this man benefit from my draft for a while longer and wondered what to do next. I didn't mind helping him recover, but I didn't think it was good manners to barely even say hello and then remain on my wheel. Then I decided to do what I've always wanted to do. With my arms on the bars, I flicked my right elbow forward. This is a gesture that race riders make to indicate to others behind to come through and share the work. I see it in every race on TV. It's subtle but it's the language of the peloton. I had now just done it. *Maybe he really is foreign and will only understand this universal language.*

I glanced behind again. No reaction. I flicked my elbow once more – but still I got nothing. After another few minutes of me doing all the work, I eventually got pissed off, sat up and turned towards this sandbagging bitch.

'Are you gonna do any work or will I be giving you a lift to Donegal?'

'Hmmm' he mumbled again and coupled it with a shake of his head.

Now I was wound up. I decided to slow down, to have a little game of track-style cat and mouse in an effort to encourage him forward. This was something else that I'd always wanted to do, but it looks rather strange and unnecessary when you're not racing (not to mention how strange it would look if you're riding alone). I slowed, but still he sucked my wheel, freewheeling now.

'Ah feck off' I said at last with all the diplomacy of a terrorist. And with all

A Cyling Fan's Ride Around Ireland

the rage of a Bernard Hinault, I hunched forward and let my legs do the talking. After ten days of pretty good touring, I had developed a decent bit of power and felt alive as my pace increased rapidly. Initially he upped his pace too but he couldn't hold my wheel. I imagined powering away from him, like Fabian Cancellara at the Tour of Flanders, finding strength I didn't know I had. In fact, I didn't have it before this trip and it felt good. When I'd gotten a decent gap of about eighty metres, I sat up, turned around and discovered it was more like eight metres. Clearly I had notions of myself. Nonetheless, I took my right hand off the bars intending to sarcastically gesture my 'dropped' foe to hurry up. As I did, my front wheel got intimate with the bottom of a small pothole. I felt a deep dip and heard the rim hit its edge. The bike wobbled and as I took the impact, I was thrust forward from the saddle. My foot instinctively unclipped from the pedal and touched the ground to steady myself, but not before my balls went full force into the stem. Gut-wrenched, I managed to just about keep upright but I don't know how.

It wasn't as sore as it could've been and it wasn't the first time I'd done this on a bike. The first time was much sorer. In a way, I wanted the ground to open up, but in a way, the ground opening up was more the problem (as was my impatience and lack of empathy). Anyway, mortified about the fairly artless situation I was now in, I opted not to look around anymore. The use of sight was no longer required to know what was going on behind anyway. At first I thought it most likely a bird, but birds don't howl with laughter. The sound followed me from just a few metres away until I decided to really let my legs do the talking this time. As the 'birdsong' faded, and the extra, unwanted blood slowly drained from my slapped arse of a face, I felt grateful again to be upright and alive. All I had to do now was hide myself when I got to Donegal. I didn't want any mumbling parasite following me into any café that I might use.

◊

I hold great memories of Donegal town in my heart. In my head it's less memorable but only insofar as I can't actually remember much about my last visit. The town was my destination, almost a decade ago, for my first long distance bike touring trip. I rode up from Cork over four days to attend the wedding of a good friend Ronnie – and probably his wife's too. I'd met Ronnie, a big cheery sort of lad, in Seoul a couple of years earlier. We were young, enthusiastic and thirsty. Often, very thirsty…

Though we had jobs teaching English in Korea, the last week of each month was always a bit challenging. So challenging was it in fact, that one night I challenged Ronnie to buy me some pints. The problem was that he was thinking of offering me a similar sort of challenge, for as well as being thirsty we were also skint. Crucially our broke financial states only became known after we ordered our first drinks. To some this might have been a problem, to others, namely us, this became a 'cultural exploration'. We came to explore how much trust the Koreans would put in a pair of yapping gobshites on the other side of their bar who appeared ignorant to the concept of passing over currency in exchange for drinks. *The Chief*, a nickname we later gave the friendly owner, was very understanding when the time came to explain ourselves. We offered him land in County Offaly and a battered Honda 50 if he would agree to provide us with a tab, which we guaranteed to settle the following week. This was something he was only too happy to do.

Four hours later we were on the bar's stage creating havoc with guitars and microphones. On that night alone, we formed a band, played our first gig, set up an open mic night and 'bought' pretty much everyone in the half busy bar a drink – including each other. The following week when we went in to pay and realised that the bill was a lot less than we'd feared, we knew that we had found our regular.

That summer housed our halcyon days. We grew up, belatedly I admit, but it was a special time. The bar became a well-known 'open mic' venue in Seoul and a hub for English speakers in the south of the city. We had money (sometimes) and an appetite for distraction and we rocked out (visually at least) á la Rory Gallagher most Friday nights. Later that year, the Chief, who had costly medical bills due to his daughter being unwell and whose business was (before we arrived) struggling, said that when he saw us come into the bar on that fateful night and (though skint) order a beer, he knew that we were 'sent by God'. Not many bar owners would share his optimism. We were after all Irish, broke, thirsty and in a bar. The notion of being a gift from God wouldn't normally arise in these circumstances. We understood the Chief however. We knew that when we arrived on that fateful night and came to realise that we could order whatever we wanted without having to inconvenience ourselves with silly exchanges of cash, that indeed it was 'God' who had led us there. It was a match made in, well, heaven really. When you light a match made in heaven, you get warm memories.

Unfortunately or fortunately (I wasn't sure which), I was not now in Seoul but in Donegal. Ronnie wasn't however which was a shame as I'd have happily invited myself to stay with him. I'd decided not to stay the night this time but press on after I'd eaten.

'I'll have the lasagne, is it homemade?' I asked the good looking waitress in the café off the main… Diamond.

'Aye it is aye, do you want a few wee chips with that?'

I was suddenly taken aback by the very different Donegal accent. The last time I'd heard anyone speak (not mumble) was back in Sligo, which was in terms of distance only about sixty kilometres away, but in terms of accent, half the world away it seemed. Chips by the way, are served with everything in this part of the world, including other carbohydrates. Being offered lasagne or pizza with chips is not uncommon. It's not even uncommon to have roast potatoes, mash and chips on the same plate. As a touring cyclist, I wasn't complaining.

'Yes I'll have chips and a tea please', I added.

'Aye, get that wee man a tea Mary, will you?'

Pretty much everyone else in the world call them town squares because most of them are roughly square shaped. Donegal is different however. The Diamond of Ballyshannon is not alone. Donegal town has its own Diamond and it's so named on account of it being diamond shaped. The problem is of course, it's shaped nothing like a diamond. It's actually shaped more like an arse. 'I'll meet you down the arse for a pint', is probably not a suggestion that would be acceptable however. In these geometrically accurate times, it's better to be more linear and use something that we can all feel more comfortable with, so Donegal town's square became the town Diamond.

I also noticed a somewhat obsessive preoccupation the people had with flags, in particular the green and gold Donegal flag. Almost every business premises had one either on a pole or in their windows.

While eating I got out my map and decided to make a plan. Riding westward from here would be the scenic way to go and I figured I could also suss out some interesting climbs. The Glengesh Pass, a six kilometre climb with an almost 5% average gradient rises to about a thousand feet. It's popular in Ireland's cycling circles and its steep summit makes it an attractive climb for races like the 'Rás'. Somehow it appealed. But the weather didn't. It was now cloudier and greying by the minute. I also had an idea to get to Malin Head. I'd ridden from Mizen and rode out to Ireland's most Westerly point at Dunquin already, so I felt I might as well get to Malin and reach three of the four most extreme points in the country. It was too far to make it there today but Letterkenny or maybe even the city of Derry was doable. These places were also on the way to Malin. It would be easy to find accommodation there too and after my brief flirtation with the hotels of Ireland, I found it hard to get away from their comfort. The N15 would take me past the Blue Stack Mountains as far as Kilross; there I would make a decision on my destination. But first there were the flags.

I just couldn't accept that some people like flags. Having gotten over my own fascination with them when I was six, I've never really been much of a flag man. With this in mind, I just had to ask why there were so many and what they were for.

'I dunno, they're always there I think', said my waitress who clearly didn't seem to find it unusual.

I wasn't so sure. I was in Ulster now and flags are big in Ulster.

◊

Before I re-joined the N15 at Barnesmore Gap, I followed a narrow road out to Lough Eske's southern shore and stopped in the stillness. Its beauty took a good bite out of my time. I leaned over on the bars and waited. Even the day's last rays of sunshine came back out to pour its light on the crystal waters. The trees' leaves flapped against the wings of summer birds and I could touch the cool water below. I thought about staying there and wanted to, but reluctantly I pressed on.

This beautiful Lough Eske made headlines in 1998 when 'Eskie', Donegal's answer to the Lough Ness monster 'Nessie', was spotted surfacing on the water one afternoon. Old tales of lake monsters are common in Ireland and Scotland – maybe less so in more recent times, but that didn't stop people recount their tale on this occasion. Those who saw the 'monster' maintained that though they couldn't quite make out its form, they saw 'something anyway'. Amateur scientists from nearby Harvey's Point Hotel (aka waiters), backed up this claim. One Einstein even suggested that Nessie could have been transported in the lake water's currents which come from Scotland. Another man said 'shut up' and pointed out to Einstein that he should ease off on the lake hotel's whisky, which also comes from Scotland. Others suggested Eskie was in fact Nessie's cousin – a nice thought, if you're five. Non-believers claimed it was all a publicity stunt.

I didn't buy the monster stuff but I didn't buy the publicity stunt stuff either. Though I wasn't there at the time, I had a feeling that something probably did move on the lake. It being a holy place itself (a friary was built there in the 17th Century), something told me that it was the Virgin Mary, in statue form, who while on her holidays from Ballinspittle, decided to pop in for a dip.

Ten minutes later I was riding through Barnesmore Gap. After Grim Reaper-gate, I was being extra cautious as the signs warned me to look out for falling boulders from the mountain above. This was unsettling but I survived and at Ballybofey I crossed the River Finn and skipped up to Kilross where I had that decision to make. I was feeling good and Derry City, though further away than Letterkenny, was reachable. It was an attractive proposition for me as I'd never been there before and really wanted to go, despite having been averse to cities at the start of this trip. It was an easy decision; I pressed on towards Derry. The flat straight roads led me over the River Deele and into Convoy and from there I reached Raphoe where I stopped for a breather.

The Isosceles triangle shaped 'Diamond' of Raphoe unsettled me too. The large size of Donegal's 'Diamond' can easily trick people into believing that it is in fact Diamond shaped, especially those who are crap at geometry or are seven. Raphoe's small triangular, 'Diamond' shaped square wouldn't even trick the village idiot, who was walking around it in circles when I arrived. Work that one out.

After I topped up my water bottles in a pub and received weird looks from the locals, some of whom were busy putting up more flags, I was back on the road, which was also busy receiving wet rain from above. The lush green air and misty fields shortened the way from Raphoe. I felt the benefits again of all the other days' riding and was moving quickly once more. At the border village of Carrigans I was soaked through but I wasn't bothered. With only about ten kilometres to go I could see the River Foyle below to my right and knew that I'd soon be done.

Aware that I was about to do something extraordinary, I actually missed the moment when I passed, in technical terms at least, from one country to another. The rain was the same, the grass on the hills looked no different and the water of the Foyle that ran towards Derry had the self-same cool clearness. Neither had it changed one bit. Though I'd rarely been to the North, and never to Derry, I was now in a sense in more familiar territory. Having spent a good number of years living in London, I knew that my phone was no longer on 'roaming'. I could go to an ATM machine and not be charged the 'foreign' country fee for withdrawals. I could even visit a doctor for free if I needed to and I could use the UK currency I had in my wallet. I was only sure that I had crossed the border when the road signs hinted that I had, for I was now cycling in miles and not kilometres. It was strange that so many things like that could change. But I couldn't help think, in my natural surroundings, that all of this was nothing but officious mumbo jumbo made up by governments to determine how we go about our business. No matter what country I was in, what mattered was that the air was clear and breathable; that's all I cared about.

As I pedalled on, any confusion about the identity of where I now was was compounded by the unlikely evidence that the spray-painting gang of Dingle were probably active at this end of the country too. The signs to 'Londonderry' had been heavily doctored. I concluded that the 'de-anglicising', as opposed to the 'anglicising' branch of Dingle's road sign gang were enlisted to perform similar 'improvements' on these official signs near Derry. The 'London' part of course was covered with white paint, leaving only 'derry' visible. This was a total disaster punctuation-wise of course, as there was no capital 'D', but I was learning to let things go.

The irony of Kerry people wanting their town's name to be more English and Derry people wanting theirs to be more Irish was something I couldn't help smile about as I negotiated the outskirts of the city. The smile was quickly wiped off my wet face however when I was quoted £100 for a night in *The City Hotel*. I was fond of myself but not that fond.

'I'll leave it', I said to the apologetic receptionist.

It really was pouring down with rain now and I wasn't inclined to reconnoitre the city in it. The next hotel I saw was a Travel Lodge. I know. I really didn't want to spend the night in a Travel Lodge, but I had ridden 156 kilometres and the state of me required some immediate comfort. I bit the bullet, as it were, threw my bike over my shoulder and carried it awkwardly up the staircase to the first floor reception. The man behind the desk looked apathetic and bored. It's no wonder; nobody was around and the place had a similar atmosphere to that of an empty fridge.

'Hi. It's just me, how much for one night?'

The man, who was about my age, reluctantly checked his computer screen.

'Do you want breakfast with that?' he asked, with all the upselling skills of a seasoned McDonald's recruit.

I glanced around to a soulless breakfast room and remembered where I was.

'No. I'm not a big eater', I lied.

'Sixty pound for the night', he said.

At this point I didn't hear 'sixty pound'. I heard forty pounds less than the last place. This was an appealing figure at least.

'Do you have a pool or anything?' I asked as I stood with rainwater dripping from my legs into a newly formed puddle on the ironically coloured red carpet. The man looked slowly over the top of his glasses. The long silence, one in which he was probably trying to figure out if I was taking the piss, remained for a second or two too long.

'No', was his efficient reply.

This was expected and as I grabbed my key and headed off to find my room, I remembered the good old days of the Castle Court in Westport.

The room was sterile in its decor. Everything was white with a little tint of baby blue added for entertainment. Even the floor was colourless and the lights gave off a hue reminiscent of a dentist's lamp. It was clean however and after a shower and a stretch I was out of there enthusiastically wandering the streets of the Bogside.

I found the old city walls. It wasn't difficult as they meander around for a mile or so. I climbed up to the promenade atop and took an easy stroll. Glimpses of evening sun, returned from sabbatical, helped out with the view. These walls were built in the early 1600s as a defence for English and Scottish settlers and they served their purpose pretty well, as they were never breached. This fact gives the city its nickname – 'The Maiden City'. Another, altogether more colourful nickname is 'Stroke City', on account of the city having two names: Londonderry/Derry. These old walls also house Europe's largest collection of cannons, which is nice if you like looking at cannons. I wasn't bothered.

In its attempt to turn Ulster Protestant, the British Crown began the Ulster Plantation in the early seventeenth century. Derry became the first planned city in Ireland and it changed dramatically from the settlement which was originally founded by St. Columba in the 6th Century (when he wasn't fighting copyright rulings). It was renamed Londonderry and crucially was to feature, wait for it… a 'Diamond' in its centre. *It was the Protestants after all!*

The so called 'diamond' shape of town centres was deemed to be an attractive proposition in terms of both commerce and defence. As a result, many towns in Ulster were planned and built in this way. You might have thought this clever if you were a town planner four hundred years ago, but what kind of message does that send out to kids these days who are trying to learn about shapes? Derry's 'Diamond' incidentally is mostly square shaped with one slightly curved corner.

Not long after my stroll of the old city I was 'NOW ENTERING FREE DERRY'. That's what the words on the white wall told me anyway. This was typical – just my luck. Only a couple of hours earlier I'd forked out sixty notes for a lifeless hotel and now I was in a place that was totally free and as it happens, very colourful. I noticed immediately how giving the artists were in this area too and so I availed of the free art exhibition of murals that seemed to be on that week. The one I was drawn to took me back to Ché Guevara – in fact, to be more precise, one Ché Guevara Lynch. Ché's grandmother was Irish and his father's quote underneath his portrait, which lies between the Irish and Cuban flags, reads: 'Through my son's veins flowed the blood of Irish rebels.' Margaret Thatcher's great-grandmother, as it happens, was also Irish. Any reports however that through her veins flowed the blood of Irish rebels are unconfirmed. *I wonder if they're related?*

I like Derry. Its wholesome river and bouncy hills remind me of Cork. Its people are friendly and welcoming too. After my day, it just seemed too far to walk across the river to check out the East side, so I stayed put. I was tired and hungry and after a good dinner in a stylish restaurant by the water, I retired to my dentist lab of a hotel room in the hope of extracting a good night's sleep. I did. But I also got a blue corporate stillness that was uneasy – far from the plain peace of the road.

CHAPTER 11

*'The root of all superstition is that men observe when
a thing hits but not when it misses'*
Francis Bacon (17th Century Philosopher)

I had the unusual task next morning of having to fend for myself if I wanted breakfast. I did want breakfast; I knew that much. After I deposited my key to the same man who was still sitting alone at the Travel Lodge reception – looking now like he was terminally ill with boredom – I hit the river in search of morning coffee. The smell of bacon led me to a café near Atlantic Quay. It was early, but I already had a good feeling about the day.

After taking my order, a chirpy woman in her thirties asked me where I had cycled from.

'Cork'.

'Holy Moly – from Cork?'

'Aye' I said, showing clear mastery of the northern accent now.

'Ay away on with ye'.

'Aye' was where my mastery stopped unfortunately. It took me a couple of seconds to figure out that 'away on with ye' was the North's more polite equivalent of 'feck off' – as in 'feck off, you did not, did you?'

'Breda this mon's not half wise, he's after cycling his bike up from Cork'.

The woman was eager now to spread the news and did so by shouting it to her colleague who was preparing food in the kitchen.

'Catch yourself on Cathy, he's having you on'.

'Honestly', I said, in a now extra strong Cork accent, which I felt was necessary for proof of my roots. I now sounded like Roy Keane in some kind of passionate argument about car parks posing as football pitches.

'What ja mean 'havin you on'? Seriously, I did come from Cork... like.'

'So were ya cycling all night?'

'No ya..., not in one day. I left Cork yonks ago. I just came up from Sligo yesterday and stayed here last night....dja know'.

'Oh... I do need to catch myself on. I thought you just come straight up so I did. Aw, I get you now.'

'Breda I thought he come straight up. He only came from Sligo – so he did'.

'Aw, sure Sligo's only down the road Cathy,' shouted Breda.

'Aye I know. Sligo's only down the road', repeated Cathy, who by now was totally unimpressed by how far I'd ridden.

The two women laughed and I felt relief too at not being thought of as a teller of porkies. My coffee and bacon sandwich wasn't long in coming and I had a leisurely time watching the river's water flow gently seaward. I'd also picked up a newspaper and read an unlikely article about Donegal being a saviour for the Japanese. Since the Fukushima nuclear plant meltdowns, seaweed as a food source has become contaminated around parts of Japan. This has led the Japanese to look elsewhere for a good source of sea vegetables and their search has led them to Donegal. *I can see it now, mounds of sea lettuce on plates in Tokyo restaurants with little Donegal paper flags flying atop.*

For the second time in two days Donegal was my destination, for the morning anyway. It seemed like my departure from Mizen Head was only a couple of days earlier. In fact it was nearly ten days earlier and I was close now to Malin Head.

Before I left, I reflected again on seeing the hearse carriage after leaving Yeats' grave. It was mad really, certainly a story to tell. But it also helped me to reflect on the concept of superstition. On these shores people are generally superstitious. I'll often wave to a single magpie and if I'm in company, I'll do it discreetly. It's insane really. It makes no logical sense but it sort of has to be done.

The world of professional cycling is no stranger to superstition either. It breathes it. There exists for example the well-known 'curse of the rainbow jersey'. Every year, in each of the sport's disciplines, the new world champion wins and gets to don the rainbow jersey for the following twelve months. For a long time the folklore of cycling has suggested that winning the jersey, while it should represent fortune and greatness, actually brings with it bad luck, injury, illness, poor form and in some cases even tragedy. There's enough evidence to support this belief too.

Britain's Tom Simpson broke his leg skiing while he was world champion and as we know, later died riding the Tour de France on Mont Ventoux. In 1969 Harm Ottenbros won the jersey almost by default. He was by no means a star of the sport –a water carrier really. During the World Championship race, all of the top riders were riding against Eddy Merckx. They were intent on stopping him winning and sort of forgot to win themselves. Ottenbros took advantage but was ridiculed when he did win. Only one rider congratulated him and that was months later. While wearing the rainbow jersey, the Dutchman broke his wrist and soon after his team collapsed, leaving him out of a job. He ended up depressed, broke and sleeping on a mattress.

Freddy Maertens of Belgium (who Sean Kelly was often the lead-out man for) also won the jersey in 1976. His subsequent career slowly began to unravel and his results were never what they were before he'd won it. He resurfaced in 1981 however and won the world championships again. But this second win was followed by more disaster. He hit financial difficulties and then hit the bottle. Having been a millionaire in the 1970s, today he works in a cycling museum and earns a modest income.

Ireland's own Stephen Roche had a terrible season after he won the rainbow jersey. His knee problems meant that he couldn't even start races the following year. In fact Roche's career went into decline from then on and his race wins became few and far between.

The 'curse' doesn't always strike while the rider holds the rainbow jersey either. In the case of Americans Greg LeMond and Lance Armstrong, it could be seen to have occurred a few years later. LeMond won it in 83' but was then shot in a hunting accident in 86'. Armstrong won it in 93' and was diagnosed with cancer in 96'. Incidentally, since 96' one of his only notable results that still stands is winner of the 1998 Tour of Luxembourg. He did have a more successful career of course for a time as a creator of fiction. Albeit not marketed as such.

Many other men and women have suffered crashes and poor form after they were declared world champion, too many in fact to go through all of them. Perhaps the most devastating ill fortune of all however, befell a young Belgian rider named Jean-Pierre Monseré. The talented and exciting prospect won the Tour of Lombardy Classic in 1969 and then the rainbow jersey in 1970. During the World Championship victory celebrations his father died of a heart attack. A few months later, while racing, he himself collided with a car and was killed instantly. Five years after that Monseré's seven year old son was also hit and killed by a car while out riding his bike. That's three deaths and three generations. And some people say bad luck comes in threes.

With breakfast finished, my new Derry friends came with the bill and to see me off.

'Where are you going to now?' asked Cathy.

'To Malin Head, heading north,' I pointed.

'Oh aye, that's in the South.'

It took a second for this to register and make sense but I knew what she meant.

'What's up there?'

'Probably not that much to be honest,' I said hesitantly.

'Well good luck and take care'.

'Thanks'.

She was right too. I was headed due north but also heading for 'the South'. I understood, but I'm just glad for Cathy's sake that I wasn't foreign or something, as there'd probably be an awkward conversation needed to explain how in Ireland going north could lead you to 'the South.'

◊

Almost immediately I was climbing out of Derry on the Culmore Road heading for the border. It wasn't far away but before I crossed it, I passed close to the point where eighty years earlier, one Amelia Earhart landed her plane after being the first woman to fly solo across the Atlantic. Nicknamed 'Lady Lindy', on account of Lindberg being the first man to do it five years earlier, Earhart crossed the Atlantic in just under fifteen hours. This isn't bad really considering I once got a Ryanair flight from Spain which took sixteen hours (waiting) plus three hours (flying) and it wasn't even 1932. Anyway, Earhart had actually expected to land in Paris. Instead of the Champs Elysees however, she found herself in the *champs de Gallagher,* a farmer's field near Ballynagard. It didn't matter. Strong winds had blown her off course and to be honest, she was really lucky. Had she landed a couple of miles to the north, she'd have landed in Muff, a village in the South, and that would have been very hard to explain to the folks back home for quite a number of reasons.

Earhart was a huge star in America and her story was followed very closely by the press and public. The headline *'Earhart lands in Muff'* is one that the *New York Times* or some such publication will never know how close it came to having to deal with. For my own part, I was about to land in it myself. At least it wasn't raining.

There's a little village in Essex called Ugley, a small hamlet called Broadley Common (it's very ordinary) and another tiny hamlet called Cold Christmas. These are all places that I would regularly go through on training rides in England. I'd always have a little chuckle when I'd see their signs. However this was my first time in Muff, so to speak, and as with most people's visits, I suspect, it didn't last very long. In less than two minutes in fact, I was back skirting the banks of Lough Foyle with (and I'm really not making this up) a clear view of Grania's Gap to my left!

Amelia Earhart never got a chance to return to Ireland. Just five years later, while attempting to circumnavigate the globe, she and Fred Noonan (her navigator) disappeared. Neither her aeroplane nor her body were ever found, despite a huge search mission that covered a vast area in the central Pacific including Howland Island, where she was supposed to land. Though she probably just ran out of gas after miscalculating her position, these kinds of events always seem to fuel the imaginations of the conspiracy theorists. We've already seen this with Britain's Kitchener and Malaysian Airlines 370 is a more recent example. Even after so many years, the enigma of her disappearance has given rise to all sorts of propositions. One theory was that she faked her death, changed her name and returned to the U.S. incognito. Some believed she may have made it to Saipan where Japanese soldiers killed her, thinking she was a spy. Others felt that she may have gone to Saipan on a reconnaissance mission to test its suitability as a potential pre-World Cup training facility for the 2002 Irish football team. There, it was believed that she fell off the island and drowned after being hit by a ball kicked from a car park. This theory was later proved false; balls would not have arrived until much later...

Eight Kilometres of relaxed pedalling with good views of Lough Foyle brought me from Muff to Quigley's Point. There I cleaned my bike at a petrol station and oiled the chain. These things just had to be done, especially after so much rain. My first stop of the day would be at Carndonagh where I planned to view the seventh Century St. Patrick's Cross and for some reason, I was feeling almost excited by the idea.

The cloistered road rolled towards Glentogher. Yellow gorse dotted the hilly land like crumbled egg-yokes on a green plate. The sun warmed me from beyond gold and silver clouds. I could smell peat again too faintly, and I knew, not from maps, but from the sacred silence, that I was on a peninsula once more. There is a binding quiet on Ireland's peninsulas. It was here too on Inishowen – a calm fated emptiness.

I came through a glen with the Slieve Snaght Mountain ahead. Just off this road St. Patrick's well can be found. In pagan times well-worship was a common practice all over Europe. Rather than discourage its continuance however, early Christians pretty much embraced the practice and used wells for baptisms. St. Patrick, as we all know, is famed for 'driving the snakes out of Ireland' but the snake is really a metaphor for a druid. The word 'naddred', which means druid, was also the ancient Gaelic word for serpent. By performing baptisms, St. Patrick was in essence limiting the number of druids that would come about, so he was really 'driving the druids out'. Here at this well, he baptised Prince Owen who was the son of Niall of the Nine Hostages, a High King of Ireland. It is from Owen that Inishowen and Tyrone (Tír Eoghan) get their names.

Wells are also thought of as places where various ailments can be cured. The holy water is believed responsible for this. There are many wells all over the country dedicated to St. Patrick but at this one, near Glentogher, the water will cure warts apparently. Luckily I wasn't in need of a visit. Nor was I attracted by the thought of going to an ancient wart clinic. I opted instead to push on towards Carndonagh. Incidentally, St. Cleer's holy well in Cornwall and the 'Well of the Mad' (Tobar na nGealt) in Camp, County Kerry – where the Milesians arrived unannounced – are both wells that are said to cure insane people. Lunatics will be lowered to the water by the ankles and will be dipped in head first by 'non-lunatics' so as to receive the curative powers, which let's face it, is an action that encourages thoughts about irony. Still, I'm sure for some it has a placebo effect at least.

Twenty minutes later I was dropping into Carndonagh where coffee and more food was again required. I found a little café by the town triangle and ordered cake from a short, roll-up smoking Frenchman who appeared to be the proprietor.

'Can you tell me where the cross of St. Patrick is? I believe it's here in Carndonagh.'

'Ze what?' he asked with a concerned look that seemed to say, 'I'm only learning English'.

'The Cross. Carndonagh Cross. Où est lacrosse?'

'Ah lacrosse, eh, like ze hurling?'

'No. No, not lacrosse.... The cross.'

'Where is the cross?' I tried again a little louder this time...

'Ze crossroads, non?'

'I know what you mean,' interrupted a local woman who unlike the Frenchman was remaining calm.

'It's just out that road a wee bit,' she advised pointing down another street.

'Ah, oui oui, ze cross. Just down ze road... a wee bit', added the Frenchman,

A Cyling Fan's Ride Around Ireland

who now had developed the strangest Franco-Donegal accent I've ever heard – the only one I've ever heard in fact. He also gave me a smug look, as if to say 'how clueless are you?' which I must say, I found amusing.

The Donagh cross was easy to locate after all and it was a real treat. It's one of the oldest crosses in Ireland, dated around 650AD and can be found surprisingly close to the road outside a church which was founded by St. Patrick. What makes this cross special is that it is one of the best examples of how ancient/druidic or Celtic art has fused with Christian stories. It's a sculpture really; the Celtic interlacing is similar to that found in some ancient texts and the carved figures, though basic, tell us something of Christian tales. This cross really demonstrates a transition from one period to the next in Irish history.

I sat nearby in the sunshine and took in the scene around it too. I think I'd have preferred this relic to be in some field out in the middle of nowhere. Having a fourteen hundred year old cross so close to commercial premises and the road felt odd. Then again if the cross itself symbolises change, I suppose I'd just have accept it. It did look and feel incredibly special, a real work of art – *and if this cross could talk...*

◊

As well as driving druids out of Ireland, spreading Christianity and founding churches, St. Patrick (or St. Patty as Americans call him) also invented green beer, parades, casual projectile vomiting, roaring along to songs of *The Pogues*, fighting your mates and bar brawling (a form of fighting, usually someone else's mates). These traditions of course died out but have made a comeback since the 1990s and are known to reach their climax on St. Patrick's Day. The traditions can be found all over the world, from Boston to Brisbane – in fact anywhere really where it says 'Bar'.

Other traditions often related to parades include wearing green clothing, driving tractors covered in shit (actual shit) through main streets (Co. Cork 2013 & 2014) and the lesser known tradition of sitting alone on a chair, next to a table, on the back of a lorry, and drinking whiskey from a bottle placed on the table, while occasionally waving to thousands of confused onlookers (Trafalgar Square 2005 and possibly other years, I never returned to find out).

Hairstyles associated with St. Patrick's Day festivities include the cow's lick look and the comb-over. Also, some people like to dress up as leprechauns, which they mistakenly believe gives them a licence to act like moronic muppets for about twenty four hours. *St. Patrick gave us a lot really.*

I hopped back on the bike and spun north from Carndonagh for six kilometres or so to Malin village. I was getting close now to my destination, Malin Head, Ireland's most northerly point. The sun, like a growing child had gotten bolder as the morning became the afternoon. At last I crossed the causeway bridge at Malin and arrived at its 'Diamond'.

Malin is not Milan. Let's get that cleared up straight away. It does have a pleasant tree-lined Diamond however which (you really don't need me to tell you) is also totally triangular in shape. Malin folk are flag lovers too. It seems the fact that the village lacks flag-poles hasn't prevented them indulging their passion. I'd noticed that someone had actually nailed Donegal flags to the trees instead. They flapped carelessly in the breeze all through the village and gave some hope that something might be going on. I stopped, took a sip of water at the corner of the Diamond and tried to suss the place out. It was quiet, nothing was going on really – but then again it was the Inishowen Peninsula and everywhere was quiet. *What's the story with all the flags?* And then the answer came. I'd forgotten that the GAA season was in full swing and that Donegal had won a big match on Sunday when I was in Westport. The flags were out to show support for the football team. It was obvious.

'Hi, which way is Malin Head?' I asked a woman who was crossing the road near me.

'Just out that road about twelve kilometres', she said pointing to the massive sign in front of me that read 'Malin Head 12 kilometres'.

I waited for her to ask me how long it had taken me to cycle from Mizen. There was surely no other reason for a cyclist with a rucksack on his back to be in Malin other than to be doing Mizen to Malin or that trip in reverse. I had a slight Cork accent too. It was fairly obvious what I was doing. I waited expectantly for the inquiry and the inevitable appreciation.

'Can you not see the sign?' she asked, with a touch of sarcasm and a dismissive snicker. Then after looking at me like I was stupid, she continued across the road without another word, locking her car confidently with her remote control key fob.

'Thanks'.

Maybe she's a bike hating motorist. Just breathe...

I started to ride again and headed towards the road to Malin Head, but by the time I got to the end of the Diamond, I did something quite surprising. I turned my bike around and began heading due east instead. I had decided not to go to Malin Head after all. What? Why?... Well it was simple really – kinda. I'd been considering doing this for the previous few kilometres and concluded that there was actually no real reason for me to ride out to the Head and then ride back. If I had done it, I would not have done it for me. I'd have done it only to be able to say that I'd done it.

Some people do this ride to collect money for charity and that's very noble. Others do it as a sporting challenge and to break records and that's fine too, but I was about to do it for no other reason than to be able to say I'd done it. I guess I realised that I just wasn't bothered about what others thought. I wasn't riding my bike around Ireland to impress people anyway. I was doing it because I love riding my bike. The destination didn't matter, nor did the number of kilometres clocked or the gradient of the mountains climbed. I just wanted to breathe the air and feel the freedom of the road. I was doing this trip because I had said I would do it out loud, I wanted to do it and I could do it. That was it really. Now within this trip I had ridden my bike from Mizen Head to Malin village and just twelve kilometres short of the perceived 'finish' (of one part of the trip at least), I decided not to bother 'finishing'. Making that choice was the best feeling in the world. I made it simply because I could. In some ways that may seem difficult to understand, but I felt I had achieved more by turning around than I would have by reaching the top of the country. The freedom to stop was more important than the 'achievement'.

And what were the consequences of not 'finishing'? There were absolutely none...

◊

It was Wednesday. The days were passing quickly but on Saturday cycling's Olympic road race would be finishing in London. All eyes were going to be on Mark Cavendish, the overwhelming favourite to win on home soil and I would be making sure I got to see it too. I figured I'd be on the East coast by then and would have to find a way to watch it. Cavendish was the sport's latest world champion and wearer of the rainbow jersey. Riding for Sky, he had set out three major goals for his season. The first was to win the Milan-San Remo Classic for a second time. He wanted to win it in the rainbow jersey too but it wasn't to be. He was dropped well before the finish. The second goal was to win the green jersey/points jersey at the Tour de France. While nobody could use the words 'Team Sky' and 'failure' in the same sentence when it comes to the 2012 Tour, Cavendish must have been disappointed not to have won this jersey for the second year in a row. So now his last major goal was to win the Olympic road race on the Mall in London, the day after the opening ceremony. Would he win? Or was the curse of the rainbow jersey going to have its say? I was looking forward to finding out.

But first I had a lot of work to do. From riding northward towards the South out of Derry, I was now riding southward towards the North and duly followed the signs for Moville. From there I would have a short jaunt up to Greencastle where I hoped to get a ferry across the Foyle and back across the border. The ride back was relatively easy and easy on the eye too. The green hills wore a coat of purple heather and the high teenaged sun was getting brazen now. The silence strengthened too and I barely saw a car on the road for twenty five kilometres until the Foyle again became my flowing friend.

At Greencastle I didn't have to wait long for my ferry. It was inexpensive and very economical for my legs too. A rough calculation concluded that I would cut out at least fifty kilometres by not having to go back down to Derry and then north again towards Coleraine. I followed a few cars on and within a minute the vessel's engine's deep growl indicated we were moving. By now I wasn't roaming anymore with my phone network, so a quick look at google maps allowed me to confidently conclude that I'd make it to the Giant's Causeway on the Antrim Coast before evening. This was going to be good.

The short sailing delivered us to Magilligan pier and I was followed off by a chorus of coughs from the convoy of cars. Unlike the day before when I crossed the border for the first time, here I really did get the sense that I was in a different country. On the flat Point Road I encountered some road signs that essentially warned me not to get shot. Red flags and lights if seen, apparently would indicate that firing would be taking place 'on the range' – that's the firing range that I was riding through the middle of. I realised that I was now in Magilligan British Army base/HM Prison. In the distance too I saw what appeared to be a red flag. *Bollocks. I'm gonna get shot. And I hate flags. It's the flags' revenge... Just keep going; they might miss.*

I put my head down and really did batter the pedals. It's not often you ride around and see signs warning you about guns being fired. I was in Northern Ireland too, so they probably weren't bullshitting. It's hard to know how you'd react in this situation. I wasn't used to it and after seeing the Grim Reaper a couple of days earlier, I wasn't taking any chances. Eventually I got beyond what looked like the entrance gate with its tall watchtower. Alas the red 'flag' wasn't a flag at all but a 'Stop' sign and I could feel the main road approaching. Relief ensued and I shifted to a smaller gear. *I'm still alive...*

The feeling of being in a different country stayed with me and was reinforced almost immediately. I found myself on the A2 and Seacoast Road and I really could have been in any Mediterranean Country. The sun was hot now. The golden sands tanned the coastline and there were people strewn across the beaches showing true obedience to the holiday gods. In truth, I really wasn't expecting this.

When I was young and growing up in Cork, I was always a bit puzzled by Northern Ireland. Whenever I watched the news, I mostly noticed two things about the place: it was always either raining, or on fire. Sometimes it was raining and on fire which, to be fair, is never great. I also had a vague idea (probably from my parents' excitement) that certain stuff was considerably cheaper up north. Visits to my Granny at Christmas who lived in Dundalk, would sometimes include skips over the border to Newry to buy these 'bargains'. Unfortunately cigarettes and petrol were the alluring products – not much use to a seven year old, and if adults can get excited about buying cheaper petrol, then that tells you all you need to know about the 1980s.

Since then the North has always remained a mysterious place for me and I was really discovering it for the first time now. Hot sandy beaches and the faint jingle of ice cream vans was not what I had imagined Northern Ireland to produce on this trip, or on any trip really, yet here I was on the north coast and I had exactly that in front of me. There was only one thing for it – more seaside fish and chips.

I rode uphill all the way to Downhill from the west (I'm not even making that up) and at Downhill I pulled off the road and found a humble looking chip shop near the beach.

'Fish and chips twice,' said the older man who'd arrived before me.

'Right oh', the young woman behind the counter nodded and she went off to fill the chip pan. I noticed a 'Buy British' sticker with the union flag near the cash register. This left me in no doubt as to which side of the community I was being hosted by.

I waited and this man eyed me suspiciously but said nothing.
'What can I get you?' asked the girl when she returned.
'Fish and chips.... once' I said, showing again total mastery of the dialect.
The woman paused. 'Do you mean one fish and chips?'
'Yes'.
After a bit of shifty silence, the owner of my companion's second portion of fish and chips arrived.
'Hello', he said to me.
'Hi'.
'You're cycling'.
'I am'
'Aye, I used to race bikes myself way back in the fifties and sixties. What was the name of the bike I had?'
He searched his memory and I immediately thought of Donal back in in West Cork who was just about able to inform me that he was a 'champion' bike racer. Somehow this man was much more believable.
'A MacClean racing bike – that was it. Great bikes they were.'
The two old gents smiled as I told them I'd heard of the name but I'd never seen one.
'They'd be rare nowadays', the second man added.
'Aye', I said.
'Where are you from?' asked the first man.
'Cork..., but I live in London' I added – for balance.
'I'm just on a holiday, cycling around. I haven't been here much before'.
'Aye, you'll be doing the Antrim coast then?'
'Aye, I might'.
'That's a nice wee spin all right'.
'I've heard'.
'Well you look after yourself. I hope the weather stays dry for you.'
'Good luck,' they said together as they got their food and headed off.
This is amazing, I thought. *It's not raining and nothing seems to be on fire here. And people are friendly. Everyone is friendly. And it's cheap – £4.20 for fish and chips. That would be €8 at least in the South. This is good. I like this place. Okay, eat the food and get over it.*
And I did – on the baking hot sand of Downhill beach.

◊

The smell of the sea as well as a good helping of enthusiasm stayed with me when I was back moving, but I had a problem. My front wheel was squeaking relentlessly, like a doomed mouse caught in a trap. I knew it wasn't serious. It seemed to be coming from the hub but after a while it started to drive me bonkers. There were no more calm silences to tune into – just squeak-squeak-squeak on each slow rotation of the wheel. *I'm going to have to sort this out.*
A quick glance at the map and I figured I could get to Coleraine easily,

where I hoped to find some kind of bike shop or someone who'd lend me some oil spray. Again I put my head down and earphones in and rode hard towards the town.

It was half-frenzied when I arrived and the sun lit every corner. Some folk were clopping around in a hurry, all important with nowhere to go. Shopping and getting sunburn were others' preoccupations and there were plenty of flags flying too. These were mostly union jacks with the odd orange flag thrown in – *interesting*. I found a bike shop. The smell of WD40 and new rubber enveloped me as I bounced in.

'It's just dry,' said the owner when I told him my problem. He produced a can of oil which seemed to be an extension of his body and gave it a light spray – 'perfect'.

'You're a legend' I told him and I meant it. He'd given me back my peace.

'Aye, away on with ye' he said, seemingly not too keen on having much praise showered on him by an Irishman wearing skin tight shorts.

I remounted and after a small round of the town, I headed out the long and straight Cloyfin Road. I was making good progress but it was well into the afternoon and thoughts about where to stay began to surface. I pushed on to Bushmills, a village in County Antrim, the tenth county that I had ridden through so far. There I stopped for a look.

Bushmills is a village situated on the Bush River. It only has a population of about fifteen hundred people, but it is known worldwide for its famous whiskey. Bushmills' Distillery (or at least the act of distilling there) is nearly two hundred years older than America. Founded in 1608, it's considered to be the oldest distillery in the world. When I stopped, there was a lot of activity on the smart main street, but I was surprised at how small the place is. Surprising too is that the village is actually twinned with Louisville in Kentucky, a city that has a population approaching one million. Of course what they have in common is the golden hooch and probably not much else; Louisville produces a third of the world's bourbon.

I didn't hang around long and on leaving the village I learned that the Giant's Causeway was only two miles away – heaven.

I passed a few B&Bs on the road up to the Causeway but I held out for a hotel and I was glad I did. The Causeway Hotel is an old country house hotel and the sixty quid quoted for bed and breakfast was exactly what I wanted to hear. When I got to my stately room in the old part of the house and saw that I pretty much had a view of the Causeway itself (or at least the cliffs around it) I thought back to my breakfastless stay in the dentist surgery Travel Lodge in Derry and cringed. That was city trappings, but I was still glad to have seen Derry. I showered, stretched and had a little rest. It was evening now but the sun was still baking the cliffs and I wanted more of it.

Next to this hotel is the National Trust's newly opened Causeway Visitor Centre. Now we all know what happened at the beehive huts and Gallarus Oratory in Kerry. Because of that farce, I was feeling a little shy when walking towards this Centre. In fact I hung around outside for a few minutes and tried to get an idea of what was in there. It was all new and shiny and I could only really see myself reflected in the glass, so I finally opted to stroll into the lobby to get a better idea. When I saw the £8.50 ticket price to gain access to the Causeway, my shyness turned into an allergy. I did what any self-respecting person with an ounce of awareness would do – a U-turn followed by a beeline for the exit. I was, in a word, troubled.

'What do I get for £8.50?' I asked one of the many 'Guides' who were swarming around outside holding ropes and programmes and making it look like they had authority or even something to do.

'You get access to the causeway plus an interactive show with pictures and an audio guide', he answered.

This all sounded lovely, but really it isn't that lovely. See, when you hear the word 'interactive' (especially when it comes to tourist traps), what that really means is that you can press buttons. Button pressing is a much sought after activity in this modern world and unfortunately some people can't cope if they haven't pressed a button for a while. At this venue, the buttons, when pressed, will make some information on how the causeway was formed appear on a nice colouredy screen. Searching on Google however and using your ability to read will give you exactly the same. Pictures are great too, but why would you show someone a picture of an elephant if they were standing beside an elephant? It really doesn't make sense. Also, audio guides are for the less literate, the blind and those who only speak Japanese. I wasn't in any of those categories, but the most important point of all about this 'guide's' answer, is that while the visitor centre may well provide 'access' to the causeway, so do many other parts of the area, and they provide it without relieving you of about ten quid. My allergic reaction made me instantly hungry.

An official looking notice which read 'Northern Ireland's Best Pub' lured me toward it. Having not been in all the other pubs in the land, I'm not able to confirm or deny whether *The Nook* is actually the best pub in the North, however it did serve one of the best Irish Stews I've had. And the tasty prawn tempura starter, washed down with a pint of ice cold tap water, came to not much more than £8.50.

I spent dinner reading about the Giant's Causeway's sixty million year old hexagonal rocks that were formed from hardening lava. It was interesting and informative and it was all there on the National Trust website. The Giant's Causeway itself is a UNESCO world heritage site as well as being one of the ten 'Wonders of the UK'. The eleventh incidentally is the admission price, which I'm sure has left a lasting impression on those who have paid it.

I had a drink outside the pub and chatted to some European tourists in the late evening sunshine. Much talk centred round the eleventh wonder and it became clear that everyone had the same plan – to walk down to the causeway beyond the ropes after the visitor centre closed at 8pm. This was my plan too and it felt good to know that nobody was going to allow any elephants that might have appeared in the area to go unnoticed, as it were.

Of course nobody actually has to pay to see the Giant's Causeway. The whole place is designed to give you the impression that the only access is through the visitor centre. This is not the case. The rocks have been there for millions of years and they are owned by the people, not the government, or the National Trust, or a private company – the people.

It must be pointed out too that the science explanation of how the Giant's Causeway came about is only one explanation. It is after all a causeway belonging to a 'giant' and the story in legend is the far more interesting one. Finn MacCool, an Irish giant, was at odds with the Scottish giant Benandonner. Finn is supposed to have built the causeway as a route to travel to Scotland on, where he would be able to beat the crap out of his adversary. He refused to swim, as he didn't want to get his feet wet (giants aren't perfect) but it was actually Benandonner who made it over to Ireland to tackle Finn.

When he arrived for their planned duel, he went to Finn's house. There he found that Finn's wife Úna was charging £8.50 to enter the house, so Benandonner naturally waited outside. From inside Finn saw that his Scottish foe was much bigger than him and (clearly shitting himself) came up with a cunning plan to trick the Scot. He decided to pretend that Úna was his mother and Úna was to wrap Finn in a blanket and pretend that he was her baby – the idea being that if Benandonner saw the size of Finn's 'baby', he would assume that Finn was a lot bigger, a giant among giants, and would quickly cut his stick. Remember, babies in those days had long hair and beards so the plan was an obvious one. And it worked! Benandonner saw the 'baby' and decided to do one back to Scotland. Finn escaped unharmed.

The moral of the story of course is that if you don't want people to come into your house, charge them £8.50.

I finally made it down one of the paths to the causeway sometime after 9pm. I was far from being alone. It was clear that many others had the same idea and then I realised that we were all about to witness a sunset, the like of which I've rarely enjoyed.

On the horizon above the sea, the giant among stars was falling slowly beyond a wide and cloudless sky. I wandered around the rocks for a while, amid the clicking of cameras and watched groups, couples and solitary souls take their seats for the show. When it started, and the sun began to drop below, my thoughts went with it and in its place emerged a void of peace. Millions of times on these precious rocks, the sun's fall has enchanted and calmed. And the silence of its movement is red music, for all the tiny giants of this world.

CHAPTER 12

*'Remembrance of things past is not necessarily the
remembrance of things as they were'*
                                           Marcel Proust

God forbid that anyone would ever ask for a 'Full Irish' breakfast in England or indeed a 'Full English' in Ireland. Terrible confusion could ensue, but it's the same thing, more or less.

In Ulster, they call it an Ulster fry. Let's all be clear about this. It's a fry-up, a dirty greasy heart attack inducing one and in Ulster they even fry the bread. In fact they even bake potatoes in the bread before frying it. It's called potato bread. It's useless for your arteries but great for morale and it'll be found everywhere, even in country hotels like my one. Inclusion of this bread is really the only difference from other regional variations of the fried breakfast. I didn't have a fry-up though. I had more pan-fried rainbow trout with a slice or three of this 'taytie bread' and it was champion stuff. We'd spun back round already to meet the rising sun and I had the Antrim coast to ride on my bike. Could the world be any kinder?

It was early when I left. The air was cool over empty roads. I rolled along the Causeway route feeling sleepy but the cliffs and the ruined castles around Dunseverick were an attraction that coaxed me into a more wakeful state. The sea was stirring too and the many seabirds showed off the cloudless day.

I joined back up with the A2 at Whitepark Road for a short time, but stayed close to the red sands and cliffs until it brought me to Carrick-a-Rede rope bridge. This is a small *Indiana Jones* type bridge that connects to a tiny island. It's a big attraction on the Causeway coast, but there was nobody there when I arrived. It was too early. Not being a fan of shitting myself, my default state when faced with rope bridges generally, I wasn't really that bothered. I hung around at the steep entrance for a bit but there were no signs of life. The view of Rathlin Island was a joy however and I paused to take it in like I would my face in a morning mirror. My yawns would've suggested boredom, but I was anything but bored.

After a while I skipped on to Ballycastle and shot past the tall Victorian houses there which overlook the sea. This is a tidy town on the Antrim coast wherein Marconi was also active. The first commercial wireless communications and the first ever radio reporting of a sporting event (a sailing Regatta) were transmitted from Rathlin Island to Ballycastle back in the 1890s. There is a plaque in the town to commemorate this. There's even a park (Marconi Park) named after the man. It wouldn't be Ulster of course if there wasn't a non-diamond shaped Diamond slapped in there too. This one was surrounded by businesses that bear its name. There was 'Diamond Cabs', 'The Diamond Bar', 'Diamond Fish & Chips' and the bloke standing alone on the grassy knoll when I glanced over, I can only assume was a diamond geezer. I'd have liked to hang around and make friends, but I had a lot of cycling to do and the Glens of Antrim were calling.

As well as Rathlin Island, it's possible to see Scotland and the Mull of Kintyre from the Antrim coast. It's only thirteen miles away and it felt strange for me to be looking across the water and seeing the Island of Britain. It was after all where I lived.

Interestingly, the ownership of Rathlin Island was disputed by Scotland and Ireland until 1617. Randal McDonnell, the first Earl of Antrim settled the issue by pointing out that the Island had no snakes on it and as a result, had to be Irish. Amazingly this was accepted. My flat has no snakes in it either, I hope, however I don't think Hackney Council would be too impressed if I claimed that because of this, it could possibly be part of Ireland and therefore exempt from Council Tax. No?

As a tourist attraction the Glens of Antrim are often overlooked in favour of the Giant's Causeway. This is a mistake. The beauty of this area (it's an officially designated area of outstanding natural beauty) is a match for any of the fine places of Ireland. There are nine glens in total and I already found myself near Glenshesk coming out of Ballycastle. For the next twenty or thirty miles I would be skimming past and riding through some of these Glens. Here nature creates a canvas of colour that I was lucky enough to view from the road. The red sandstone, the pepper and apple green hills, the black basalt and yellow ochre of the coast, the baby blue sea, the white limestone and the lime green trees were all glowing in the morning sun. And I was too. This is what I came to find.

Author C.S. Lewis who penned the *Chronicles of Narnia* spent a lot of time in Antrim and was clearly inspired by the landscape as well as the folklore and legends of the place. His children's stories are known the world over. Belief in fairies and the Otherworld was strong in Antrim's glens and the world of fantasy certainly finds its way into his work. Traditionally boys in Antrim were often dressed in petticoats and made to look like girls because it was believed that boys were more at risk of being kidnapped by fairies. I can only imagine how confused any boy would be at being told to:

'Put on this auld wee dress, will you? Or the fairies will come and take you away'.

And I'm not sure what the holy wells in this area are known to cure, but it's unlikely to be paranoia.

Now I haven't read the stories of C.S Lewis for a very long time but with titles like *The Lion, the Witch and the Wardrobe,* you can see plainly how wardrobes,

A Cyling Fan's Ride Around Ireland

like witches and lions, might've been a concern for young people. Obviously they were liable to dispense some items of clothing that may have been a worry...

Anyway, after a good long spin down the A2, through forests and past excited waterfalls, I bypassed Cushendun, crossed the Glendun River and landed in Cushendall. Immediately this little village felt familiar. The mural celebrating one hundred years of the sport of hurling added further colour to the already bright Georgian style streets. I stopped outside the old Curfew Tower and took a drink. The day was hot now and I had the feeling that my arms and neck might burn. This was a good complaint considering the weather I'd had, but I wasn't sure about adding the weight of a full bottle of sun cream to my luggage. I still had mountains to climb.

'I'll have the summer salad,' I said to the waitress in the yellow café after I'd decided to have an early lunch.

'Do you have any taytie bread?'

'Aye but that's only for breakfast'.

This reply came with a look of real confusion.

'You can't serve it with the salad?'

'No', she said bluntly as she began to make coffee.

I took a seat outside on one of the scorching iron chairs and while my arse was cooking, I saw my waitress talking to an older colleague. It seemed the shock of being asked for taytie bread for lunch had spread. I was unimpressed.

During lunch I read about Oisín, Ireland's greatest warrior poet. Oisín was Finn McCool's son. It is thought that Finn first met Oisín when he found him naked on Ben Bulben (he must have refused to wear a dress and got kidnapped by fairies). Anyway, on meeting the beautiful Niamh when he was older, Oisín ran away with her to Tír na nÓg (the land of eternal youth). When he got back, he found that he had aged three hundred years but he still used the skills he had learned and the secrets of Tír na nÓg to open a Botox clinic in Dublin 4. He actually became an excellent plastic surgeon and made a killing in Dublin during the Celtic Tiger era. Unfortunately, when the economy also went tits up, as it were, Oisín emigrated to America where he became a builder and played hurling at weekends when he wasn't trying to avoid US Emigration.

It was a sad end to a great poet. Oh yeah, and then he returned and died and got buried in a field of stones right here in Cushendall... or something.

The salad was great, even without the taytie bread.

I filled up my water bottles in the café, threw caution to the light breeze and crossed the street to buy some sun cream at a chemist's. I don't really need to tell you what happened as soon as I rubbed in the lotion. That's right; the sun did one, like Benandonner hot-footing it back to Scotland, and it seemed to happen as if on cue. It had been a very promising morning up to that moment, but getting a couple of really good days in a row is pushing it when it comes to Irish weather. At least the smell of the cream reminded me of happier times and the clouds rolling in didn't look like bursting.

◊

After Cushendall I found myself on the Antrim Coast Road proper. This is regarded as one of the most beautiful coastal routes in the world – one of the reasons why it was chosen to feature in the 2014 Giro d'Italia. It was built by William Bald, a Scottish Engineer over ten years from 1832. Before it was built, the small farmers who lived in the Glens could not access market towns easily and often had to sell their produce in Scotland, as it was comparatively easy to get to by boat. In harsh winters they would often be cut off for weeks at a time.

This new road offered little or no climbing and that was a relief for me too. I passed Waterfoot and skirted the North Channel on the Garron road. For a few miles the rising crosswinds were a bit of a pain but I made good time and got into a decent pedalling rhythm again, covering almost twenty miles over the next hour or so.

Soon I was in pretty Carnlough, at the foot of Glencloy and I whizzed past the Londonderry Arms Hotel. Once a coaching house owned by Lady Londonderry, the hotel was inherited by her great grandson Winston Churchill in 1921. It was an appealing focal point of the village and I was glad that there were a few villages en route, as this road, though spectacular, is improved by the option at least of a break. That break would come at the next village – Glenarm, or so I thought.

When I got there, Glenarm was suspiciously quiet. The only sounds were of the union flags flapping in the breeze and the swish of the lowering tide against travelling sand and stones. I was hungry again; the lack of taytie bread in Cushendall had proved problematic. But nothing was open and to be honest, I just wasn't feeling this place.

Seven more miles of riding brought me to Ballygalley where I ransacked the shelves of the local store and pigged out on the long beach. It was a feast of crisps, pasta and chocolate – stuffed sloppily into my gob in no particular order.

I was tempted to go for a swim too. The clouds had split, gaps appearing like a fractured group of riders on a Pyrenean climb. The air was warm but the water? I hoped I might discover a hotel pool later instead. Also, the thought of sand in my socks was about as appealing as the rope bridge, so I sacked off that idea in favour of that oh so popular pastime of 'just looking'.

Ah, just looking... This really is a favourite pastime of many Brits and Irish at the beach. On Sunday afternoons especially, cars are often filled with aging ham sandwich folk. We picnic *inside* our cars; the dash board becomes our spread. Flasks of hot tea wash down youth and blackened crusts, and we wallow in our bubbles watching sadly. The seats recline and sometimes half-sleep catches up, as radios make hideous sounds of matches and bad news – cancelling the silence of the world. We read too, mostly nonsense and more news. Rarely do we listen for the music of the sea and in not doing so, we wonder how on earth we haven't left these godforsaken freezing 'shithole' shores. *I should have booked that holiday to Spain.* We exist only, miserably.

The real reason why most go to the seaside and 'just look'? The water is freezing and we're afraid of it. Still, this fact deters most but never all from taking a plunge. *Do I always take the plunge or does fear grip and win?*

Of course stating the absolute obvious every time we get back out again after we take the literal plunge is always part of this process. We creep into the water screaming, clutching our shoulders and our wet shivering return is accompanied by a nod to strangers when we're frantically searching for our towels. We couple this with a desire to be 'informative':

'Oh my god... that's bloody freezing'.

The standard reply is usually 'yes, I imagine it is', but really what our new friends are thinking is *'I know it's bloody freezing you dunce – it's only March or something for fuck sake'.* Then you force out something like – 'though... it... makes... you... feel... really good...' – in between the chattering and vibrating of your vaguely electrocuting lower jaw. We never stay.

At this point these 'just looking' types smugly think *'Ooh... on the contrary, standing here dry and not shivering makes me feel rather good in fact'.* Of course these thoughts never actually become words, only a smile returns and you are left alone to dry your milk-white goose-pimpled stringy excuse for a body and wonder why you haven't booked that holiday to Spain...

We can never win... maybe...

The game of keeping things civilised is really what seems to get us through life, but sometimes it can be tempting and even refreshing to just say it as it really is, without the charade.

The Grandmother with the two children playing near me on the beach didn't look like they'd been in the water, but I decided to ask anyway.

'Been in?'

'Sorry?' said the woman.

'Have you been in the water?'

'What... in there?' she asked nodding towards the sea with a disgusted look on her face and in a thick Scottish accent.

'Yes'.

'You must be jokin... it's bloody feezin pal, do you think ah was born yesterday? Ah might be a wee bit older ken but am no stupid like.'

'Have you ever gone in?'

'Have ah ever gone in? Aye, ah course ah've gone in, when I was wee, but now that ah know that it's freezing ah do nay bother. I'm no stupid'.

I suddenly felt like I was on the wrong end of a bollocking. Actually, I was on the wrong end of a bollocking, for asking what in hindsight, was a fairly half-witted question – two fairly deficient questions in fact.

I thought it prudent to hit the road at this point and as I said my goodbyes I couldn't help but think again that the woman was wondering what day care centre the guy on the bike had been let out of. As I wiped the sand off my padded arse and hurriedly tried to cycle away on the beach, my rear wheel spun a little and kicked a chunk of drying sand into the family's picnic.

'Oi oi, what the... watch the bloody sand will ya? ... Are you taking the pish pal?'

These were the last words I heard, repeatedly, as I managed with some toil to regain the road. I rode now like I was being chased. Though the angry hollers from the woman got fainter the further away I got, I was afraid to look back – just in case she was looking for a fight or something. It all calmed down a mile or two later but it occurred to me how tempting, even refreshing it is when people just smile, create the charade and don't say exactly what they're thinking – just to make things civilised of course...

◊

One of Ballygalley's main attractions is the 17th Century Scottish style stone castle (now a hotel) on the main road. Not only do its owners claim that it's the longest standing residence in Ireland, but it is also considered to be the most haunted castle in Ulster. Many ghost stories are told about the place and mediums who have stayed, report that there are often more spirits there than guests.

We know that poitín is unlikely to be stocked as that's a spirit officially banned in the North. However I'm sure there are all types of brandy and whiskey products keeping these mediums in touch with the ghosts as well as, I'd imagine, the voices in their heads. Again, I didn't fancy sticking around too long, lest I might bump into some freak. Nothing related to the Otherworld would surprise me now and there was also a chance that the Scottish woman could catch up with me too. The town of Larne was luckily only three miles or so away.

I say luckily...

I knew little about Larne but something told me that I'd be seeing a lot more flags flying there. Still, I was interested to know what the folks there were like. I felt I might have something in common with them. You see some people in Northern Ireland love the outdoors. They love going for walks and sometimes like to bring their drums with them, so that they can be noticed and appreciated. They love it so much in fact that there's even a Parades Commission which was set up to help people from all communities to get together and parade as one big happy family. St. Patrick would have been proud. Various groups involved in the outdoors and the marching include the Irish Ramblers Association (IRA) and the Ulster Drumming Association (UDA). These organisations just love spreading the love of walking. In fact, they'd even march through your back garden if they could get away with it.

Some love the colour orange too, like at the ginger-fest all the way back in Crosshaven. I'm not sure they'd look out of place at Dutch corner on Alpe d'Huez or even at the Glasshouse in Sligo wearing their orange sashes and banging those big orange drums.

Anyway, it was July and the marching season was in full swing – so to speak. Now that I was here, I was hoping to come across a parade or two and I was looking forward to soaking up the friendly festival atmosphere. I figured I could chat to the people cheering at the sides of the road and if I was lucky, being an outdoorsy sort of bloke, I thought I might even get a chance to join in the marching.

When I arrived and came off the coastal route, Larne was all traffic lanes, roundabouts and industry. It had all the charm of Milton Keynes and it had enough flags to keep Britain stocked out for the Olympics. I reached the large Circular Road roundabout and there in front of me was Finn McCool's massive shiny helmet... Or so it seemed.

Actually in the centre of the roundabout was a huge golden regal crown made of plastic or wood; I wasn't sure but it was definitely shiny. It looked like it may have been some kind of Art installation, but to be honest, it was more like something found in a lucky bag belonging to a giant among giants. It didn't matter what it stood for (I later found out that it was there to mark the Queen's Jubilee); it was just plain ugly – like something out of a Damien Hirst 'art' factory. In fact, I was surprised it didn't send cars careening off the road. If the sheer bad taste of the thing didn't make you shut your eyes, at least looking away due to the glare was a likely and costly response. It was certainly a surprise and definitely did its job in leaving a mark.

There was no sign of any marching going on in Larne either, a further disappointment for sure, but I pushed on through the Bank Road and found that I was on the quiet hilly route bound for Belfast already. *Oh well, I'll just have to make do with the rolling hills, the shimmering streams and the generous views...*

◊

When I was growing up in the eighties, folk songs and ballads were a staple in the car, particularly on long journeys. Pushed into the cassette player were compilation tapes usually titled *'Various Irish Artists'* or something similar. One of these often-played songs was *'Carrickfergus'*, a hauntingly sad ballad about missing the town of that name. The song features all three of the major themes of Irish folk songs: the perceived pain of emigration, self-pity and of course – boozing. This ballad, like Andy Irvine's more modern song about Miltown Malbay, sparked wonder for me about the town. It left me with a desire to at least check the place out. The painful longing for Carrickfergus expressed by the speaker in the lyrics, is enough to convince anyone that the place has at least some merit. The fact that the song is so popular and was recorded by so many artists including Joan Baez, Loudon Wainwright, Bryan Ferry, Van Morrison and others, helps convince us too. I was excited.

In the town itself there is an impressive 12th Century Norman castle by the eastern shore, but I arrived from the north side where I got a good close up of the large Tesco with its overcrowded car park instead. I was also treated to an array of orange flags from the Ulster Drumming Association (UDA), some of which were flying outside St Nicholas' Catholic Church. I couldn't help think how clever, almost genius this kind of target marketing was. It was clearly an effort to encourage mass-goers to take up marching. We all know how nice a Sunday stroll can be. Why not do it with the neighbours and get the drums out as well as the flags? Of course all of this added to the colour and vibrancy of the town already provided by Tesco. It was sure to tempt tourists from all over to stop and spend a few pounds in ...well Tesco, and I can only imagine how pleased other members of the community were at knowing how inclusive the UDA can be. It warmed my heart, probably like the whiskey had warmed the heart of the narrator in the song.

Of course we should never trust a song where the speaker admits to being currently, and in fact almost always off their face from drink.

'For I'm drunk today, and I'm seldom sober'.

Warped memories of the reminisced about town are always likely to surface, for as the old saying goes –'when drink is in, you talk utter shit'. In these songs the reasons the exiled had for leaving the now pined for town in the first place: lack of money, food or work (or because of some imminent arrest warrant) are often quickly forgotten, especially when drink stirs the emotions. Suddenly the place they've left is the most romantic, soulful and abundant in the world, where people shite £5 notes, grow spuds out of their ears and rattle off poems and songs like a free juke box in your favourite pub.

Another classic example in song of this phenomenon is *'Dublin in the Rare Oul Times'*, a ballad made famous by *The Dubliners* – 'Oh the years have made me bitter, the gargle dims my brain'. Too right lad. Would these celebrated days be the same rare old times when people lived in filthy tenements, ate thin gruel and walked around shoeless? Yep,' the good old days', no, 'you don't see days like those anymore'. Thank God we don't.

In a few years they'll be writing ballads about how great it was to be in negative equity, when the beautiful ghost estates kept us all entertained and it'll be generally agreed that 'we had nothing, but jaysus we were happy'! My arse...

When I reached the main promenade of Carrickfergus and thought of the comparative cosmopolitanism of Belfast, contrary to the opening lines of that song – I really wished I wasn't in Carrickfergus. *Be careful what you wish for.....* It was time to move on.

Luck returns for the cyclist after Greenisland. The long traffic heavy route all the way to Belfast is avoided because of the bike path that takes us closer to the shore of Belfast Lough. This path is a cyclist's friend and I pedalled on toward the city, past the Harland and Wolff dockyard and eventually into the centre. I hadn't necessarily planned to stay in Belfast but now that I was here, with a decent day's riding behind me, I was full of hope and happy about it.

◊

The buzz of Belfast city grabbed me straight away. I discovered that I wasn't quite done with the metropolitan yet. My newly developed penchant for hotels was about to reach an alarming climax too as I rode straight to the Europa Hotel on Great Victoria St. Inside I chucked my bike over my shoulder and strode nonchalantly towards the reception desk. I'd always wanted to stay at this hotel. It's almost as famous as the city itself and I figured I'd earned it.

'Just me,... one night,... how much?'

Taken aback by my lack of pleasantries the youngish woman quickly checked her computer.

'No problem, that's £80 for tonight'.
'Does that come with breakfast?'
'Of course' said the woman.
I was slightly relieved to hear this price. It was really only twice the price of a B&B or as I like to put it, one night for the price of two, but it was probably the best located hotel in Belfast and it's not often you get a chance to stay in the most bombed hotel in the world.

'I'll take it'.

After accidentally charging £800 to my card, a transaction that left me shaken, the woman spent a good while apologising until my breathing returned to normal and I regained my strength. Eventually I made my way (less nonchalantly) up to my room.

In the seventies and eighties, my room's location – above the fifth floor and at the back – would have been the most sought after at this hotel, because it meant there was much less chance of the windows being blown out by a bomb. Nowadays, the close up view of a long grey wall is less fashionable. Still, the rest of it was pleasant enough.

I took my time and luxuriated in a hot bath for way too long before having a lie-down and a change into my man-about-town gear in readiness for a night out. Unfortunately, after several days touring, this gear amounted to a filthy pair of shorts and a damp odorous t-shirt. It was more man-about-to-ask-for-20p than man-about-town, and I even had a slight concern that if I hung around the lobby too long, I might be asked to move on. At least I'd had a bath.

That habit of checking into hotels and then disappearing without really considering the hotel itself as a good place to hang out is an easy one to break. It's easier after you've ridden 86 miles to get there on a bike, and can't be arsed walking anywhere else anyway, but when the hotel in question is the Europa, it's easier still. I went to the café and ordered tea, hardly the beginnings of a riotous night on the town, but it was a start. I figured I'd need to eat too and I could visit at least one tourist attraction; I was after all a tourist.

It was evening now but the sun was still warming the streets from which the smell of soft tar was rising. I considered having a picnic down by the Titanic museum. Bread and maybe some lettuce (iceberg) would've been easy to get and I'd heard there were some famous butchers on the Shankill Road. I wondered if they'd cut me a few slices of salami, but I had a sinking feeling that they'd be shut. It was getting late. I'd probably missed the boat on the Titanic museum too. But after the price of the Causeway Centre, missing the boat on the Titanic is probably not the end of the world.

There was only one thing for it – the Kathmandu Kitchen on Botanic Avenue. On my only previous visit to Belfast I'd gone there with a friend. The Nepalese food was divine. If it ain't broke...

But before heading out, I considered the fascinating history of the Europa hotel. If it wasn't for the fact that it housed the Northern Ireland correspondents of the international press corps, the place probably wouldn't have been bombed half as often as it was. In total, around thirty devices have gone off in and around the building. Detonating bombs, literally on the doorstep of the world's media, was sure to get coverage and that's what the paramilitary organisations wanted. They weren't trying to kill the press, but were just sort of making sure they took note. What better way than to blow the glass out of their bedrooms?

The Irish Ramblers Association (IRA), that other outdoorsy group were often responsible for this. So into the outdoors were they, that sometimes they encouraged guests outside in the middle of the night by waking them with loud bangs using Semtex. Even if only wearing pyjamas, guests were given an interesting and often unforgettable outdoorsy experience. In fact, it was less outdoors and more no doors at all really when they reached the ground floor. But luckily that's where the fun ended. There was generally no obligation to go on any night marches beyond evacuating the building.

Despite these interruptions over the years, many famous and celebrated people have stayed at the Europa including Julia Roberts, Brad Pitt, Lionel Richie, The Clintons and of course John Delaney, the Chief Executive of the penniless Football Association of Ireland (FAI).

Delaney, who pays himself more than the salary of the US President and more than his counterparts in Spain and Italy combined, was possibly planning the Rep. of Ireland's 2002 pre world cup visit to Saipan while a guest. But again this is unconfirmed; it's unlikely that anyone actually 'planned' the Rep. of Ireland's 2002 pre world cup visit to Saipan – not even Amelia Earhart!

◊

Much like the rest of Ireland, Ulster is a great sporting arena. It boasts some of the best golfers in the world and has a great history in motorsport, football and rugby. Unfortunately it's not been a noted hotspot in the sport of cycling – not until 2013 anyway.

When I was in Belfast it hadn't happened yet, but a few months later Martyn Irvine became World Champion after winning the scratch race on the track at the World Championships in Minsk. His gold medal and rainbow jersey were added to the silver medal that he'd already won from the individual pursuit competition only an hour earlier. Irvine who is from Newtownards near Belfast became the first Irishman to don the rainbow jersey since Stephen Roche won the road race in 1987. So, would Irvine now be subject to the curse of the rainbow jersey? Well, a few weeks later he did break his leg riding the Tour of Taiwan...

That same week, when Irvine was beating the world on the track, it was announced that Belfast would host the start of the 2014 Giro d'Italia. This was a great coup for cycling fans in both Britain and Ireland and it was something that I for one was chuffed about. But does good fortune come in threes as well as misfortune? Winning silver, gold and the Giro all in one week would suggest it does .But is Francis Bacon right about superstition ; do we mostly 'observe when a thing hits, but not when it misses'? I'm keeping an open mind on that one.

I like Belfast. It's a charming city and its mixed architecture gives variety as you stroll through the streets. I walked around by City Hall (the flag atop hadn't been removed yet) and through some of the pedestrianized shopping lanes. It has the feel of a British city (the same high street stores are omnipresent in UK towns) but there was something distinguished about the place too.

Belfast incidentally is not as old a city as you might think. In fact Carrickfergus was a much more important and larger place until Belfast began to grow significantly from the late 17th Century. It is probably best known for producing linen and for its shipbuilding industry but while famous racing cyclists from Belfast might be few and far between, its contribution to cycling couldn't be greater.

In 1887 John Boyd Dunlop, a Scottish vet living in Belfast, invented and developed the first successful inflatable or 'pneumatic' tyre. Dunlop encouraged racing cyclist Willie Hume to use it and when Hume won almost every race he entered with this new tyre, it soon caught on. The Dunlop name became a household name over the next century after commercial production of tyres began in Belfast in 1890. John Dunlop himself never made a huge fortune out of his ideas because he sold the patents. In fact he later moved to Dublin where he developed bicycle frames but his contribution to cycling and indeed motorised transport is unquestioned.

My legs and stomach colluded to send me off for dinner soon after my stroll. I found my spice smelling haunt and ordered lamb bhuna which was of such remarkable quality that I can only assume it came from the famous Shankill butchers, or some such reputed purveyors of fine meats. The restaurant was quiet save for two Asian couples who appeared to be on a double date. I'm not sure what is custom, but the one curry and the basket of poppadum shared between all four of them seemed a bit scanty to me. I have no doubt that the four courses I devoured amounted to more food than what all four of these diners had combined.

After eating, I peeled myself off the chair and headed straight back to the Europa. Night had fallen and so did my enthusiasm for anything other than bed. I thought about stopping off at a cocktail bar and ordering an 'Irish Car Bomb' with an extra thick southern Irish accent – for the craic. Then I realised that I was supposed to be a mature man and that I valued my life more than having it ended by someone who had an apprenticeship done as a meat victualler.

In any case, as I walked passed one bar, the unconvincing advice to the bouncer to 'fuck clean off' by a now ex-customer, as he was being escorted into the middle of the road, turned me off.

Bed was truly the better option.

CHAPTER 13

'People who enjoy waving flags don't deserve to have one.'
Banksy (Artist)

I like lounging around busy city hotels in the morning. What's better than that hour bedecked with newspapers and strong coffee? It's great when you're on holiday but when you've got to get on a bike and ride for hours, reaching a more chilled state can be challenging. I was enjoying the hum in the Europa's lobby but it didn't last long.

Breakfast, a hearty (attacky) Ulster fry was happily settling within as I considered whether it was a Protestant or a Catholic fry-up. It having been christened an 'Ulster fry' and not an 'Irish Fry', I suspected that it was of the Protestant persuasion. I was perfectly fine with this. Being a bit of a Buddhist monk myself, albeit one with a weakness for fried bacon, who'd sent himself on a journey of discovery atop two prayer wheels turning out countless mantras for the saviour of all Ireland and the world, I was happy to allow my food be of a non-Buddhist persuasion. *I never did get those prayer wheels properly ordained, but then again Saint Imor of Killimer (idle murder suspect fella) never took Holy orders either. I think I'm safe enough.*

To be quite honest, I know I'd probably had Catholic breakfasts in the South, but by god you could've fed me fifty of these Protestant ones – like in a kind of Coke/Coke Zero challenge (one is great fun but bad for you, the other is just great fun) and I'd never have known the difference. *The sheer wonder of it all...*

In the polished lobby Northern accents mixed with the lighter squeaks and 'ooh la las' of some French tourists and I was reminded of the small matter of touring that I had to do myself. Soon I was checked out and back on the road, full of caffeine and stocked with half swiped slices of fried potato bread that were slipped shyly into the back pockets of my jersey.

This time I did have an idea about where I would end up that evening. A phone call to my Aunt cleared the way for a night's stay at her and my Uncle's house near Dundalk. Berni and Bernie (I know, it sounds like some kind of puppetry double act) are pretty good craic. Actually they're probably funnier than most double acts, so I was looking forward to hanging out as well as not having to fork out for a bed. It was always likely that I'd ask a favour from some friend or family member at some point on this trip. The east coast is where most people in the country live, so it's the most likely place to pay a visit.

Dundalk was a good bike spin away though. For now, I switched between Van Morrison and guitar band *Two Door Cinema Club* on my ipod while making my way through south Belfast' trafficky suburbs. I was in County Down now and both my music choices hailed from the county so it was apt. I'd thought about playing *The Undertones* too for kicks, another Northern band – so hard to beat, but they haven't released anything for a while. A good band these days is hard to find, but the lively beats of their modern replacement kept my legs going and the miles kept clocking.

There are many ups in Down, highlights of the county that could make anyone's morning. Unfortunately Carryduff wasn't one of them. It was plain enough – another greyish Tesco town that looked like it needed a holiday. I stayed on the A24 and before long the rolls of green reappeared. I was pleased to be back again in the airy quiet, heading for Ballynahinch.

Of course it's not really fair to blame Ulster for heart attacks, be they the consequence of fried breakfasts or harshly timed building evacuations – certainly not nowadays anyway. In fact, since the 1960s Northern Ireland is known for quite the coronary, I mean contrary. County Down itself is the birth place of Professor Frank Pantridge C.B.E (aka 'The Father of Emergency Medicine'). Pantridge invented and developed the portable defibrillator at the Royal Victoria Hospital Belfast in the 1960s. This is a device which is used to give an electric shock to heart attack victims in order to restore their optimum heart rhythm. Most ambulances in the world now carry them and from the mid-sixties a Belfast ambulance carried the very first one, prompting people to regard the city as 'the safest place in the world to have a heart attack'.

This fact is interesting because Belfast from the 1960s was a place where taytie bread fry-ups were cooked in lard. They were probably washed down on weekends with swigs of Bushmills and followed up with a smoke of a few locally made Rothmans cigarettes too. There was also the excitement of some occasional marching to consider as well as the building evacuations, so when you think about it, Belfast was really probably *the most likely* place in the world to have a heart attack… *'Necessity is the mother of invention' and all that.'*

The A24 road finally led me into Ballynahinch. Not to be confused with Ballynahinch in County Galway, this place is bigger and is an improvement on Carryduff. After not bothering to reach Malin Head a few days earlier, I had pretty much ignored the idea of reaching Ireland's most easterly point as well – which incidentally is Burr Point on the Ards Peninsula, not far from where I was. I was heading due south now, all the time aware that I was in a sense on my way home. Every pedal stroke from here on would take me closer to Cork, the place where I'd started. I was pleased about this but only because the task I'd set myself, to ride my bike around Ireland, was all the time nearing completion. It wasn't that I'd wanted it to end; I just knew that it would have to.

Off the busy A24 road I found a sleepier route that more or less runs parallel. But this further reminded me that good things often come to an end, as a short while later it merged again with the A24 at Dundrum. It was good while it lasted. But what I was learning about good things is that more comes, just as often.

Not to be confused with Dundrum in County Dublin, this old port village on Dundrum Bay is an even further improvement on Ballynahinch. It was pretty and offered the smell of the sea. I was now grazing the coast and I knew I had the Mourne Mountains ahead of me. *More comes.* This ride was getting better.

A few miles after Dundrum, I arrived in Newcastle. Upon arrival, I slowed to take the place in. Famous for its football team, magpies, Anglo-Saxonish dialect and scantily clad women, I'd never been to Newcastle before and was eager to learn more. The sun was showing too, something I wasn't expecting as I'd heard it was often grim up there. I'd also heard of the *Geordie Shore* but I wasn't expecting it to be so long. Stretching for five miles on the South Down coast, Newcastle's beach and promenade is a true gift. It's also nestled under the Slieve Donard Mountain, the highest peak in the Mourne range. One of the first things I'd noticed was that it really does 'sweep down to the sea' as the lyrics of the famous Percy French song suggest. Poetry was alive in front of me.

I'd ridden over thirty miles from Belfast already and I'd made up my mind to stop; tea and cake were a must and besides, I had my touring rules to obey. After crossing the trout filled Shimna River, I hopped off the bike and began negotiating my way on foot through the crowds of people.

Everyone knows the dialect is hard to understand here and I was looking forward to using a few of the phrases that I knew from ....Ant and Dec on some of the locals.

'How's about you big mon?' asked the tall, tattooed and heavy set owner of the roadside bar as I parked up and took a seat outside.

'Way aye man', I said.

'Ah'll ave a tea an a canny bit a cake pet,' I continued, conscious of how accurate my Newcastle accent really could be.

I felt certain to be understood as I'd also learned a few phrases from a guy I knew from Sunderland – which is the same place really.

This man however looked a bit puzzled. He might have even looked a bit angry.

'Tea and cake is it?'

'Aye' I said, pointing to a picture of a scone on the menu.

'Righto', he said, coupling it with a suspicious enough look.

As I looked around at the scantily clad ladettes strolling down the beach, I had a feeling that the heat was getting to me a bit. I wondered too if I would see singer Cheryl Whateverhernameis herself, and for a moment I thought that I did see her on the beach playing volleyball. I was about to ask the café owner if he often saw her around but he seemed a bit moody when he returned and sort of bundled everything clumsily onto the table. *I'll leave it,* I thought.

I felt better again after the tea. I think I may have had a touch of the hunger knock as well as being affected by the heat. When I looked back to the beach,

A Cyling Fan's Ride Around Ireland 153

the volleyball players had completely disappeared. It was like as if they'd never been there in the first place.

I noticed I'd forgotten to eat the taytie bread in my back pocket too. A quick scan of that revealed it had sweated itself into a doughy ball. I did think about keeping it, taytie bread was not easy to find in the South, but I resisted and left it on the table for the nice man to clean up.

It was time to move on but just as I was contemplating leaving, with absolutely no warning whatsoever, the RAF's Red Arrows flew right over head. The roar was loud and quick and left everyone peering skyward. But why were these planes flying over Newcastle near the Mourne Mountains? Then the penny dropped. Later that evening London was due to open the 2012 Olympic and Paralympic Games. I assumed that this was the reason for the fly-past– to mark this occasion. In their wake they left a trail of blue, white and red vapour, in vertical bands, a representation of course of the French flag. Maybe this was a gesture to French people – *'Unlucky, we know Paris had wanted to host the Games but we won and so we're honouring you in this way for being a good sport...'* In any case, the people of Newcastle didn't seem too bothered by the fly-past. Everyone continued on as normal as soon as the aircrafts disappeared across the Irish Sea.

This was really noticeable and few seemed to have gathered especially for the occasion. I was probably more interested than the locals. Being a resident of Hackney, which was an 'Olympic Borough', I lived and worked not far from the Olympic stadium. I was curious to see the Opening Ceremony myself and was glad I was headed for my Aunt's house where I knew the sports-mad family would be eager to watch it too. But I couldn't get away from how unconcerned the people here were about the whole thing. The planes were asking us to look towards London. London was 'calling', but it all seemed to fall on deaf ears.

For me everything pointed to the last verse of the Percy French song *'The Mountains of Mourne'*, a song that warns of the superficiality of London and although I would have enjoyed being at this world event (if I'd been lucky enough to get a ticket), I felt that this place here was more than a match for any in the world. It's no wonder the people here weren't fazed.

'That if at those roses you venture to sip
The colours might all come away on your lip
So I'll wait for the wild rose that's waiting for me
In the place where the dark Mourne sweeps down to the sea'

I rode on along the coast for a time, watched constantly by the muted mountains. A freakishly heavy rain shower forced me to take cover under a huge oak tree at the edge of a field. Luckily it didn't last long, as I just had the feeling that the farmer watching me from his jeep wasn't too pleased I was on his land.

Soon I came to the village of Annalong which was like a shrine to King Billy with its bunting, flags and metal 'orange arch' stretching across the road. This arch instructed all who passed under it not to forget the battle of the Boyne and other such 'glorious' occasions. I've seen some bizarre things in my time but this was definitely up there.

It was a pleasant bike ride however. I was riding the outline of Ireland and if the mountains were silently watching, the sea was its groaning opposite. It felt like the road was the peacemaker between the two, but I wasn't sure if it was bringing them together or keeping them apart.

◊

Ten miles later the beautiful Carlingford Lough made its entrance into my world and soon after the village of Rostrevor. When leaving Crosshaven over ten days earlier, I knew that I'd encounter some kind of wild and whacky festival or other somewhere on this trip – something maybe to match the ginger festival that the County Cork village hosts. As I spun into the enlivened Rostrevor and jumped off the bike in favour of another tourist stroll, I realised that this was *the* place.

The '26th Fiddlers' Green International Festival' was in progress and judging by the pale faces of the line of musicians camped outside one pub, who were face deep in the hair of the dog, I figured all sorts of shenanigans had been had the night before. The twinkles in the eyes of others suggested mischief and that more was to come too. I wanted to stay.

This is an Arts festival celebrating mostly traditional music. With bands like 'Folk the Recession', it had all the ingredients for a typically Irish denial-style assault on frugality. Let's 'folk the recession' and just sing our way out of it. I thought there might be something in this idea, but I wasn't sure.

The frolicking fun lasts for eight days and the word 'international' suggests a truly international flavour and not just that Mick hitched up from Monaghan and Malcolm rowed over from Mull kind of international. But for all the excitement, I didn't hold out much hope for 'Folk the Recession'; I mean what are they going to do when the economy sorts itself out? *Write songs about the old days – 'Rostrevor in the rare oul' times' – when we were in negative equity, but didn't give a shite and said 'folk the recession' to the landlord and the bank manager and the bailiffs and stuff...? Can you really sing your way out of recession?*

What I'd observed about Ireland were the social changes that had been occurring over the past few years. Everyone it seems is some kind of amateur economist. On radio and TV it's all anyone appears to talk about (apart from the weather of course). Money, equity, banks, deficits, house prices, cuts; these are the words that hang now from Irish lips – constantly. Before it was 'session', now it's 'recession'. When one brings economics into an Arts festival – even just with a simple and humorous band name like 'Folk the Recession', a title that delivers not only information on the state of the economy, but also advice on how to handle it – it says a lot about where Ireland is as a nation. For now, I, like the couples in their parked cars at beaches, was 'just looking', but I was also increasingly wary that 'Folk the Recession' were among the few managing to get paid for folking the recession...

A quick scan of a borrowed programme from a reveller revealed that *The*

Fiddler's Green Festival featured all sorts of goings-on. Banana boating, 'literary' pub crawls, a duck derby, festival bingo (my favourite) and indeed the musical delights of 'Deirdre and Gerry', were all real attractions for me. It had all the ingredients of a Father Ted style festival really, and I was genuinely sore that I couldn't stay. These kinds of events are so particular to Ireland it seems, and are something that I really miss.

Aside from hosting mad festivals, Rostrevor is near where Patrick Murphy, a well-known genuine 19th Century Irish giant came from. Murphy really was one of the tallest men in the world and by the 1850s he was making a living out of being so. Claims about his actual height varied however. Some said he was 8 feet and 10 inches but when he was actually measured by a doctor in 1860 he was only 7' 3.4". This tells us much about the people of this time. Apart from their fascination with giants, they were either:

(a) Full of shit, or
(b) Unable to use measuring tapes.

It's no wonder the legends of the likes of Finn McCool and Oisín survived so long in Ulster. It's probably (a)...

When I remounted my bike, I pushed on pedals of melancholy out of Rostrevor. I was genuinely sad. I'm not sure why, maybe this festival was rooted in nostalgia for me, but I knew that this place, like Lough Gill in Sligo, would be a place I'd return to.

◊

Little boat trips are true treats. They can prove very accommodating when you're riding your bike around the country and I was about to take another one. At Warrenpoint, a short flat jaunt down the A2 from Rostrevor, I waited at the pier for the return of the small passenger boat that spends its days crossing back and forth over the mouth of the Newry River. My destination was Omeath, a small village in 'the South'. This little vessel takes bikes and a handful of people but not cars. It's a short trip too and thankfully it cuts out a good twenty kilometres of riding. The alternative is a long stretch into Newry before a traffic heavy ride towards Dundalk.

I crossed the boatman's palm with the Queen's money, not a lot, and waited to be transported back to where that money is no longer good. I was once more very aware of the transition I was making but again once over the water, the air and the apple-green hills were the same – chilled and breathing. It was soothing and remarkably similar to the land from where I'd just come.

What this place needs is flags, I thought as we neared Omeath at the far side of the river. *Lots and lots of flags – and marching bands, and parades, loads of them too...*

Remounting my bike wasn't necessary when I got off the boat. Waiting for my arrival was a charming country café.

Feed me....anything....please ...just feed me

And in the most immaculately unaffected County Louth accent, as if reading my mind, the lady behind the counter, who I guessed owned the place announced:

'This poor man looks starvin, lord bless us and save us.'

'What'll you eat?'

'Food', said I, an unfussy response.

'I'll do ya a wee steak sandwich, will I?'

You will and there'll be nothing wee about it.

'Sounds good', I said and I took a seat at a large round table. There were maybe six other people afternooned in the café, all in pairs or alone reading newspapers. It was quiet. Not much was being said, but I had the feeling that all eyes were on me, this curious man who'd just gotten off the boat from 'the North' – with a bicycle.

'Have you cycled far?' asked an older woman who seemed least able to resist asking me a question.

'Today... from Belfast, but I've ridden up from Cork and am riding around the whole country,' I said proudly.

'I'm heading to Dundalk now.'

'Jesus Mary and Joseph, he's heading to Dundalk', said the woman as if translating. This appeared to raise a few eyebrows.

'My god I'd never be able for that,' admitted the woman.

The other women agreed and the men, almost simultaneously, took sips of their tea. I wasn't quite sure if she meant she'd never be able to go to Dundalk or she'd never be able to cycle there from Belfast. This worried me slightly. Had Dundalk deteriorated since the days I spent visiting my Grandmother there in my youth? Whatever the case, I felt they had some level of admiration for my effort and I was full of appreciation.

My tea arrived and I got busy squeezing the soggy teabag and breathing in the hot vapour of home.

'How far is Dundalk?' I asked the woman whose name I gathered was Joan.

'How far is D'dalk, lads?' she translated again.

A few of the men scratched their heads.

'Which way are you going?' asked one man from a corner.

'The quickest way,' I said. 'Whichever way is the quickest way.'

More head scratching followed and then a long drawn-out pause...

'This way is the shortest way, if you go up this road,' said the man gesturing behind his head.

'Okay, thanks' I said.

'But it's not the quickest way,' he now added.

This confused me and most of the café. Suddenly a debate started as to which way would be the best way for me to get to Dundalk. The café owner and waitress joined Joan and the five other customers in several side conversations and all of them sounded like they were related to my question. I listened to a few, quite stunned, and it was true. Everyone bar the chef was now involved in the debate.

'Not at all, Carlingford way is much longer', added one woman.

'Aye it's longer, but he'll never get up those hills on a bike if he goes the other way,' said Joan.

'That's what I'm saying Joan,' added the other woman – 'If he went Carlingford way, it'd be longer, but it'd be easier, and it would take less time. He asked what the 'quickest' way is.'

'Sure he'd never get up that hill on a bike if he went the long woman's grave way,' Kevin, the man in the corner declared, clearly not hearing Joan's argument and forgetting that he'd already suggested that way himself.

'Of course he would Kevin, isn't he after cycling around the country but?'

Kevin didn't look too pleased that the other woman, who was also called Joan (as if things weren't confusing enough already), had disagreed with him.

The long woman's grave way... Sounds interesting and I think I remember my grandmother mentioning something about a 'long woman' years ago.

At this point all I could make out was that there were two ways to Dundalk. One was hilly and shorter and the other was flat but longer. Eating was my priority now though and I wasn't going to make any decisions on an empty stomach. The café left me in peace to eat my food and everyone settled back into the way they were before I'd arrived. Though I'd just gotten off a boat, it was easy to forget that Omeath is quite a rural area, but I was enjoying the attention. I felt I'd needed some interaction.

After a while and when my face had been suitably stuffed, I reasoned that it was time to ask my second burning question.

'So what's this long woman's grave business anyway?'

'Kevin, you went to school, you'd know that,' advised the owner.

'Ah,' said Kevin, 'I forget'.

'She was a big tall woman – 7 foot 4,' added another much older man who also sat alone in the dark opposite corner to Kevin.

'She was not, she was 7' 6''', added Joan (the younger).

'Adrienne, you'd know wouldn't you?' said the café owner to Adrienne who was just returning from the loo. Adrienne looked a little younger than most, but had an air of elegance, someone who was the wise woman of the group. She commanded respect and everyone looked to Adrienne.

'Know what?' asked Adrienne.

'About the long woman's grave'

'Oh yes', she said, in a slightly less rural accent. She settled herself back into her chair and began to tell the story of the long woman's grave. Even the men had put down their newspapers now and had gathered their ears to listen, like children round a fireside in times gone by.

'Well, she was a big tall woman – 7 foot 2'''

'Near enough,' said the old man from the corner.

'She was not, she was nearly 8 foot', said Kevin, suddenly remembering.

'Whist,' said Joan (the older).

Oh for feck sake... Here we go again. These people are straight out of 1860s Rostrevor.
'And didn't she marry Finn McCool?'
Oh no, here we really do go again....
'Anyway' said Adrienne, clearing her throat and preparing to start the story again, but there was another pause followed by another confused question.
'And wasn't she from Argentina or somewhere?'
Suddenly it appeared that out of the blue, just when we expected much, Adrienne was failing to deliver some vital information about the long woman. In fact, Adrienne was failing to deliver any information whatsoever about the long woman.
'No' said Kevin authoritatively. 'She was foreign alright and she was promised a whole haype of land if she married Finn. She was going out with him ya see. So she said that was grand anyway and decided to marry him, but when she arrived, didn't she see that the land was only auld shite marshy land; twas no good for cattle'.
'Jaysis she dropped a bollock when she saw the land', laughed the ghostly old man in the corner.
'That's right. And didn't she drop dead then with fright or something?' asked Adrienne again.
'And that's where she is buried' added Joan,' in the grave up in that mountain.'
More debating and arguing followed, but the general consensus was that that was the story – more or less. I felt my question had animated the place for a time at least. I'd have loved to have stayed around longer, if only for the entertainment, but I still had a promise to keep.
'Good luck in your trip' rang round in a chorus from all at the café soon after. I bid my farewells and was almost instantly dragging my sorry ass over some truly steep gradients. I'd opted for the short but hard route where, as was promised, I eventually came upon the long woman's grave. The views of Dundalk Bay and back to Carlingford Lough were sublime and of course I stopped to read the story of the long woman which was carved out on a huge headstone at the graveside.
Eagerly I read, wondering who in the café had been right and it quickly became apparent that, well...none of them were. At 7 foot tall, Kathleen O'Donnell was the mysterious 'long woman'. She was just three inches shorter than her also exceptionally tall new husband, Lorcan O'Hanlon (not Finn McCool). O'Hanlon was the son of a Chieftain and O'Donnell was of noble birth – so they were deemed a good match, not just in terms of height.
Though considered Spanish, with a name like Kathleen O'Donnell, it's obvious her home town of Cadiz was like an ancient Costa del Sol type place. She moved there no doubt when her old man needed a hideout after he'd made a killing supplying cocaine to the streets of Limerick and Dublin during the first Celtic Tiger era (aka The Celtic Wolfhound).
In truth Kathleen really was Spanish. She lived and in fact was born there. But she was a descendant of the noble Ulster O'Donnell clan and she did arrive

back to her ancestral home to marry Lorcan. He enticed her, or so the story goes, by announcing that she would be queen of all the land she could see from the top of the mountain at Aenagh (where I was standing). Unfortunately, when she arrived at the top, she could only see mist and no land at all. The weather was shite. This was an experience that I knew only too well from the Beara Peninsula. Anyway, having only just experienced this drizzly misty manky-grey kind of dampness for the first time (after all she was from Spain), Kathleen couldn't quite cope with it. Not only that, but she also suspected that she'd been duped into a misleading marriage arrangement and as a result, she dropped dead into a hole – which then became her grave. Lorcan, distraught, killed himself pretty much straight after. *Eejit...*

Of course this was an altogether different story to the one that was debated in the café, where the eight foot tall Argentine wife of Finn McCool 'dropped a bollock' when she realised that her cattle wouldn't survive on the bog-land of Dundalk Bay. Still, it's not like the original story is actually more believable is it? I was certainly satisfied with both.

◊

Half an hour later I was in Dundalk. I knew the town reasonably well having spent holidays there as a child but before I went out to my Aunt's house, I thought about doing something that I'd always wanted to do. A favourite poem, learned at school and written by the late Patrick Kavanagh called 'Inniskeane Road July evening', was calling me. I love the opening lines –

'The bicycles go by in twos and threes
And there's a dance in Billy Brennan's barn tonight
And the half-talk code of mysteries
And wink and elbow language of delight.'

These lines, which capture the youthful anticipation of an outsider, have stayed with me for years. I wanted to go to Inniskeane on a July evening and try to re-live this scene. I figured I may never get another chance. The village, though in a different county, was only ten kilometres away. I'd easily make it out and back in time for dinner. And so off I rode, in the direction of County Monaghan and in search of Patrick Kavanagh.

But with each pedal stroke, my enthusiasm waned. After just a few minutes I felt that I was making a mistake. I loved these lines and I wanted to experience them, but they were written decades ago and were about a time that's long gone. I reasoned that the village probably had few bicycles and instead of country roads with people, likely had half-finished ghost estates or some such abhorrent reminder of a collapsed property market. I stopped.

I can't do it. From now on every time I read or remember the poem, I will think of Inniskeane Road July Evening 2012, and there'll be no 'dance in Billy Brennan's barn' and no 'wink and elbow language of delight'. There'll be nothing like that and the images I have from the poem will be replaced and ruined by rude reality forevermore.

That's what I told myself anyway. The real reason might have been the lack of being arsed to ride 10k out the road and 10k back. I'm not sure.

In any case, like an injured dog, I slowly turned away from the dropping sun and rode back to Dundalk. The pensive mood continued when I found my Grandmother's old street. She's passed on now but I allowed a few minutes to remember redbrick childhood afternoons. Often us kids were instructed to go out and play, but not with X-Boxes or phones. No. With 'the traffic' no less. This was certainly one regular suggestion offered by my Aunt when we complained that there was nothing to play with. Nice…

Ah the old days, when we had nothing but we were happy – thumping the shite out of each other and dragging one another round the summer streets by collars and trouser legs until darkness fell or someone started bleeding – again. 'God be with the days…'

Anyway, the added bonus of staying with family of course is that having dinner together is always part of the evening. I was damn sick of eating alone and though I don't mind being alone, it's good to mix it up a bit. It's more than good, it's essential to mix it up. Berni, my Aunt, was busy cooking when I ambled in. Bernie, my Uncle was even busier getting in an early evening nap on the couch.

'Ah you're here,' said Aunt Berni. 'How was your cycle?'

'Great, Newcastle is lovely, not grim at all and I was just at the long woman's grave. She was only seven foot you know. And Belfast was good, stayed in the Europa and it didn't even blow up. I ate in this Nepalese place and it hasn't rained for a few days and I'm a bit tired but I'm grand and thanks for having me and holy shit the Antrim Coast is amazing isn't it? And I was just in a café in Omeath and…' On and on and on it went.

I don't think even I expected so much gibbering, but I realised that I hadn't really spoken much or to very many people in the previous couple of days. This was the one drawback of staying in hotels; conversation is less likely unless you really make the effort. I needed conversation now and I was lucky to have an understanding extended family to take it all in, whether they wanted to or not.

Of course this non-stop mouthing woke my Uncle.

'Well.'

'Well.'

'Where are you after cycling from?'

'Belfast.'

'Feck off, are you serious? Berni will ya get a chair, he needs to sit down'.

In doing so Berni was multitasking now and though not best known for her culinary skills, I was confident that her homemade beans on toast (or whatever she was making) would be okay if left unattended while we watched her find me a chair. 'Old fashioned', would be a way of describing Uncle Bernie. That theme continued when I handed him a bag of washing and he insisted Aunt Berni would have it done by morning.

Of course dinner was great. After a good shower I was treated to a Thai green curry and a carb fest of rice and real homemade bread, which was all surprisingly claimed to have been really 'cooked' by Uncle Bernie –though the actual task of cooking had been 'outsourced' to Aunt Berni. *Maybe he wasn't so old fashioned after all.*

Bernie had recently developed an interest in Oriental and Indian cuisine. In the few years since I'd seen him, he'd also taken up yoga and started making trips to Indian ashrams and Chinese temples. Often he would bring back spices too and he tended to meditate a lot. He managed to meditate anywhere he could in fact, and usually did it lying down with his eyes closed. He said it helped him concentrate – though Berni found the snoring distracting.

Over dinner I also learned of his new found love of Korea and he confessed that he wouldn't mind being a Buddhist monk. Aunt Berni thought that would be a great idea and encouraged him to go away and become one. She said that he was already nearly bald so he wouldn't have to worry about shaving his head and she needed a bit of peace herself. He agreed it would be great, as he wouldn't have to listen to her. It was a perfect family meal and it was great to be in the company of people who were so dedicated to themselves after so many years of marriage.

The yapping continued until I'd burned the ears off my hosts with more stories of my trip but before long we were all happily stretched out in the lounge ready to watch the Opening Ceremony of the 2012 Olympics. I was pretty excited.

On the couch the realisation of how tired I was after my day in the saddle hit, but also after the several days in the saddle. The cumulative effect was noticeable. It was hard getting out of bed and doing a long ride over and over again, though I loved it all.

'Berni... where's that foot spa? asked my Uncle.

'I don't know, you had it this morning,' said Berni, but she managed to jump up and locate it nonetheless.

Without hesitation, Bernie's shoes and socks came off and into the foot spa basin went his tired feet.

'Ah...this is great, if you've been on your feet all day'.

And I'm sure it was. Bernie of course, who is semi-retired, had to go into the office for an hour before his meditation, so it was with great relief that he could relax now with a good foot soak.

'Where are you riding to tomorrow?' he asked.

'Dublin or Wicklow', I said.

There was a long pause. It was maybe a time for reflection more than just a mere pause, though I'm not sure that the irony of the situation had fully hit.

'I'll make you breakfast', he said. 'I have to get up early anyway; my massage is booked for midday.'

'Thanks Bernie, but really you shouldn't go to so much trouble.'

'It's no problem, sure toast and a bowl of cornflakes will do, won't it? That doesn't take long.'

'Aye it will; thanks'

'Grand...'

And so it was with all the comfort of being surrounded by my own people that I settled in to watch the Opening Ceremony of London 2012. We were all gobsmacked by its artistry and the performance of it. I loved the music too, and when Alex Trimble of County Down's *Two Door Cinema Club* sang *Underworld's* 'Caliban's Dream', I knew that I loved this event. It was poetic and dreamy – a near perfect expression for all the world through the vehicle of sport.

And in lieu of war, it's probably the only time where flag carrying, if not waving, is just about okay... maybe.

CHAPTER 14

*'A nation exacts a penance from those who dared
to leave her, payable on their return.'*
                                                                James Joyce

My uncle Bernie was true to his word next morning and appeared in the kitchen shortly after me. He helped with breakfast by pressing the switch of the kettle and pointing to the cupboard where the cornflakes could be found. Later I put some water in the kettle (necessary if you want it to work) and began to plan my day.

Dublin or Wicklow was my intended destination, but I felt that Dublin was the more likely. I didn't really care, but I did care about watching cycling's Olympic road race, one of the first events of the Olympics which would be taking place in Surrey and London later that day. I figured I would need to be stationed in front of a TV by about 3pm to enjoy the final kilometres and so any television rather than Dublin or Wicklow was my real destination.

'Thanks Bernie for all and for putting me up,' I said as I finished eating and got ready to head off.

Only silence returned however and I noticed that Bernie was now meditating again on the couch in the adjacent room. Instead of disturbing this sacred time, I found a pen and wrote a note.

> *'To Bernie and Berni, (the best B&B in Ireland), thanks for everything.*
> *Ps. The element in the kettle seems to have blown but there's a pot on the stove in which you can probably boil water.'*

I left the note on the island counter and stole out of the house to the fresh morning. It was Saturday, a sports fan's Sunday and with the Olympics starting, it was going to be like Christmas day every day for the next two weeks. The sun wasn't shy about making an appearance either. Result.

Almost instantly I was on the old Dublin road passing the village of Blackrock. I felt strong on the bike and knew there weren't many hills on this spin. I knew too that it couldn't be more than eighty or ninety kilometres to Dublin. This road also offered a comforting hard shoulder and though the sea was next to me, the long straight sections warranted a bit of music – to counter monotony as much as an aid to get the legs going. Van Morrison again? Why not?

Louth (or Lú in Gaelic) is Ireland's smallest county. It's named after Lugh, a well-known mythological Celtic god figure. The whole county in fact is rich in mythology and folklore, the long woman's grave story being just one of many.

Lugh, who was Cú Chulainn's father no less, is believed to have joined up with the Tuath de Danann to help them fight off the Fomorians, who were semi divine gods of chaos. As you might expect from being Cu Chulainn's dad, Lugh really was special. In fact his talents knew no bounds. Much like Kim Jong Il of 1990s North Korea, he was just brilliant at everything and he made sure you knew all about it. Also like Kim, Lugh had control over the weather and an ability to develop deadly weapons – seemingly out of nothing. Lugh also held a harvest fair on the 1st day of August and this became the Celtic festival of Lughnasa (Lúnasa). In England August 1st is known as Lammas day.

Tailtu was the name of Lugh's mother and it is at Tailtu Hill (Teltown) in the neighbouring county of Meath where the Lughnasa festival actually began. As part of it, and presumably to honour his mother, Lugh developed the Tailteann Games, or if you prefer – the Irish Olympics. These games really did exist and are thought to have lasted longer than the ancient Greek Olympics, predating them by a thousand years (some say around 1800 BC). From 1922 the GAA (Gaelic Athletic Association) tried to revive the games and succeeded at least in having a sporting festival of the same name – The Tailteann Games. It didn't last very long, but the initial meeting was a success.

Cycling fans will note that Ireland's premier bike race – the Rás Tailteann (or simply the Rás/An Post Rás), which started in 1953, also takes its name from Lugh's mother Tailtu.

History, as we know, has a habit of repeating itself. Aside from Kim Jong Il and the fanciful claims in the style of Lugh, the Taillteann Games of 1924 were created to encourage Irish people and those of Irish ancestry from around the world to come home to Ireland to celebrate their roots. They did this through sport and the arts (the Games were an Arts festival too). This was really the original 'Gathering'. The more recent 'Gathering' of 2013 was the Irish Tourist Board's push to encourage Irish people from all over the world to return home to celebrate whatever they wanted. It too was generally regarded as a success, but it wasn't the first 'gathering'.

I pushed on past Castlebelingham and crossed the White River at Dunleer before landing in the town of Drogheda. The old industries of County Louth have been replaced by the Hi Tech, Services and IT industries which are now to be found all over the county. Some of the bigger names, Pay-pal, E-bay and Xerox are based in Dundalk but Drogheda too has its share. The place was unrecognisable from what I remember of the last time I was there in the 1990s. It's certainly one place the building boom has helped.

Before crossing the Boyne River, close to where the famous battle took place, (where William of Orange of the BNP beat 'Papist' James II by producing a bigger flag than him... or something), I stopped for coffee.

'How far is Dublin?' I asked the waitress at a service station café.
'Oh I am sorry, I am Polish. I don't know… but maybe it takes one hour.'
Forgetting that Polish people don't know how far Dublin is from Drogheda, I thanked the woman nonetheless and comforted myself with knowing that I was probably or nearly halfway there already. It looked about halfway on the map anyway but on a bike it was certainly more than an hour.

I sat contemplating where I was, which was close to an area very rich in Ireland's Neolithic past. The ancient monument sites of Newgrange, Knowth and Dowth as well as the old monastery town of Kells were all a relatively short bike spin away. I thought of all the fine places around Ireland I'd been to and reasoned that not going to these sites would be close to criminal. I'd need to justify leaving them out as they are such a huge part of Ireland's past. Had this Olympic bike race not been on, I certainly would be heading to the passage tomb at Newgrange at least.

The Newgrange monument, built around 3200 BC – like the Dolmen in The Burren – is also older than the Pyramids of Egypt and Stonehenge in England. I'd never been. For a few minutes over coffee and croissants I toyed with the idea of sacking off watching the road race. It was probably going to end in a sprint finish anyway and Mark Cavendish was most likely to pop up in the final hundred metres to claim the gold medal. Would it be worth watching? I have nothing against Mark Cavendish, but watching him is exciting for all of ten seconds. He's fast – maybe too fast. *What to do?*

By the time I'd finished my break, I'd decided that Newgrange had been there for 5000 years and would likely be there again next year. The 2012 Olympic Games were only on once and I'd have to wait another four years to see anything like it again. It was an easy decision in the end. I was definitely Dublin bound.

Crossing the Boyne, I was aware that I was now firmly in The Pale. The Pale, or 'English Pale' was an area around Dublin under English control from the middle ages. This was the only part of Ireland at that time which was under direct English rule and ownership. Back then, even Drogheda sometimes hosted meetings of Parliament. Ireland beyond the Pale was mostly controlled by the native Irish and was often seen as less civilised – possibly even borderline barbaric.

To this day some Dubliners seem to have an understanding that this is still the case, often assuming folk who are not from Dublin (or at least the Pale) to be spud burping dysfunctional muck savages. That might even be putting it kindly. This attitude towards country folk is common to residents of most capital cities to be fair. Nonetheless, I was eager to see if Dublin is as enlightened as it thinks it is and if its denizens are generally a more attractive lot. I was born there myself, but at the age of just six months, realising that Cork was far superior, I instructed my parents to move there. They did, and life began in earnest…

◊

It's impossible not to notice the towering steeples of the impressive Gothic Church of St. Peter as you spin through Drogheda. Curious tourists wandering inside might find more than they bargain for, as the actual preserved head of Ireland's most recently canonised saint (Saint Oliver Plunkett) sits there on display in a glass case. He was hanged, drawn and quartered by the British in 1681 after being convicted of high treason. It was all a set up however and Plunkett became the last Catholic martyr of the English Reformation. His soul might be in heaven, but his head, whether he likes it or not, is most definitely in Drogheda.

On quitting Drogheda I found myself in County Meath, or the 'Royal County', so named as it was once the seat of the High King of Ireland at Tara. The crosswinds near the coast were getting up and a few clouds had now camped above me, so I decided to continue my ride more inland and away from the coastal wind. I headed for Bellewstown, a place of real sporting significance. This is where the first racecourse in Ireland was established. The first horse races known to have been run there were held all the way back in 1726.

I rode on glancing into fields trying to imagine what horseracing was like 300 years ago, but it was also fairly apt, I reflected, that wind speed would concern me in County Meath. Why? Well because one of its sons was Sir Francis Beaufort, Royal Navy Rear Admiral and inventor in 1805 of the 'Beaufort scale'. This scale measures wind speed by observing the effects that wind has. The effect it had on me was to force me to change course –not inconsiderable – but I don't know where it would fit on the scale. Knowing my soft dislike and exaggerated fear of crosswinds, I doubt it would be above 'light breeze' but it was enough for me to take action.

In any case, moving inland was a mistake. By doing this, I unwittingly also avoided the flat terrain and gave myself a series of annoying mini mountains to drag myself over. One near Naul was particularly steep but the line of ancient oak trees led me to a height where a fine view of Dublin Bay appeared in front of me. It was probably worth it, but my lungs were screaming.

My time in Meath was short. I soon arrived in County Dublin and kept pushing for a while yet until I came close to the airport. It was now lunchtime and I was getting hungry again, but I couldn't get the Olympic road race out of my head. The riders would be on one of the laps of Box Hill in Surrey by now and I was nowhere near a TV. I panicked and decided to stop for a long lunch where I would ask some kindly publican to put the race on. Then I would relax, watch it and make my way into Dublin City later – simple. A sign offered me the way to the village of St. Margaret's. This will do, I thought. But it didn't do at all.

There is seemingly no pub in the village of St. Margaret's. Yep. I'll say it again – there is no pub in the village of St. Margaret's. Most Irish villages have more pubs than could ever possibly be needed. In fact pubs are the most common business premises in *every* village in Ireland. But here I was, the only time I actually needed a pub, and there was none. There was a church of course, wherein I could have prayed for a pub, but there was no pub. *Clearly there should be protests...*

As you can imagine, I wasn't really inclined to get too familiar with St.

Margaret's. The road I took from there zigzagged past the airport, through Finglas and towards Glasnevin. I thought of stopping at a couple of pubs on the way into town but the ones I came across were shameful looking places. Though I had a light lock for my bike (designed more for slowing than stopping potential thieves) I knew that it wouldn't be much protection around Dublin. Time was ticking and I was now getting into a proper panic. There was nothing to do but phone my mate Gary for advice. He would be glued to the race and would be one of the only people in my world who would understand my predicament. Also, he lived in Dublin, which was handy.

'Alright lad', he said in his usual condescending manner when he answered.
'How's it going? I'm in Dublin.'
'And?'
'And... I need advice.'
'Yeah'
'Where am I going to watch this bike race?'
'Where are you?'
'I don't know, I think I'm still in Finglas but I really can't say.'
'What's it like?'
'Eh...'
'Is it a bit shit?'
'Well there's not much going on and I've been in more attractive places', I said diplomatically.
'Yeah, you're probably still in Finglas.'
'Where do you live?' I asked.
'Stillorgan'
'Where's that?'
'Down south, close to Wicklow, come down and watch it here. It's no problem.'
'I would but it'll take ages to get there. I might miss the race.'
'I know... that would be a ball ache.'
'What'll I do? I can't decide. It's like my brain's gone numb. It's been happening a lot lately. I have to watch this race, but I'll never get to yours on time.'
'You will. Just keep riding. Go over the river and ride for twenty minutes, then call me again. '
'Are you sure?'
'Yeah you'll catch the last 20k of the race anyway. I'm watching it now.'
'Okay, I'll come down but if I miss it, this whole bike trip is ruined…. Okay maybe not but you know…'
'Shut up and ride your bike.'

And I did. With renewed energy I slipped my chain into a big gear and tore through the streets of Dublin's north side. Unfortunately the rain had the same idea; an angry shower ripped down, bouncing off the glossy tarmac. I had no choice but to check my speed which probably wasn't a bad thing. Before long I found Dorset St., turned left into Temple St. where things began to look familiar, and wound my way down to the top of the handsome O'Connell St. I had now arrived on Ireland's premier street, one of the widest in Europe and it was rammed with crawling trams and tooting traffic. Just as I began to move on after stopping at lights, I felt a sort of hardness on the road and looked down. 'Bollocks' – of all the things to see, the miserable, defeated and pitifully empty state of my front tyre let me know that it was flat.

After two weeks of riding, on every conceivable type of road – up mountains, over bog roads, dual carriageways and hard shoulders – here I was on Ireland's main thoroughfare, Dublin's O'Connell Street, and at the only time on my trip when I was actually in a hurry, I punctured. The chance of this happening at this time is quite slim. The chance of it happening on the main street of the main city after I'd ridden well over a thousand kilometres around the country is even slimmer. Astounded, I shook my head but punctuated it with a smile and half a laugh. In the big scheme of things a puncture is nothing and the race I wanted to watch wasn't that important, I could see that, but there was still time. I reasoned too that a puncture was inevitable and it was as likely to happen on O'Connell St. as any other stretch of road, but it was strange that it would be on Ireland's most majestic stretch.

I phoned Gary.

'I'm not coming.'

'Why?'

'Puncture...'

'Will take ten minutes to fix and I still won't know where I am going. I'll grab a hotel, watch it in my room and fix it later. What's happening in the race anyway?'

'Team GB are controlling but they are under pressure.'

'Okay. Enjoy.'

In search of a hotel, I wheeled my bike around and walked it past the Rotunda Hospital heading back round towards Dorset St. The Rotunda is in fact the oldest maternity hospital in the world and is incidentally where I was born. It's so named after its circular shape and dome. Actually this was quite a strange moment. I'd had a feeling that I was going around in circles, in more ways than one – in many more ways than one. Here I was at the round Rotunda, I was turning my bike around, I was making a natural loop back around to Dorset St. and of course I was riding my bike around Ireland. I was spinning in a whirlwind of circles and I had a feeling that something was changing too. I was changing. Though I was physically going round in circles, I knew from this trip that I'd never be afraid to take on a challenge again. I felt that I'd no longer do things in my life that didn't fulfil me. I wouldn't repeat things and expect different results. And I'd no longer just talk about doing things; I would actually do them. I knew instinctively that in this place I was breaking the rut – the cycle of going round in circles. From now, I'd move forward instead.

On Dorset Street I found a decent modern hotel. I was checked in by another French woman and hauled my wounded bike into the lift. Eager to watch the race, I plunged into my room and grabbed the remote control, almost forgetting to bring my bike in from the corridor. I flicked through the channels. There was no Eurosport and a crisis loomed – but not for long. The BBC offered hope and when I changed over a voice announced that they'd soon be returning to the Olympic road race. *Thank you.* I sat back in my damp clothes and waited. Tick-tock – my fix was coming. *Relax...*

Over the next hour I watched Ireland's three riders make no impression in the end game of the 250 kilometre race. Team GB weren't much better. Much had been expected of favourite Mark Cavendish. Maybe he owed Britain a penance. Her exiled cycling heroes rarely had the opportunity to race on British roads. In fact, the last major one-day bike race on British soil was probably the 1982 World Championships held at Goodwood. For this Olympic race, thirty years later, Britain wanted gold and all eggs had been placed in Cavendish's basket – but it wasn't to be. The (some would say cursed) world champion's third and final major goal of the year had eluded him like the other two. This anticlimactic start to the Olympics was compounded by the fact that probably only Borat would be celebrating at the end. Swiss rider Spartacus (Fabian Cancellara), who looked strong, crashed in the final kilometres leaving the door open for Kazakhstan's Alexander Vinokourov to attack towards the end and win.

'Alexander the Great' certainly was great in this race. He wasn't however in 2007 when he was caught blood doping at the Tour de France. After a suspension he returned, but not many were impressed by this comeback as he refused to admit to any wrong doing. Many were afraid to move on.

My faith in cycling was tested as I reluctantly watched the post-race interviews. *Was this worth sprinting into Dublin for? Is the sport of cycling stuck going round in circles too?*

But I knew that this was all just a story. I was the reader, not a character or participant in that world. I could detach and I liked it that way.

◊

My aversion to cities had waned further now as I was pleased to be in Dublin. After I'd cleaned my bike and sorted my wheel, I set off in search of a bit of 'craic' – the Pale is 'superior' after all. I was going to call some friends and let them know I was in town, but I opted instead to let the city decide my fate. A map from reception indicated that I was just around the corner from Eccles St. This is one of the more famous addresses in world literature, as it was where the home of Leopold Bloom (a main character in Joyce's Ulysses) is set. It's also where the day and the journey around Dublin begins and ends for Bloom in the novel –the start and end point of the circle, his circle.

I kicked on down Parnell Square and took shelter from another shower in the dim porch of the Rotunda. The greasy road seemed to take it well. Little rivers formed and flowed down either side. It occurred to me, as the ding of church bells filled the air that most people who leave the Rotunda never go back. There's no need.

As the sun cut through parting clouds and lit the sprayed street, I left the

Rotunda for the second time, maybe a little wiser, *a participant now*. This was my world and I'd be moving forward, with the option at least of silence.

◊

Dublin is an easy city for the solo traveller. Company or entertainment is only a pub away. I held off for a time though. I'd been a tourist in Dublin before but revisiting a few places is always a decent option.

The river led me westward to the Ha'penny Bridge. The official name is the Liffey Bridge and though it was made in England, this cast iron saviour for pedestrians is very much a Dublin landmark. I'd always thought that it was named on account of it being shaped like a ha'penny. It is arched after all. The fact that it's actually shaped nothing like a ha'penny doesn't matter (there are triangular squares in Donegal called 'diamonds' remember). No – the real reason is that up until 1919 it was a toll bridge. Users were initially charged a ha'penny to cross it and there were turnstiles at either end. Today some people still try to charge a 'yowrow' or 'any bit of spare change a'tall', but that's more in hope than expectation and I managed to sneak through.

From Temple Bar I crossed up to Dame St. and arrived at Christchurch Cathedral from where I moved on to Dublin's second Cathedral, St. Patricks. These cathedrals are pretty much next to each other and between them have a very rich history. Jonathan Swift, writer of *Gulliver's Travels* was Dean of St. Patrick's for thirty two years from 1713.

'Strongbow' (Richard de Clare) commissioned Christ Church in 1172 after he invaded Leinster. He was a Norman Knight who helped Diarmait MacMurrough regain his land in Leinster and who later became King of Leinster himself. I have heard he was helpful in many other ways too. For example, one day while sitting under an apple tree, a falling apple landed on his head and gave him, amongst other things, inspiration. There and then his thoughts gravitated towards a 'theory of fermentation' and within a few minutes he had invented cider! This was a real breakthrough as cider was more clinical than other drinks and could leave the drinker inebriated for longer and at less expense. To this day Strongbow cider can be seen providing refreshment for many Dubliners all over the city, including those camped on the Ha'penny Bridge…

Indirectly, Strongbow's influence can be seen around Dublin in other ways too. In 2013 while promoting a movie, actor Tom Cruise was accosted by the Irish Ancestry Police and was made to become Irish. As part of 'The Gathering', someone had commissioned an examination of his heritage. Low and behold, it was revealed that it doesn't matter if your Irish accent is criminally shit, you can still be Irish – sort of.

Cruise's ancestry was traced back to Strongbow's time and in fact Cruise is a descendant of one of Strongbow's own Norman Knights – Augustino de Cruce. What's interesting is that the other side of his family are from Dorset in England, which proves that Tom is actually English and French and not really very Irish at all. He's probably less Irish than Margaret Thatcher or Barrack Obama in fact.

Some might even describe him as an alien. One wonders if the scientologist might even describe himself as an alien. Still, these inconveniences couldn't stop the Irish Department of Foreign Affairs (the clue is in your name guys) from claiming the biggest ego in Hollywood, a man who follows a 'religion' which holds that our real ancestors were murdered extra-terrestrials from 75 million years ago, as 'one of our own'. Thus, Cruise's penance was to accept a presentation of a Certificate of Irish Heritage. Nice work...

After some forgettable sushi in a quiet Japanese bar that was as cold as the sushi looked, I crossed back over College Green and made my way up Grafton St. I considered a drink in Davy Byrne's pub. This pub is another Joyce landmark as it is where Bloom eats lunch during his walk around Dublin in Joyce's novel.

Ulysses is set on June 16th 1904, a date which has become known and celebrated as Bloomsday. It is also the date on which Joyce first 'walked out' with Nora Barnacle and is the reason for Joyce setting the novel on that particular day.

Their encounter had become more than just a date however, especially for Joyce. Rather than take Nora to a café, he walked with her down towards the sea, to the quieter suburban area of Ringsend. Annually, in cities around the world, but mostly in Dublin, Bloomsday is celebrated by thousands of people. But not all I'd imagine are really aware of what they are actually celebrating or what actually took place that evening in Ringsend. There and then, probably the most famous hand-job in literary history took place. Nora wasn't at all shy about sliding her fingers inside her companion's trousers and giving Joyce a bit of 'a frigging' – prompting him to remark that he had been now 'made a man'!

'What'll it be?' asked the pretty brunette tending the bar in Davy Byrne's when I finally walked into what is now a modern and flashy establishment.

Make a man of me...

'Eh... I'll just have a lemonade', I said, fully aware of how ironic this request was considering my thoughts.

'What kind of lemonade do you want?' enquired the barmaid impatiently.

'What have you got?'

Bored, the young woman listed the various non-intoxicating products of which there were many and did so increasingly as a means to highlight how laborious answering my question really was.

'Maybe I'll just have a sparkling water,' I said pensively.

If looks could kill...

Aside from being a tasteless and futile drink which nobody should ever order anywhere, this annoyed my hostess further as it was now clear that her listing labours had been in vain.

By now others waiting at the bar were also getting impatient. I felt suddenly under pressure – something that unfortunately often makes me indecisive.

'So you'd like a sparkling water...' said the woman, loud enough for one or two regulars to hear and I imagine sneer at.

'No.... Sorry... an espresso please,' I replied.

I'd ordered this in the hope of redeeming some morsel of manliness.

'Aw for feck sake' was muttered. If I didn't hear it, I certainly lip read it.

'Anything else?' she asked
'No... Not really'.
The following ten minutes were sat in silence. I stared at the wall and the wall stared back frowning. Any hope of impromptu recitals from *Ulysses* by the eccentric regulars had now vanished along with my credibility and the long shot of being 'made a man'. I sat at the bar and fiddled with my phone like a teenager, giving the impression (to no-one really) that I was attending to some pressing business.

Note to self: never try to choose a new ring tone for your phone in Davy Byrne's pub again...

◊

From Duke Street I strolled up towards St. Stephen's Green. The evening had become fully summerlike now with the sun feeding the trees as well as the gathering of Goths and Punks who were entrenched at the main gate into the park. There were at least twenty of them, all teenagers or young adults. Some were fingering flagons of cider (Strongbow no doubt); others were just fingering – fingering whatever they could get their fingers on really. Others were crying.

Crying, I have noticed, is a common pastime for teenaged Goths. Sometimes it's 'just not fair'. Often people 'don't understand' but it always seems to be that they 'just want to be original' – and dress the same as all the rest of their friends. I felt for them, lost souls cast out from pubs if not society. I felt an urge to offer an encouraging word to one who was wailing wildly, but when I heard the words 'my mum said I could have the car, but she hates me', I backed off knowing it's better not to get involved in family feuding.

St. Stephen's Green was blooming with evening strollers among beds of smiling flowers. There were others too who were anxious to relieve me of a few more 'yowrow', but I declined each offer. I began to feel that as a business enterprise, the market had become a little saturated for these street folk. Diversification was clearly the answer. I thought of maybe sitting one or two down and going through a business plan with them. Strategy was needed. Relocation might be an option too, as there were probably untapped markets out there in smaller towns and villages. It had therefore crossed my mind to advise one or two to maybe go someplace else. The sheer numbers of them steered me towards this consideration but then out of nowhere, a wave of compassion passed over me and I resisted.

One man in the park, who didn't seem too enthused about an American tourist using his camcorder, hid in the bushes for fear of being filmed. His patience didn't last however and after a few minutes he advised the tourist to –

'Put the bleeding camera away or I'll stick it up your hole'.

This passed over the American who was engrossed in filming but it was a source of amusement for the picnicking couples who were strewn across the lawns. Being unenthused myself about seeing a camera fly up the arse of a fellow tourist, I retreated to the relative safety of Grafton St.

It is a worrying and noticeable fact that Dublin is marked with addicts and homelessness. No doubt the economic woes are at least a contributing factor in this and it's not hard to feel for these souls. In order to cheer myself up, I decided I needed a bit of comedy. The International Bar on Wicklow St. is a favourite of mine. Nightly, Ireland's rising stars and established stand-up acts entertain tourists and locals alike in the intimate venue. I've never had a bad night there and I wasn't going to start now.

After a drink and a toasted sandwich at the bar (the food staple of the Irish pub), I wandered upstairs to the dimly lit comedy room. I settled down the back at a table filled with giggling students and was instantly welcomed. Noticing that I was on my own, some were keen on finding out why.

'I'm cycling around the country', I said, in a tone that suggested that this was normal.

'You're what? That's mental. Lads, that's mental. Yer man is cycling around the country', announced one clearly impressed young woman.

'Go on ya mad thing,' advised another.

'Aw Jaysis I'd love ta do that', confessed someone else.

'Cheers everybody,' shouted another excited lad who'd just been handed a fresh pint – 'to the lunatic on the bike'.

'The lunatic on the bike', came the chorus.

My new friends were all recent graduates from different Universities in Dublin and had all the enthusiasm for life that you'd expect from those in their early twenties. It was cool to observe their youthfulness, but we all came to laugh and that we did.

During the course of the night, five comedians from all over Ireland dished out a fair amount of wit that has so often been associated with Dublin. At one point, one audience member was asked where he was from.

'County Longford' he admitted, somewhat in hope than expectation.

'Oh Jesus Christ,' came a shout from a concerned local man who felt certain that this fact would lead to carnage on the piss-taking front (Longford is not so fashionable). Unfortunately for the local, the area of Dublin where he was from, was expertly ascertained by the comedian and was revealed to be an area of Finglas. Half the room, led by the paid wit, promptly turned on him and reminded him of his roots with enough clarity (mentioning pie-ball horses, shopping trollies and shiny tracksuits) in the process, to make the unlucky man think twice before ever opening his gobsmacked mouth again. For everyone else it was an uproarious twist – which put Dublin's superiority complex firmly in its place. For me it was pure pleasure...

When it was time to go I was advised by Layno and Opto, two of my new friends, to get a cab back to my hotel.

'It's dodgy down O'Connell St. at this time,' warned one.

'You might get mugged. There's a lot of junkies around'.

Junkies... Really? ... You don't say...

Having not been in the city myself for a good while, I was unaware of this mugging problem and I was certainly open to the idea of not getting mugged. It wasn't a very long walk back and I like walking almost as much as I like cycling, but I was mindful that the shady Wicklow Mountains, though sound asleep, were looming in the south and I knew I'd be riding them next day.

A cab suddenly seemed appealing. I thanked the students, who were intent on going clubbing, and said goodnight.

When I hit Dame St., I jumped into a roof-lit car. Inside I felt a little embarrassed that my journey would be so short, but I don't think it was anything out of the ordinary for the cabbie. When he pulled up at my hotel, I handed over the €10 fare – a penitential tax for not knowing Dublin too well. The cab ride took barely three minutes and cost the same as the three hours of laughing I'd just had. Somehow I'd managed to buy into other people's fears – something I wouldn't normally do, for if I did, I'd never ride a bicycle again. *Onwards*

CHAPTER 15

'Some moments are nice, some are nicer, some are even worth writing about'
Charles Bukowski

While sleepily waiting in line to be seated for breakfast, just six hours after I'd arrived home the night before, I noticed that the hostess was asking guests for their nationality. When informed, she would take a paper flag of their nation from a box and place it in a little vase on the tables as she sat them. I scanned the room and saw Belgian, Italian, French and American flags on various tables. The couple in front of me were Australian but didn't seem too upset when the hostess produced a flag of New Zealand. I haven't learned the difference either.

'Close enough, mum's from New Zealand so I guess I'm half Kiwi,' said the woman to her husband before laughing.

'Where are you from?' asked the hostess, when she returned to me.

'North Korea', I said. 'Pyongyang.'

'Ha ha! ... No really?'

'Really' I said, as I bowed my head slightly and smiled.

Hesitantly she looked in the box and with more confusion than regret, informed me that she probably had no North Korean flag. I waited.

'What does it look like?' she asked.

'It's blue and white with a red star in it.'

'I've got a Chinese flag. Will that do?'

'Not unless it's on the menu', I said.

At this point, seeing that I was holding up the queue, the tall and well-dressed duty manager intervened.

'North Korea is it? Go way outta that...'

'We have a South Korean flag though,' he said a little impatiently as he picked it out of the box and gestured me to follow him. I did and took a seat next to some hungry Americans as I watched my flag get shoved carelessly into the vase. Bowing again, I sat down to consider my new nationality.

I hadn't really expected flags to feature so much on this trip and it never occurred to me how much use people actually appear to get out of them. I just don't like flags. It's not a flag-a-phobia, it's just that they're totally stupid. This mini fiasco did nothing to change my opinion. Rather than celebrate diversity, which I think they are intended to do, flags really just reinforce difference. In fact anything that celebrates diversity really only reinforces difference. Oh and stereotypes. The Americans next to me were probably no hungrier than anyone else in the room, but one look at their flag and I had them down as greedy overeaters. And having the North Korean flag beside them would have been interesting I thought – if they'd have had any clue what country it represented. Oops... stereotyping, there I go again...

In 2014 when Europe won golf's Ryder Cup, a Northern Irishman from Rory McIlroy's hometown of Holywood decided to celebrate by flying the European flag. This could well be the most inclusive and least offensive flag in the world but it still riled a neighbour who, believing it was some kind of Islamic flag, complained to Police that it was offensive! In short, flags just don't bring out the best in people – including me.

I needed coffee. My half Korean brain was still flitting in and out of reality and when I got it, I eased myself into some bacon and eggs. It was Sunday and I had a mammoth bike ride ahead of me. Again, I wasn't sure where I was going to end up, but there was definitely a lot of mileage to cover. I gave myself just two days to get back to Cork. That would total sixteen days on the road, my limit, or the exact number of days one would have in a two week holiday.

The Wicklow Mountains were going to be tough, so I packed up on carbs too. My first port of call however would be Dundrum in south Dublin. Why? Stephen Roche. That's why.

◊

In 1987 Stephen Roche did the improbable; he won the Triple Crown of cycling. Only one other man has won the Giro d'Italia, the Tour de France and the World Championships in the same year and that was the greatest cyclist who has ever lived – '*The Cannibal*', Eddy Merckx, who did it only once in 1974.

Roche grew up in Dundrum and spent his youth riding in the Wicklow Mountains. After his miraculous year, a monument was commissioned which commemorates his extraordinary feat and I'd read that it was erected in Dundrum village.

Growing up in Ireland in the 1980s wasn't very glamorous. I wasn't a mad football fan, so watching Roche, Kelly and America's Greg LeMond (another hero) ride in far flung and exotic places like Nice or San Remo was something I veered towards. It might have been hard riding, but it certainly looked glamorous.

When I got my first racer, as a city boy, I wanted to escape and rode off discovering places around Cork – places like Belgooly, Ballydehob, Ballygarvan, and Shanbally. Okay, admittedly these were more 'far out' than 'far flung' places (where 12 year olds drove tractors and had beards) but it was all I had. Of course the word 'glamorous' would rarely marry with these rural spots, but isn't it the journey and not the destination and all that?

Anyway these cyclists of the 1980s are responsible for my long-time interest in cycling and as Dundrum was en route, I felt it right to pay homage to a boyhood hero and take in this Roche monument.

After I left the United Nations of breakfast eaters, I hit the city's early morning streets. Seagulls had replaced people, all pecking the footprints out of flattened chips left by last night's revellers. The only other people around were sleeping junkies and those with nowhere to go. I could see traffic lights down the length of O'Connell Street and beyond. A soft mute breeze tickled the litter but there was nothing else on the road.

I got going quickly and felt surprisingly good. Before the suburbs came, I took in the soothing statue of Patrick Kavanagh as I crossed over the Grand Canal. This slightly made up for not going to Inniskeane. I was glad to acknowledge him too on this trip, but soon I found myself south of the city and in Dundrum.

This was a village in its own right but it has been hugged into the city by the outstretched arms of a growing urban Dublin and is now a suburb itself. There were signs of life too, which was encouraging because when I arrived at the shopping centre where I believed the Roche monument was placed, there was no sign of it at all. I rode around for a while but couldn't find it anywhere.

'Do you know where the Stephen Roche monument is?' I asked a man out walking his dog.

'Sorry?'

'Stephen Roche'

'No my name is Lech, I'm not Stephen.'

'Don't worry about it,' I said and moved on.

Another man, who sounded like a Dubliner, had no idea who this Roche character was at all. I was getting concerned now. Surely the last twenty five years weren't a dream?

'The Stephen Roche monument; do you know where it is?' I finally asked an old lady by a bus stop who I just felt would know.

'Oh yes, I remember that. I think it was there,' she said pointing to an area of bushes by the shopping centre's perimeter fence.

'They took it away I think, maybe moved it, but I'm not sure where they put it.'

'Oh that's a shame.'

'He was a good cyclist; didn't he win Tour de France? But he split up with the wife I heard. That's terrible. She was a lovely young one.'

Her knowledge certainly made up for the others' bewilderment, but she was almost as stuck in the past as I was.

The countryside was close. I could sense that too and I pedalled off heading south again. I wasn't too disappointed that I hadn't seen the monument. I'd done my bit after all and there was always Google images.

Stephen of course isn't the only one of his family to have made a contribution to the cycling world. He got the bug from his parents who were touring cyclists. His brother Laurence rode the Tour de France in 1991 and his son Nicolas is a top pro who has ridden with Alberto Contador and now with Chris Froome at Team Sky. It's his nephew however who has brought the family the most success in recent times. Dan Martin, whose mother is Stephen's sister, won the Liege Bastogne Liege Classic, the Tour of Catalonia and Stage 9 of the Tour de France, all in 2013 alone. The Roche genes, if not the monument, are still very much on show.

There are other Dublin families steeped in cycling. The Kimmages and the McQuaids have all made varying contributions to the sport. But there is one other Dubliner who came before all of them.

Shay Elliott was an equal and contemporary of Tom Simpson and a pioneer for English speaking riders in the often intrinsic European peloton. Elliott was the first Irishman to wear the yellow jersey at the Tour de France; he won stages in all three Grand Tours as well as a semi-classic and a silver medal at the World Championships. He was the hero of my heroes and he would be the next man that I would try at least to pay homage to when I came to the Wicklow Mountains, for without him, there may never have been a Kelly, or a Roche and maybe not even a LeMond.

I rode down to Stepaside, passing close to where Leopardstown racecourse is. There I could feel the mountains breathing before me and the road began to rise almost immediately. Flanked by woodlands of evergreens, I caught up with a cyclist who was on his Sunday morning ride.

'Hi, are you out for a long one?' I asked.

'The wife's been away all week, so I've been out with the lads a lot. I'm wrecked but I needed the air. Not a long one, no. Where are you off to?

'Kilkenny maybe, I'm not sure', I said.

'That's a good spin – about 90 miles from here. You're doing a bit of credit card touring is it? I used to do that myself, until the wife took the credit card'.

'I am, but I haven't ridden in the Wicklow Mountains before, so I'm not really sure which way to go. Do you know the Shay Elliot memorial?'

'I do, that's past Laragh. A lot of climbing, I'll probably ride as far as Roundwood if you want to ride with me.'

'Definitely, thanks.'

This was great. I now pretty much had a tour guide –for some of the way at least. Dermot seemed strong on the bike but he was also just out to loosen his legs so we clipped along at a relaxed pace.

'Have you been to Enniskerry?'

'No, I've been to Ennis and Kerry but never both at once.'

This piece of brilliant wit didn't go down too well. Dermot looked at me like I was a bit dim, which I felt was at least arguable.

'I'll take you there. It's where all the show-offs hang out and drink coffee instead of riding their bikes.'

'Sounds good… I mean ha ha, yeah show offs… ha, bloody show offs… hate them'.

We rode along in silence for a while, over Two Rock or Three Rock Mountain (I'm not sure which), but these are part of the collective Dublin Mountains. At the village of Glencullen, Dermot mentioned something about a giant's grave being nearby, but I'd had enough of that crap and gave the most unenthusiastic 'really' I could come up with. This served only to solidify the impression of dimness he was now most certainly forming of me.

A few kilometres later we dropped into the square at Enniskerry and true to his word, many cyclists were lounging around sipping cappuccinos and admiring one another's barely ridden bikes. It was a sight to behold, like the start village before a stage of a fancy race. We stopped briefly and glanced around the square. The smell of coffee drifted temptingly in the air but neither of us were ready for a break, so we rode on amid the sounds of Sunday bells.

We were finally in Wicklow now and from Enniskerry began climbing once more. I'd read about an old narrow military road that ran from Dublin right into the heart of the Wicklow Mountains. It was built from 1800 by the British as a means of gaining access to rebels and insurgents who were hiding out as well as running a campaign of guerrilla warfare in the mountains. The failed rebellion of the United Irishmen in 1798 was the catalyst for having the road built and I was interested in riding a bit of it at least. We were now riding parallel to it, on our own narrow road and along the edge of Wicklow National Park.

'You'll join up with the military road at Laragh', informed Dermot. 'It's a great spin.'

I was excited to be back in mountainous quiet again, the perfect antidote to a night out in Dublin. Almost twenty or so kilometres later we arrived in Roundwood. This time it was time for a break – for me anyway. I asked Dermot if he'd join me for coffee.

'I can't, the wife is home this afternoon and there'll be blue murder if I don't tidy the place up, ah sure ya know yourself. '

Being unmarried, I didn't know myself, nor was I too enthusiastic about finding out – not yet anyway.

'Well thanks for the little tour. I wouldn't have really known where to go'.

'Don't worry about it. Go straight on at Laragh and then you turn right to head for Glenmalure. The Shay Elliot memorial is at the top of the pass. Enjoy. Take care.'

In an instant Dermot was riding the other way. I felt like I'd lost a comrade. But the thought of food and coffee took over and the village of Roundwood offered a couple of options. I chose the café with the most bikes outside. When I parked up and entered, the sound of cycling shoes clopping off the wooden floor filled the place. Most of the twenty or so people there were cyclists, though some were settling in for the day with the Sunday papers and pots of coffee it seemed. I just did what I had to and moved on. There is always that sense of urgency when you're doing a long ride. You never want to get too relaxed. Also, I figured I'd pay a visit to Glendalough.

◊

Meaning the Glen of two lakes, Glendalough is probably Wicklow's most popular tourist attraction. Like so many of the places I'd visited on this trip, it too has been a monastic settlement since the 6th century. Of course it would have to have a saint associated with it too; this is Ireland after all. Saint Kevin is our man, founder of the monastery, hermit, ascetic, lover of animals, eater of no meat whatsoever and dude with an awful lot of patience.

I rode on for almost ten kilometres through thick woodland to Laragh, where I turned right for Glendalough which appeared soon after. The tall round tower lets you know you've arrived – if not the muddle of gift shops and tourist buses.

So, this Kevin fella was actually a bit of holy celebrity. Initially he lived by one of the lakes in a tiny cave (St. Kevin's bed), where he did nothing but pray and meditate for seven years. During that time he is supposed to have had a blackbird land on the palm of his hand and build a nest. For fear of disturbing it, Kevin stood totally still (for ages...proper ages) until her eggs were laid. This demonstrates a fair amount of patience but also a talent that could have made him a fortune as a statue busker on Dublin's Grafton Street.

Missed opportunities aside, it was animals more than people that he was attracted to most (presumably because they don't talk) and he remained at Glendalough before coming out of isolation to teach. Teaching of course was a curious career move for one who was more of an animal than people person –unless of course the pupils were like what Wittgenstein described as 'three quarters human/one quarter animal'. Anyway, there must have been some attraction. After all, it was a job that ultimately gave him decent holidays, plus a guarantee of Paddy's day off. Result.

Actually Kevin not only didn't like people generally, but he in fact hated women. One unfortunate young lady got stung when she took a shine to him and thought there'd be no harm in throwing the leg over. Kevin, no doubt figuring she was a bit of a dirt-bird, rewarded her efforts by pushing her into a growth of nettles. Ouch...

What impresses me however is Kevin's vegetarianism. I mean it must have been hard eating only salads all day. Being constantly hungry is also not easy and of course vitamin supplements weren't readily available back then. But I suppose his lack of energy probably suited the hermetic lifestyle and if he got lonely there was no shortage of trees to hug – so long as they were male trees of course. I guess it wasn't all suffering for Kev. As little else is actually known about Kevin, we can probably assume that with his vegetarianism at least, he was only going through a phase.

In reality, aside from maybe the misogyny, Kevin was probably well ahead of his time. Or indeed maybe we've gone backwards. Talking to animals and trees is something that would probably get you locked up for today. Curiously however, if you walk into a church and talk to a statue, or sit chatting to ones that 'move' in West Cork, that's completely normal.

I did genuinely hold Kevin in high regard when I sat reading a little about him at Glendalough, but hanging around for very long was not something I fancied doing. The large numbers of people searching for 'peace' in the gift shops is an irony that goes a little too far. The place's purpose of course is to help create an environment for quiet contemplation. I had a look at St. Kevin's Cross, of which legend has it that if you can wrap your arms around it, your wishes will come true. I didn't even try. In fact I headed off without even seeing the lakes or the other attractions of Glendalough. But as I'd discover later in the day, my wishes would still come true...

◊

Another right turn back at Laragh and I was finally on the old military road. Here I climbed out of oak and beech woodland and up towards the Glenmalure Pass. This was steep in parts but manageable. I was a lot stronger on the bike than I'd been two weeks earlier. The climb is not very long, about 3.5 kilometres, but it has an average gradient of about 7.5%. It seems a lot longer however when you're not completely sure if you're on the right climb.

I kept pushing and hoping that this wasn't in vain. I'd followed Dermot's directions but there weren't many signposts on the roadside so I just rode up in hope. Finally, as the clouds greyed, I came to a clearing and spotted of all things, a car park atop the mountain. Just to the left of the road was a small headstone. I stopped and read: *In Memory of Shay Elliott – International Racing Cyclist*. I'd arrived.

Elliott had had a colourful life, but things were to fall apart very quickly at the end of his racing career. Though his racing results were good, he was a much better rider than these results suggest. It was not uncommon at that time (or indeed now) to throw races (or at least not fully compete) in exchange for payment. Shay made a lot of money as he was a feared and respected rider. Often riders could earn more from a race by not winning than they could by winning. He was a trusted *domestique* too for the great Jacques Anquetil – so it was often his job to help others rather than try to win himself anyway.

Near the end of his riding career, Shay invested all his hard-earned money in a hotel in France (Hotel d'Irlande), but his friends and employees were to run it into the ground and financially ruin him in the process. He was betrayed over and over again by those he trusted. His marriage ended too and he finally returned to Dublin where he set up a panel beating business. Unfortunately his father died not long after he returned and Shay took it hard. Two weeks later he shot himself. It's not fully clear if it was an accident or not. Most believe it was, but it was definitely a tragedy and a sad and premature end for the father of Irish Cycling, a great pioneer of English speaking riders and Ireland's first real cycling hero.

I stood in silence for a while and paid my respects knowing that Shay's legacy lives on. There is of course Ireland's second biggest one day race, *The Shay Elliot Memorial*, which takes riders over this climb and the Rás pays a regular visit to the area.

I nodded to a couple of hill walkers as I got back on my bike and headed off down the other side of the pass. I'd done some good climbing and was pleased with my efforts. Though I was only about 1300 feet up, it was a good height for Ireland.

I thought about Shay again as I rode off. Had he been too trusting of people? Or were they the ones who lacked trust? I wondered if Bradley Wiggins would return the favour of trust to Chris Froome in the following years' Tours de France. Time would tell.

I dropped down 800ft and for some reason assumed that my climbing was done for the day. I'd wanted to do the Glenmalure climb and had now done it. I didn't really think much beyond that. In my head I had decided that there was nothing left to do but have a nice long, mostly downhill spin all the way to Kilkenny – far from it. Dropping down into the valley, I passed close by the Glenmalure Lodge pub before crossing over what I figured was probably a tributary of the Avoca River. Here the road began to rise a little and then that 'oh shit' feeling came over me. It didn't help that some smartarse cyclist had spray-painted on the road the words 'Welcome to Hell!' I knew then that I was screwed and that the tough previous climb had just been the appetiser; I was now on the Drumgoff/Slievemaine climb that leads up to Aughavannagh.

Over the course of many minutes, I toiled my way up this climb. Every now and then I saw that the smartarse had sprayed more 'information' on the road. 'Not even half way there', and 'losers quit' were some of his taunts. I did think about stopping too but rose to the challenge – probably thanks to these very taunts.

It was just me, in the wilds of Wicklow, the 'garden of Ireland', hurting. The evergreen woods got denser the further I rose. My rucksack felt heavy too as I picked up the pace and set my lungs and legs on fire. Warm sweat trickled along my beating neck and when a light drizzle drifted down I was happy. It cooled me. Only two cars had passed on the climb and both drivers, coming down the mountain, slowed and gave me that *'have you lost your mind?'* look. At times it felt like I had.

Finally the road began to level off. I'd just ridden what was the steepest and hardest section of road in my entire trip. I was 1550 feet up at the summit, about 200 ft. higher than the Conor Pass climb in Kerry (though I did start this climb at 500 ft.). I reckoned it was just over 4km long and it was steeper than the previous climb, but it was done.

I stopped and took in the views. The sun was pouring a salvo of light through the high clouds and it lit the distant land like spotlights on a stage. I could see for miles too. Dublin was back to the north but there were no clues at all that a city could be there. Silence reigned once more. I had 70k ridden and the hard part done, but Kilkenny was another 95k away.

The lonely old military road led me back off the mountain where cautiously I swooped down, delighted with what I was sure was going to be a very long descent, but there was yet more climbing before that happened. I was pleased nonetheless to be riding on this historic route.

After the failed rebellion of 1798 the British were worried about rebels hiding out in the Wicklow Mountains, but also about another landing of French soldiers. Bantry hadn't worked out for the rebels. If not for the weather however, it could have been a different story. Not only did the British army build this military road from Dublin but they built four barracks along the route too. I didn't spot any but they are nestled into the sides of the mountains and are now in varying states of repair.

One man, Michael Dwyer, a member of the United Irishmen, was the thorn in the side of the British Army at this time. He and his men fought a guerrilla campaign from the woodland and misty glens of this mountainous region. In truth, he scared the bejaysus out of Crown Forces and caused chaos for them. For five years he evaded capture and continued attacking groups of soldiers and yeomen. Eventually he did a deal with the Crown and was offered free passage to Australia. Thrown into the deal was 100 acres of land, which might indicate just how much the British feared him.

Some believe that Dwyer 'invented' guerrilla warfare and demonstrated how effective it could be from his remote hideouts. By 1813 however, he was made Chief of Police at Liverpool, New South Wales, an appointment which might have turned a few heads, if not coats, but he was fired a few years later for being too pissed to do his job. He ended up in debtors' prison after he had to sell off his assets, including a pub, as a result of being sued for aggrandizing his farm – which had now grown to 'over 600 acres'. Dwyer fell ill in prison and died of dysentery in 1825.

It seems Ireland has had as many inventors as it's had saints, but in this case, once again we might be witnessing an example of not letting the truth get in the way of a good story. Dwyer was as much loved amongst the rebel Irish as he was feared by the British, but in terms of 'inventing guerrilla warfare,' he did nothing of the sort. Guerrilla warfare can be traced back to 6th century China, but the term –meaning small war – was coined by the Spanish in the 1700s.

As Wicklow is the 'film making capital of Ireland', it's not difficult to believe that a movie about Dwyer and his men is in pre-production. *Guerrillas in the Mist* is due out sometime in the future, probably after royalties from armies around the world are paid to Dwyer's estate for his great 'invention'.

◊

Finally I started dropping fast out of the mountains and was swallowed whole by the soft scenery around me. The military road soon ended. I wasn't sure exactly where, but the route has a total length of 34 'Irish' miles. Road signs in parts of Ireland still used Irish miles until 1926. The Irish mile was longer than the statute mile – measuring 1.27 statute miles. It was often said that four Irish miles was the equivalent of five English. Similarly, in Scotland the Scottish mile (the most famous probably being the Royal Mile in Edinburgh) is 1.12 statute miles. It's from these old and similar variations that we probably get the expression 'a country mile'.

Anyway, close to bonking from lack of food, when the road finally flattened out, I knew I needed to eat. Any country pub anywhere was needed and after what seemed like a fair whack of country miles later, leading up to a long straight stretch of road, I stumbled upon Rathdangan. It was immediately clear that I was now very much in the interior.

Rathdangan has a crossroads and a pub. That's it. It's more like the backyard of someone's farmhouse than a village and the silence of the place, a hopeless rather than contemplative silence, scared me. I didn't just want food, I needed it and it was not entirely obvious that food was available. Sheepishly, I opened the door of the pub and became its fourth customer. The other three were a priest, who was entertaining his girlfriend or housekeeper or both in a quiet corner; the other was a pint-filled man at the counter whose eyes never left the hurling match he was watching on TV.

'Come on Kilkenny ta fuck', encouraged the man, fairly oblivious to those around him.

'Where am I?' I asked the woman who came out to serve me.

'You're in Rathdangan, Wicklow, not Carlow, Wicklow. Carlow is down the road here,' she said pointing and looking at me with some curiosity.

On learning that sandwiches could be made and chocolate and coffee was available, I felt relieved at being in Rathdangan, Wicklow – not Carlow.

Let's be brutally honest about this; Carlow isn't Ireland's most popular county. In fact Carlow town is probably the very capital of 'the interior'. Nobody ever seems to know anyone from County Carlow; I've certainly never met anyone from there. This is possibly because nobody will ever admit to being from there, or because nobody from there ever leaves the place. Either way, it rarely makes it on to the list of Ireland's shit counties, but not because it's any good, simply because people forget that the place exists – which, let's be honest, is even worse than being just ordinarily shit.

It does exist however, and in order to get to Kilkenny, I had to ride my bike through the place. This was unsettling and it didn't help that the woman behind the bar was so eager to disassociate Wicklow's Rathdangan from the neighbours.

In no time, I had devoured a 'round of sandwiches' garnished with Tayto Crisps and a 'Purple Snack' chocolate bar, all further staples of the Irish pub. I burped my goodbyes, not forgetting to give the priest a knowing nod of respect and rode off towards County Carlow.

It was a surprise and a relief to ride up to Hacketstown, an old and charming place, seemingly untouched by modern housing. The clear rivers and patchwork green fields were a postcard and I began to realise that maybe Carlow County wasn't as lacking as I'd first thought. This led me to reflect on the true beauty of Ireland and how even the ordinary places can be so pleasing. While rolling along in the direction of the capital, Carlow town, it occurred to me that I had experienced almost everything I had wanted to on this trip. I'd engaged with Ireland and it offered me all that I had expected and more. Just one thing was missing however – a rainbow.

For decades now, rainbows have been as much associated with Ireland as leprechauns or pubs. I'd seen everything else, (okay maybe not leprechauns) but all the other Irish clichés, both old and new had been there. I couldn't decide if the rainbow as a symbol was a reality or a myth. Obviously I'd seen them before, but I hadn't seen one on this trip. I figured seeing one might just make the whole journey complete. However with only a day and a half left, and it not actually raining, the chances were fairly slim.

Out of Hacketstown I headed east and rolled along mostly flat roads at a good speed for about an hour. They were quiet roads too which suited me as I began to feel tired, allowing my mind to drift off into olden time fields. Without much fanfare, I arrived in Carlow town. Unlike Hacketstown, it was as I expected – grey and lifeless. Ashen rows of 80s three-bed semi Ds marked the town's outskirts. I didn't really need to see much more so, devoid of curiosity, veered left before its centre and headed back out following the signs for Kilkenny.

After another flat and lonely section of road that skimmed County Laois, I led myself to Leighlinbridge. Here, needing sugar badly, I stopped for something sweet. The whiff of petrol on the station forecourt ushered me inside. By now I was wrecked. The hours of climbing had stretched the day long.

'How far is Kilkenny from here?' I asked the man at the counter.

'Would it be 20k?'

'Oh it would... handy', he said in his drawn flat midland brogue.

'Handy'. I smiled. This meant it was well over 20 kilometres but could be any distance you want it to be really. I knew deep down it was probably over 30, but I just couldn't stomach knowing that it might over 40. I had a feeling that the man probably didn't want to let me know exactly how far it was, hence the vague answer. Maybe, after seeing how spent I looked, he was being kind.

Outside I shoved an opened packet of *Liquorice Allsorts* into my back pocket and chewed my way into the distance.

Just one stretch of road at a time

Only a few kilometres later, it happened. The sky had been darkening for a while, but I rode on flanked by old stone walls unfazed. Before long, a sharp shower of ancient rain gushed down, darting into the grit. I pulled over to the grass margin to get my jacket. As I did, the flat field next to me lit to a deep lime green. At its far end appeared a vivid rainbow, perfectly formed against the grey sky. It seemed to end in the field too, but when I looked back down the road its complete arch hung above the trees. What's more is that above the bow, was its only slightly faded shell. It was a double rainbow and I stood stunned under it.

It wasn't easy to take it in at first; the enormity, the closeness and the intensity of colour was such that I just didn't know what to think. And maybe that was it. Maybe I just wasn't supposed to think. I'd wanted to see this or something like this, and here it was in front of me. I didn't have to wait long and it stayed too. For a long time I watched the show in silence. Nothing at all passed on the road; it was empty and full all at once. I just stood, seeing spits of golden rain fall through bars of evening light, in Carlow – in ordinary Carlow. A rainbow, and yet one more, watching one another –one, but not alone, all at once.

Within the hour I was rolling into Kilkenny grinning. For one so tired there was no hardness in my face; I'd seen the magic of the world. Though I had another day on the road, I knew my journey was now complete. I'd found magic in the ordinary – a mysticism that took me straight to Yeats, an epiphany to Joyce and a rural rite to the heart of Heaney... all in a field in Carlow.

Somehow I knew I'd be kind to that county from now on – indeed everywhere... maybe.

◊

The Ormonde Hotel wasn't full as others were, but it was close to perfect and well located in the centre of town. I ambled around Kilkenny in a daze all evening. Almost eight hours of riding had landed me there, ten hours after I'd left Dublin. I had eighty Irish miles in my legs, a hundred statute ones and one hell of a country one. I ate risotto and skirted shadows outside cafés until the light of day began to fade.

Having one final stroll before bed later in the night, I noticed someone had put a Kilkenny Hurling jersey on a statue that was placed between the pillars of the Tholsel (old town hall). I'd garnered from the celebrations I'd heard earlier, that Kilkenny had won that hurling match they were playing, but as I got closer, I noticed this seated 'statue' was breathing.

No, this wasn't West Cork circa 1985 and I wasn't on mushrooms. It was alive. *He* clearly wasn't a statue but this man had somehow managed to fall asleep sitting perfectly straight and still on the step. He probably wasn't fully asleep, but he was certainly plastered and palsied, and the curried chips trailing up his front did well to blend into the lined gold of his jersey.

Carlow had surprised me – it's true, but the 'interior' was alive and... well, breathing.

CHAPTER 16

'Doubt is a pain too lonely to know that faith is its twin brother'
Khalil Gibran

By watching bike racing or by touring, we can find drama or behaviour that helps us understand the world and its people. Chris Froome was loyal to Bradley Wiggins in the 2012 Tour de France. His loyalty was rewarded the following year, but not by Wiggins. Wiggo announced his intention to defend his Tour title in 2013, a decision at odds with his teammate Froome's own plans to win the Tour for himself. In the end Wiggins never rode the race and Froome showed his superiority by claiming the yellow jersey for himself. But it was no thanks to Wiggins. Maybe Froome's loyalty was misplaced all along? Had he not been a loyal servant to *'le Gentleman'*, he could be a multiple winner. Or maybe the karma for his loyalty and faith was his own win. Maybe by letting go of the 2012 race, better and more was to come, just like better and more always seemed to come on my journey. *We'll never know.*

Froome is less popular in Britain, probably because he could ride under three flags – the Kenyan, South African or Union flag. He's 'British' but he's not really British – not compared to others anyway. But does it matter? Do flags really improve our lives? What matters is that he and Wiggins are good bike riders. And whatever about loyalty and faith, they're human beings.

Human nature is flawed. Mistakes are always going to be made. And yes, the sport of cycling has doping problems, but people have been cheating since time began. It's not going to change easily. Temptation will always follow some people around. The drama for me is how individuals change – and if they do cheat – how they react to getting found out. That's where the true test of a person lies. It's normal to be flawed. It's not normal to believe your own bullshit and treat everyone like they're stupid.

Some of my own boyhood heroes have their flaws too, they're human. Cycling might seem like a troubled sport, but only because it's actively cleaning up. It knows it has a problem. But it's like 'painting the Forth Bridge'; the cleaning has to be done constantly. The job is never finished. Just like people are never totally happy. There's always a want for more. But it's there, what we want. It's in front of us all the time –on whatever stretch of road we're on. It's even in fields in Carlow.

◊

On a wet night Kilkenny glistens. Electric light runs like rivers down its marble streets. It is the 'marble city'; its black limestone, warm in summer, makes it so. Built on the banks of the Nore River, the varied architecture of the city alone would keep any half interested tourist happy. Night showers were replaced by a hot morning sun and after breakfast, feeling in no particular rush, I decided to kill an hour wandering.

I stumbled upon Rothe House, a Tudor townhouse built in the late 1500s and the only example in Ireland of one such house. Nearby is the most impressive building of all however – Kilkenny Castle. This 800 year old medieval stone structure, perfectly intact, dominates the city and was a strong symbol of Norman occupation for centuries. The Butlers of Ormonde bought the castle in the 14th Century and the family remained there until 1967. Because of near financial ruin, they were forced to abandon it before handing it over to the Irish State for the sum of £50. They simply couldn't afford its upkeep and rather than see it fall to ruin, they kindly offered it to the people of Kilkenny.

The building, which is now a major tourist attraction, hadn't opened for the morning yet (to cater for tourists) so I headed back towards Kieran Street. As I pushed a hot coin over the counter of a café, my thoughts turned to the road.

There were many reasons why I'd now come inland and away from the coast: the coast tells only part of Ireland's story and I'd ridden a lot of it already; Kilkenny itself is a big attraction and this inland route helped me stay within my two-week-holiday (16 day) limit; most importantly however, if you're a cycling fan paying homage to your heroes, you can't really do that in Ireland without visiting the inland town of Carrick-on-Suir. Sean Kelly, a native and resident of Carrick, was the sole reason for me wanting to head there. He is quite simply the greatest cyclist ever to come out of these shores. A few Dubliners might well disagree, but that's probably as much to do with the superiority complex within the Pale, than anything based on actual reality. Indeed Sean Kelly is one of the greatest ever to have ridden a bike.

Kelly's nickname maybe wasn't as colourful as *'le Gentleman', 'le Blaireau* (the Badger)' or even *'Spartacus'*. It was simply *'King Kelly'*. This is enough to leave us in no doubt as to how high a standing he had in the 1980s peloton. Kelly was the 'King of the Classics' and if he was the King, then I as a fan, am happy still to be one of his subjects.

Carrick was a good 40 kilometres away however. In fact it was 40k 'handy'. Before I got back to my hotel to pack up, I took in Kyteler's Inn. This old stone building with its small medieval windows was once owned by Alice Kyteler. Back in the early 14th Century she was the first woman in Ireland to be accused of witchcraft. She was rich and attractive by all accounts and she managed to marry a number of wealthy bankers, four in total, three of whom left everything to her in their wills before dying under mysterious circumstances.

Kyteler's fourth husband suspected foul play when his hair and nails began to fall out. Believing he'd been poisoned, he complained to Kilkenny's bishop, who happened to really dislike Alice and her family. The bishop's doubts about her meant he immediately charged her with heresy and with leading a coven of witches. So began the famous 'witch hunt'. Before she could be tried however, Alice disappeared from the dungeons of Kilkenny Castle. Of course she probably flew out the window on her broom and I'm sure when the gaoler discovered that she was no longer in her cell, it prompted the question: 'Alice, Alice, where the feck is Alice?', or something to that effect.

Anyway Alice's maidservant Pertonella wasn't so lucky. She was tortured and confessed to witchcraft –not a great move, as the confession then led to a flogging, followed by a burning at the stake – all very Hollywood. In contrast, Alice's son William got off lightly. He was charged with a whole list of things including heresy and perjury, but was only punished by being made to go to mass three times a day for a year – light in comparison, but let's be honest, still harsh...

'Where are you off to?' asked the bespectacled hotel receptionist when I finally checked out.
'Cork' I said.
'What, on a bike?'
You have no idea.

◊

I left Kilkenny on the Kells road before midday. This narrow and quiet route led me once more into old Ireland. The midlands are less travelled and retain an ancient but hauntingly lonely quality. There is something melancholic about this 'interior' too.

I came to the little village of Kells. Not to be confused with Kells in County Meath, from which the famous book comes, but this other smaller village of the same name lies a few kilometres south of Kilkenny City. Here, the horse chestnut trees, breathing in stonewalled fields, stand in their yoga pose, wise and old. It's hard not to respect Ireland's landscape. It had become my master. It *is* old and wise, but very much alive.

Kells itself is quite small but it was about to play a memorable part in my bike journey –as it was where near disaster happened. Suddenly somehow, I noticed while spinning along that my left testicle had disappeared. It had inexplicably gone upwards inside me – or so it seemed. This was quite worrying as it had never happened before. In fact, usually it goes the other way when one has reached the age of man. I rode on in mild physical discomfort, but in growing mental discomfort – uniballed.

I sort of knew now what it was like to be Lance Armstrong – the only other uniballed cyclist I was aware of. Of course this inconvenience required me to stop, and so at the edge of Kells village I pulled over to examine myself. I'm not sure if I was seen by any locals who may have glanced out their farmhouse windows, but if they had and caught sight of a man in Spandex searching frantically for his lost bollock, I can only apologise. I knew it was there somewhere, but it was not keen on coming back down. I could do nothing but jump up and down on the spot at the side of the road and hope that it would just fall down by itself. So, resting my bike against the mossy wall, I got to it. A few cars passed, but the looks I received didn't bother me. It had to be done... but it was no use.

I didn't stick around. Quickly I abandoned this idea and rode off, feeling slightly off balance now and hoping that it would just sort itself out. I told myself that this was called 'disappearing ball syndrome', that it was common among bike riders and that there was nothing at all to worry about. Still, I tried sitting further up on the saddle, then further back on it. I leaned over each side searching, always searching, until finally I just got out of the saddle altogether. Actually, I rode every which way it is possible to ride a bike successfully – but nothing.

It was an extraordinary coincidence I felt, that I should think of Lance Armstrong in little old Kells, for it is here that Ireland's own Lance Armstrong lives – Michelle Smith de Bruin. As Michelle is now a barrister, it might just be prudent to state that she has *never taken performance enhancing drugs at any time during her swimming career.* Of course spending a good chunk of your life stating that you have never taken performance enhancing drugs at any time during your career, is not the only similarity Michelle has with Lance. There are a number of others which I think would justify Michelle being known as the Irish Lance, or indeed vice versa: neither one has ever failed a drugs test; both were 'Olympic medallists'; both have been banned from competition and indeed both own less than two testicles...

Rather like me...

Michelle was a piss taker in more ways than one. In fact she was banned for taking the piss – literally. She was accused of taking the urine she had produced as a sample for drug testing and adding enough whiskey to it (presumably to mask a performance enhancing drug) before trying to pass it off as a normal sample. In doing this however, she produced a concentration of alcohol in her pee that, if it were consumed through the body in the normal way, it would have probably killed her. In short, she was done for tampering with her sample.

Only a few in the swimming world were surprised that something like this happened. Me, I had a surprise of my own to sort out, but I wasn't sure how to proceed.

Whenever something gets lost, there are of course certain tactics one can employ to help find the lost item. As Carrick got nearer and with balance still to be restored, I decided to employ some of these tactics. The first thing I did was to think back to the last time I had the lost item. But that was in the shower back at my hotel. I hadn't seen or felt it since. Then I just thought okay, try to think like a testicle: *if I was a testicle where would I be?*

The answer of course was hanging loose and carefree about me, attached but not too attached, but it wasn't there –was it? *Nope...*

Of course as an Irishman, I could have employed the 'Ask the Mammy' technique too. This had worked before when I left my debit card at home at the start of this trip. But for some reason, I chose not to go for that option this time.

Something told me to hold back, an understanding maybe that I was indeed a man now (albeit with one ball) and that I was going to have to work things out myself – for now.

I rode on but there were times indeed when, on what had become an even lonelier than normal bike ride, I thought: *I'd give my left nut for everything just to be okay...* But it was no use.

There was one more thing I could do to help find my lost item. It's a kind of a last straw option – something many in Ireland grow up being advised to do by faithful grandparents. It's the option of praying to Saint Anthony –the patron saint of lost causes – or at the very least, lost items. I thought about doing this in letter form. I don't know why, but an all-out request for help in prayer would have been a bit alien to me as I don't really pray. Also it's not like we're always in touch.

Somewhere near Kells
Ireland
July 2012

Dear St. Anthony,
It's been a while, I know. Listen, I don't want you to think that I'm using you, that I just talk to you when I've lost something. Okay... I am using you, and it's not like you're good at other shit, but it's just that I've lost something important – my bollock in fact, my testicle, one of my balls you know... and a man kinda needs both balls. I mean if God feels he needs to take one back, then that's fine, look at Lance Armstrong, but it's just... it'd be handy if I had two – or at least knew where the other one is.
I don't expect miracles but you're good at finding stuff. See what you can do. I'll facebook ya...
Regards,
Alone

My imagination had drifted into the writing of this letter and it brought me back to when I was a child and when this tactic worked. And maybe it worked again here because finally, after I stopped north of Carrick for a 'natural break', I felt my ball's triumphant return. I was saved, my progeny too. Disaster was avoided; balance restored. It had returned as I crossed into County Tipperary, another unlikely location. A slow sigh of relief, lasting almost as long as it took for the station master to open the level crossing gates near Carrick station (about 15 minutes), ensued. I was truly back in the interior; I knew that much.

'Is this Sean Kelly Square?' I asked as I stood looking at the walled plaque which confirmed what I already knew.

'It is', said the man outside Marty's tea rooms, making me more than doubly sure.

'What can I get you?'

'Coffee and apple tart with cream'. I was sort of celebrating now – the return of the prodigal ball.

I sat outside reading the list of Kelly's major wins that surround his photograph on another stone plaque which was stuck to the wall of the building next door. The man, I thought, is truly remarkable.

It's true that Carrick is not a rich town. It has never been so. It's very rural. Most of it is in Tipperary but the southern edges are in County Waterford and the number of 'To Let' signs clinging to rusty business premises tells its own story. It's impossible to ignore the rich cycling history of the town however – fan or no fan.

In 1998 when the Tour de France came to Ireland, the peloton powered through this very square as it kinked its way towards Cork and in so doing, the race paid its own tribute to Kelly. That summer I was in Edinburgh enjoying a working holiday away from College. My new Scottish 'girlfriend' Kelsey invited me out to her flat one afternoon. My excuse for not accepting the invitation was that the Tour de France was arriving in Cork and that I had to watch it on television.

'It's my home town and... I might see people I know,' I said feebly and fairly unconvincingly.

'Look,' replied Kelsey coldly. 'You don't have to bullshit me, I'm not thick. How can the Tour de France be in Cork? That's in Ireland. It's the *Tour de France* for god's sake – not the *Tour de Ireland...*'

'But you are thick', I ventured sourly before heading off to find a TV.

It was a lonely enough summer. Still, at least I got to watch the race and I managed to see it pass through Sean Kelly Square.

It's not often that a place is named after someone who is still alive. Sean Kelly Square was named after Kelly as far back as 1982, in recognition of his green jersey win at the Tour de France. By then Kelly had won plenty but it was nothing compared to what he would go on to win over the following decade.

He's not the only cyclist recognised either. To be fair to Stephen Roche, after his own *annus mirabilis* of 1987, he was afforded freeman of the City of Dublin, an honour he shares with Nelson Mandela, JFK, Mother Teresa and of course that other saint, Bono. Incidentally Bono is the only one who has actually grazed sheep in Dublin city centre, an ancient right that comes with the honour. I'll let you make your own mind up about that one.

Anyway, I sat sipping my coffee and thinking about those two heroes of Irish cycling. Between them, Kelly and Roche have won almost every race and jersey worth winning – all three Grand Tours, the World Championship, every Classic race bar the Tour of Flanders and numerous other stage races – some multiple times. Overall between them they have won 252 professional races, Kelly winning four times as many as Roche.

But what does it all mean? It's well known that Kelly is a simple enough rural man who rode a bike in order to escape the hardships of farm work. Roche too probably wasn't too enthusiastic about his manual work as a fitter which he had lined up if bike racing had failed. Both men came out of 80s Ireland which really was a relatively bleak place. It was a comparatively poor country too so it was probably an easy option to commit to the hard work on the bike; rewards were potentially huge. For me, it's no surprise that the traditionally European peloton today is being infiltrated by Colombians and Eastern Europeans (particularly Poles) – riders from countries that are not economically strong. For those with talent, a better life is only some hard training away. None of Kelly or Roche's success however came without a lot of really hard work, which I guess is the other lesson.

There wasn't much happening in Carrick-on-Suir as I whiled away a half hour in the sunshine. Just as I was getting ready to leave, I saw him. *Surely it is him*. A man dressed in a white shirt and dark trousers, aged in his fifties and with slicked back reddish-brown hair came walking towards me from the top of the square. My heart blushed. *Is this Sean Kelly? I'll drop a bollock if it is...No wait, maybe not*. But as the man got closer I realised that it was not Sean Kelly, nor was it his twin, but just some bloke who really only looked like himself and nobody else. It was all a sort of mirage brought on by thinking too much about bike racing. It was time to go.

◊

I climbed out of town and started my journey through a new county – Waterford. Dungarvan was my destination for now. That too was another 40k away – 'handy'.

The road rolled for a while. Dancing red fuchsia flanked it too. The Comeragh Mountains appeared on my right, with their distant and purple haze of heather. The sun too was on and off and I rode for a while through a long spectrum of light. Relief was overriding when I passed below and not over the Comeraghs. My legs would have been outraged at the very thought of more climbing. I'd done enough.

It occurred to me that I'd just been in three counties in a very short space of time. Kilkenny and Tipperary are inland and rural – like shy and awkward cousins. They are unassuming counties but their people (or at least their people's descendants) throughout history have given much to the world. Without Kilkenny folk we may never have had *Coca Cola*, *The White House* or *Disney* (Walt Disney). Similarly, Tipperary's people have given the world *The Financial Times (FT)*, George Orwell's Big Brother concept and at least two American Presidents – Ronald Regan and Barack Obama.

I kept going, on an endless road towards the town of Dungarvan. Of course this road would end, as all of them have and it actually linked up with the busy N25. In doing so, it delivered me back to the coast. But before I got reacquainted with the sea, a tractor pulled out from a side road up ahead and continued in the same direction. I took this as an opportunity to gain from a bit of drafting. Sprinting quickly to catch it, I knew that if I tucked in behind, I would save a good bit of energy by getting sucked along in the draft. But when I did catch up, it's old exhaust spat out a trail of diesel fumes and smoke before swooping around and into an open field. There was no more drafting. My sprinting was in vain and it had taken as much effort out of me as I'd hoped to save. *Lesson learned, slowly-slowly –just one stretch of road at a time...*

'Do you know why restaurant mash is always nicer than the mash you have at home?'

'No, but I've a feeling you're going to tell me.'

I was eaves dropping now while trawling through tweets in a restaurant in Dungarvan. I'd ordered chowder and with over 80k done I was halfway home.

'You see', said the man in the know, to his increasingly interested friend, both of whom were at the next table.

'They put as much butter into the mash as they do spuds. The ratio of butter to spuds is almost the same. Sure no wonder it costs a fortune.'

'What do you mean? So we're aytin butter really with just a few spuds mashed in?'

'Exactly'.

'Jaysus'

'Things are never what they seem.'

In 1951 Dungarvan man Ernest Walton was awarded the Nobel Prize for physics along with his colleague John Cockcroft. Long before this (in 1932), they jointly discovered how to split the atom, which in effect ushered in the nuclear age. In a sense, Walton had helped show the world how to blow itself up. The world of course has been threatening to blow itself up since – which isn't great really. He is still the only Irish Nobel laureate to have received the prize for anything other than literature. Clearly science therefore isn't our strong point and when we do have a go, what do we do? We discover a way to blow the planet up. Maybe we should stick to writing poetry.

I sat eating my late lunch and looking out over a darkening Dungarvan Harbour. I thought about Ernest Walton in between reading nonsense from the cyber world. Everything seemed quite complicated, which was all much in contrast to the simple bliss my two fellow diners appeared to be experiencing. *Mashed potatoes with loads of butter* – this was the extent of their worries. At least that's what I told myself. I vowed to live a simpler life from now on – *just one stretch of road....*

Thankfully, like most counties, Waterford has also given the world some simpler and slightly less dangerous things too – *Cream Crackers* being just one of them...

By the time I'd gotten close to Youghal, just 50k or so from home, I was soaked. The rain had come quickly as the clouds suggested it would, but I really didn't care. What got to me more was the N25 road. I'd ridden it before and it's just not a pleasant bike ride. It's noisy. The constant rant of stressed out traffic wears you down and it's not what I had gotten used to on my trip.

It wasn't a pleasant ride for Chris Boardman either in the 1998 Tour de France. While wearing yellow, on this road the Englishman suffered a touch of wheels and a fall that took him down and into one of the stone walls just east of Youghal. One minute in beautiful sunshine he was rolling along leading the Tour. The next minute, after a lapse in concentration, he was unconscious and out of the race entirely – becoming the (unlucky for some) 13th yellow jersey wearer in history to withdraw from the race and giving us all a lesson on how unpredictable life really is.

I put my head down and started to hammer the pedals. With a little tailwind too the kilometres came and went. Youghal is a pleasant Victorian seaside town but only if you can see it. I could see nothing but fat rain bouncing off my handlebars and out of fast forming pools as I sailed through.

This place too has many stories. One of Youghal's famous residents was Sir Walter Raleigh who was generally credited with bringing potatoes to these shores. Spuds are still – some four hundred years later – quite a hot topic, as I noted in Dungarvan. And why not?

I was now back in County Cork – home essentially and despite the rain, the feeling of achievement, the anticipation of my old bed again and the knowledge that I didn't have to ride my bike far the next day spurred me on. I felt good, picked up the pace and splashed towards the city.

◊

Cork, known as the 'Rebel County', is big. Its ego however is a lot bigger. If Cork were a person it would probably dwarf Tom Cruise and Bono's egos combined – which as you can imagine would barely fit in the Atlantic. Cork City is known as the 'Real Capital', which of course it isn't. That would be Dublin, unless you're talking about 'literary capitals' which is obviously Listowel, 'outdoor capitals' – Westport, or indeed 'music capitals' – Miltown Malbay. Cork people are friendly though, if slightly deluded. They feel independent even if they aren't. They're like the Catalans of Ireland. They almost have their own dialect too and an accent that would make even those Geordies in Northern Ireland sound posh. Real Corkonians don't drink Guinness and they resent having to go to Dublin to play All-Ireland GAA finals. In fact, they resent having to go there for anything as they believe there's no need for the place at all. But they're a happy enough bunch too.

Of course Cork has its own saint. St. Finbarr was special. He was to be made a bishop by the Pope, but the Pope wasn't important enough, so that honour was passed on to God himself. Finbarr therefore was made bishop directly from heaven. When he died, it is believed that the sun didn't set for a whole two weeks. This might give us some clue as to how Corkonians have acquired notions about themselves.

'You're mad to be out in that rain on a bike,' said the woman in the shop in Castlemartyr where I stopped for a sugar hit. This was my final stop and I knew I had come full circle. Things were starting to repeat; I was back in County Cork and was again being told by an old woman how mad I was to be riding a bike in the wet.

'Sure it's only a drop of rain', I said dismissively.
Something had definitely changed.
Ten kilometres more and I bypassed the town of Midleton. Famous for

producing whiskey, it has the largest pot still in the world at the old distillery and they've been producing the stuff in the town for nearly two hundred years. I was now at the polar opposite end of the island to the last whiskey producing town I was in – Bushmills. This can be a complicated country, but I couldn't help thinking that our differences are really very few.

The road became a yellow gorse lined dual carriageway now. I had planned on riding the back roads from Midleton straight to Cobh, where a river ferry would take me across the harbour to where I started this journey, but I had just one more thing to do. It was a kind of last minute decision, but I had to do it in Cork City.

◊

On the night of 5th of September 1987, Stephen Roche and Sean Kelly slept together. Seriously, they did. Well they slept in the same bed anyway. They were in Villach in Austria for the World Championship road race and due to some administrative cock-up, they had to share a bed. The idea of the top two cyclists in the world sharing a bed before the World Championships wouldn't even be imagined today. But it happened in 1987. When the two cuddled up together and whispered goodnight, little did they know that less than 24 hours later, one of them would be World Champion and the new owner of the rainbow jersey – but it would be the 'wrong' one.

Roche who had won the Giro and the Tour earlier that year was there to ride for Kelly. His job was to help his compatriot win but when both men woke and saw that it was raining, they reasoned that they could discount half their rivals straight away. They simply weren't bothered by the rain as they were used to it; many of their rivals were. Thus Roche became interested.

I remember the race well because it was the first race I ever watched live on TV. Not a bad one to start with, but I remember it not just because a man in green had won, but because the opposite of what the commentators told us would happen happened. Roche won the race and Kelly finished fifth – albeit with his arms in the air as well. The 'wrong' man had won. For me, this race was not so much about national pride, but it was where the penny dropped that bike racing was not all about strength and speed. It was about tactics too and it was about being smart. I realised that cycling had layers.

The first time I ever saw a bike race as a spectator and got hooked on the aesthetics of the sport was about a year before –1986. The location was St. Patrick's Hill in Cork. My dad dragged us into town to see Sean Kelly. 'He's a great cyclist', I was told. 'Get your coat.'

My dad could have picked any five random words from an English dictionary and it would have made just as much sense. I was nine years old and I had no idea what I was going to see. My only concern was whether or not this outing would involve eating sweets and if so what kind and how many.

The Nissan Classic Tour of Ireland ran from 1985 – 1992. It was Ireland's cyclists' penance for leaving their country and making a success in foreign lands.

The nation naturally wanted to share a piece of this success and maybe it's no surprise that the race ended around the same time as the careers of our heroes did. Nonetheless, hundreds of thousands turned out throughout the country to cheer on the riders. For them it was a Tour de France atmosphere all over again.

That September day in Cork, I was led by my older brother and father right into the heart of the action, up St. Patrick's Hill. It's a breathtakingly steep walk to the top – especially when you're only nine – but there were thousands of people all heading in the same direction. Complaining wasn't an option.

The first thing I noticed was how wet the rain was. This was clearly a shit idea, but at least it was free. Even then I had a sense of economy and things that were free in the '80s were generally good things. As the time passed, I began to notice other stuff. Cold metal barriers lined the roads and there was a constant passing growl of head-lit green motorbikes and fancy new white cars that looked like spaceships. They were Nissan Bluebirds...

Out of nowhere a man with an English accent announced what was happening in the race. Actually he announced it from the Tannoy speakers that were duck-taped to the roof of his car. When he did, he plugged the whole place in. A live and sudden surge of excitement coursed through the crowd. I still had no real idea what was going on. The single common word hanging from mouths was 'Kelly'. It was 'Kelly' this and 'Kelly' that. But everything changed when out of the sky sprayed this thunderous noise. I looked up and saw what I had rarely seen before – a helicopter.

'A helicopter, look, it's a fucking helicopter' (swearing in Ireland in the '80s wasn't much frowned upon).

This was like a scene out of *The A-Team*. I realised too that there were TV cameras everywhere. 'Jesus Christ' I said to my brother, as I grabbed the lapels of his jacket. My face wore the expression of Marco Tardelli when he scored that goal for Italy to win the World Cup in 1982 – 'We're going to be on the Tele... the Tele,' I cried as I shook my head pleading for it to be so.

Soon the riders arrived. Phil Anderson led up the hill, roared on by the crowds. St. Patrick's Hill is not a long climb but with a gradient of 25% at the top, after a long day in the saddle, it's an awful kick in the nuts. That day the punishment was four kicks. When a group with Kelly turned the corner in pursuit, the place lost it completely. I did too. I lost my innocence and a cycling fan was born – 'catch the fucker Kelly'.

The dazzling colours of the jerseys even in the wet, was totally new. The black and white of an eighties childhood was suddenly warm and glowing. Even the convoy of team cars with bikes on the roofs following the cyclists was impressive. It was like the Paddy's Day Parade – only faster, and without the shit stuff. I had found what I was looking for, though I didn't really know that I was looking for anything. There was no turning back now. Everything from then on was focused around cycling and how to go about getting a racing bike. I wanted more of this.

Anderson won that day but Kelly won the yellow Jersey.

'So he lost, but he still won?' I asked my dad on the way home.

'Isn't it great that you can lose and win at the same time?'

The sheer wonder of it grabbed me. We stopped for chips on the way home too. Things just got better.

'Dad, can we go again next week?'

As St. Patrick's Hill was where my love of cycling began, I felt it might just be the place to finish my tour around Ireland. After riding from Kilkenny through Carrick-on-Suir, I felt, in true cycling spirit, that I'd give myself one last kick in the nuts before finishing. I now knew what it was like to ride a bike for a couple of weeks around a country, but that wasn't quite enough. Still I was wanting more.

Of course I wasn't racing and it's not necessary to be a fan of the sport to get the enjoyment and benefit of touring. I just happen to be a fan and it is the sport that led me to the bike. The bike has led me to many things and places in return. But most importantly, it's a meditation and a soft link right into the world around us, a world in which participation is possible. For the two weeks I spent riding around, I learned an appreciation of myself, the country, its beauty, its people and also an appreciation of the bike – the simple two wheeled invention that makes the world okay.

I kept pushing hard on the pedals all the way into Cork. I was almost spent by the time I hit the quays. The silver-grey rain continued to fall and my rucksack felt heavier with each light rise in the road. As I turned from Patrick's Quay into Bridge St., I had one kilometre to go. I rode back down MacCurtain St., dropped to the small chain ring and dragged myself up York Hill. I caught my breath for a few seconds on Wellington Road before dropping and spinning onto Patrick's Hill. *Just one stretch of road...*

The hill was all mine and the '80s memories rolled down from its top in streams of silver rain. I hit the kink where the gradient gets hard and hurting, hauled myself into more pain. I was aware of nobody and nothing but the front wheel turning slowly. I zigzagged for a bit, to try to ease the gradient but the wall of suffering stood still. But, *more comes* and finally the road levelled out. I could see now in my mind's eye the finish line across the road where that race finish used to be, all those years ago. This was my finish line too – for now.

Breathless and burning, I came to a stop and turned to the world. I was on top of it looking out over *our* wet city, like St. Brendan looking into *our* land of promise. This 'odyssey' was done; I was home.

After a minute I took out my damp phone:

'Mum, can I have that lift you offered me?'

'Yes, where are you?'

'I'm up at the top of Patrick's Hill.'

'How did you get on? And what are you doing up there?'

'Ah...It's a long story...'

TOURING DAYS

k = kilometres

Day 1: Cork – Kinsale – Schull 129k (80 miles)
Day 2: Schull –Mizen –Castletown Beare 122k (75 miles)
Day3: Castletown – Around Allihies – Allihies 44k (27 miles)
Day 4: Allihies –Killarney –Dingle 161k (100 miles)
Day 5 Dingle –Slea Head – Dingle 43k (26 miles)
Day 6 Dingle – Listowel –Milltown Malbay 149k (92 miles)
Day 7: Miltown Malbay –Cliffs of Moher –Salt Hill 128k (80 miles)
Day 8: Galway – Maum – Westport 100k (62 miles)
Day 9: Westport – Aclare – Sligo 102k (63 miles)
Day 10: Sligo – Donegal – Derry 149k (92 miles)
Day 11: Derry – Malin – Giant's Causeway 118k (73 miles)
Day 12: Giant's Causeway – Glens of Antrim – Belfast 131k (81 miles)
Day 13: Belfast – Newcastle – Dundalk 120k (75 miles)
Day 14: Dundalk – Drogheda – Dublin 95k (60 miles)
Day 15: Dublin –Wicklow –Kilkenny 161k (100 miles)
Day 16: KIllkenny –Carrick-on-Suir –Cork 162k (101 miles)

Total 1914k (1189 miles)

Made in the USA
Charleston, SC
13 January 2015